What the eyes see, and the ears hear,
the mind believes.
Harry Houdini

THE
MAN FROM BEYOND

HOUDINI AMONG THE SPIRITS

TROY TAYLOR

AN AMERICAN HAUNTINGS INK BOOK

THE MAN FROM BEYOND
Houdini Among the Spirits

© Copyright 2025 by Troy Taylor

Published by American Hauntings Ink
301 East Broadway - Alton, IL - 62002
www.americanhauntingsink.com

Cover Design by April Slaughter
Interior Design by Troy Taylor
Author Photo by Stephanie Susie

Printed in the United States of America

TABLE OF CONTENTS

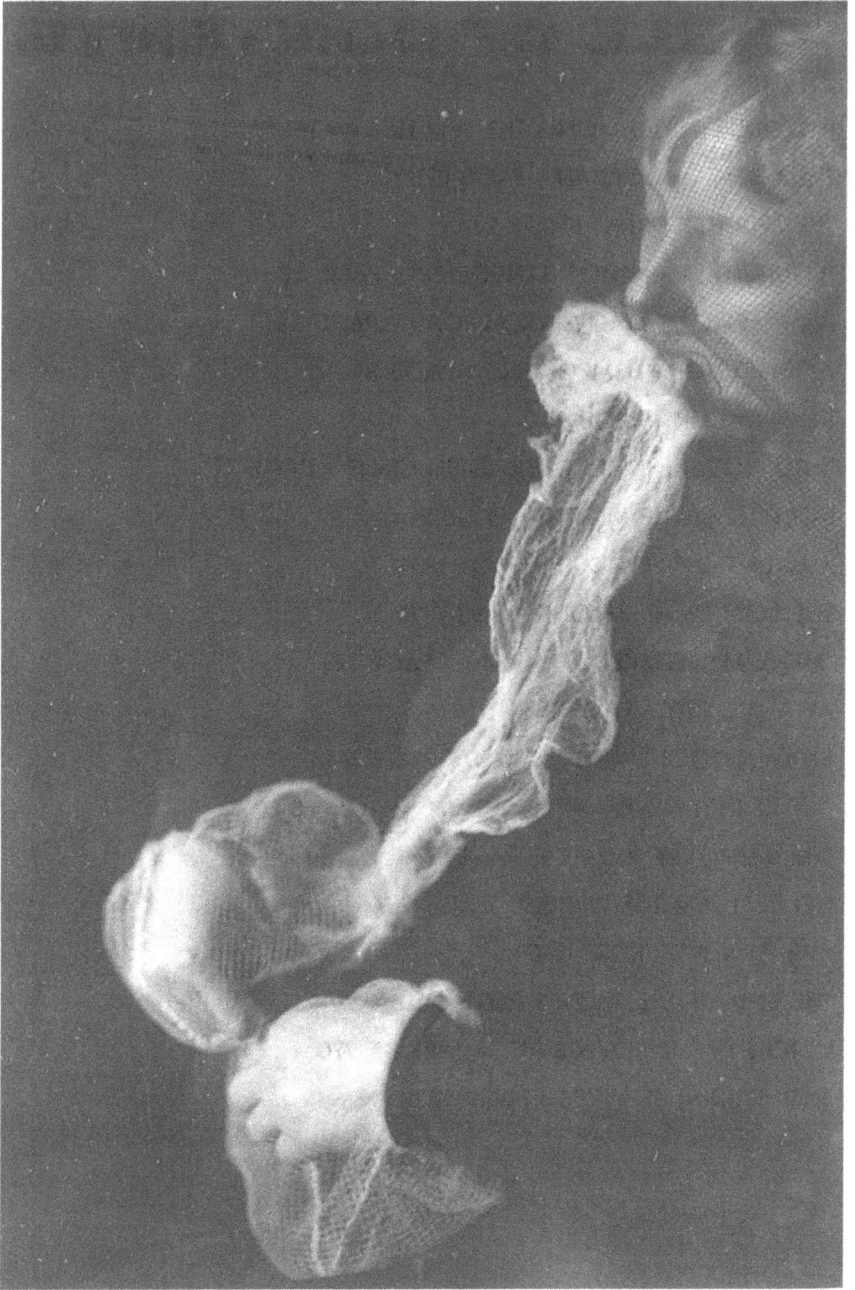

INTRODUCTION:
AMONG THE SPIRITS

SPIRITUALISM, LIKE JAZZ, IS AN AMERICAN INVENTION.

When it emerged as a popular movement in the nineteenth century, it captured the imagination of the entire country. The first followers of Spiritualism were those in mourning. Death came early in those days, for adults and children alike. But thanks to Spiritualism, the dead were no longer lost. It had been founded on the belief that the living could speak to the dead – and the dead would answer.

Spiritualism was born at a time of great religious fervor in the United States, especially since life after death was its greatest draw. Although wildly popular from the very beginning, the movement surged in popularity during and after the Civil War and World War I, times when America and the rest of the world witnessed death in numbers that had never been seen before. However, for those who attended Spiritualist séances, lost loved ones were no longer lost. They could speak and be spoken with as if they were still alive.

Spiritualism became a part of American history thanks to two women named Kate and Maggie Fox. They were young girls in 1848 when their parents rented a cottage in Hydesville, New York. The house already had a reputation for being haunted, and strange happenings began to be reported by the girls and by their mother.

Kate and Maggie Fox, the young women who introduced Spiritualism to the world

Even their skeptical father confessed to being unable to explain the odd knocking sounds that rang out in the cottage at night.

Soon, Kate and Maggie devised a way to communicate with the resident ghosts by creating an alphabet that used a certain number of knocks for letters and for YES and NO. Friends and neighbors were invited into their home to witness this astounding new development, and they walked away shocked and amazed by what they'd seen and experienced. The story of what was happening in Hydesville began to spread through the surrounding area, gaining widespread attention. Soon, what began in Western New York spread to the big cities and from there, all over the country.

The Fox sisters became famous, and the publicity around them became intense. Some newspapers called them sensations; others called them frauds. But people were desperate to see them – and happy to pay for the tickets. Newspaper editor Horace Greeley was convinced of the girls' talents and introduced them to wealthy and well-known New Yorkers, like PT Barnum, Louisa May Alcott, and James Fenimore Cooper.

Katie and Maggie even conducted a séance at the White House for First Lady Jane Pierce, who'd lost her young son while she and her husband, President Franklin Pierce, were traveling to Washington for his inauguration.

In a matter of months, Spiritualism was taking the country by storm. It's been estimated that at least two million people became Spiritualists in the 1850s -- a time when America's population was less than 10 million. The movement swept the country, long before television, radio, the internet, or any kind of mass communication.

There were Spiritualist newspapers and magazines printed, music composed, books written, and, at the height of the Fox Sisters' popularity, thousands of others also began to claim they were able to contact the spirit world. Talking to ghosts became a cottage industry, thanks to the American obsession with messages from their dead parents, aunts, uncles, cousins, and children. The living could speak to the dead – and receive a reply.

The fascination with Spiritualism remained appealing to millions throughout the nineteenth century and into the first third of the twentieth century. Tables moved around and levitated, voices were heard, spirit music was played, and ghosts appeared in dimly lit rooms. Mediums passed on messages while in trances using various methods, including spirit slates, automatic writing, and even spirit horns, which allegedly broadcast the voices of the ghosts.

Restless spirit seekers brought innovations to the movement. Many grew tired of getting messages from a ghost knocking on a table. And not everyone trusted that mediums were correctly repeating messages that magically appeared in their heads. They wanted something they could see for themselves.

That led to the introduction of a *planchette* by a French Spiritualist. The heart-shaped device was made from wood with three small wheels on the bottom of it. The point of the heart held a pencil. Sitters placed the device on a table with a sheet of paper, lightly touched their fingers to the planchette, and waited for the spirits to send them messages.

Ouija boards are still around today, but Spiritualism as we once knew it is a thing of the past

And if that description sounds familiar, it's because the device became an essential part of an American invention called the Ouija Board. It no longer needed a pencil and paper to work, as it spelled out messages using the letters of the board.

Ouija boards, of course, are still around today. But why did this one aspect of Spiritualism survive into the modern age when the movement itself did not?

The answer is a simple one -- fraud.

Many of the most popular spirit mediums of the day were caught cheating. They used accomplices to create ghostly effects, faked "spirit photographs," and cheated séance attendees out of the money they paid for the chance to speak to their dead relatives.

By the 1920s, enthusiasm for Spiritualism had started to cool for the scientists, doctors, and newspaper reporters who had been studying, researching, and writing about mediums and séances for decades.

The growing skepticism from so many directions would have worn down the Spiritualists, who'd seen another rise in popularity after World War I, if not for continued interest from the public. Even in those modern times, the public wanted so desperately to believe they could talk to their dead loved ones that they could overlook a fraud or two.

Scientists and skeptics were baffled by the public's continued belief in the spirit world. Even when blatant fraud was pointed out, believers chose to ignore the evidence. Scientific papers,

Americans remained fascinated with Spiritualism from its founding in the late 1840s all the way until the 1920s, when enthusiasm for the movement finally cooled.

letters, and reports didn't interest the public, so skeptics found a new way to reach people – they made the exposure of the fraudulent psychics entertaining.

Magicians and illusionists joined the scientists, and while they were more interested in self-promotion than public welfare, they were happy to expose the frauds. And soon, the worst of the phony mediums were thrust into the spotlight and revealed as fakes.

This earned the debunkers wide praise. The frauds who'd been exposed were no longer taking people's money or taking advantage of those who were grieving.

The magicians were successful, but not because most were so skilled at what they were doing – it was because most fraudulent mediums were so easy to expose. They were so used to those who attended their séances being gullible that they weren't prepared when magicians started showing up and stealing their secrets to recreate in magic shows. The frauds made phony ghosts, devices that created sounds, wax hands that touched people in the dark, and a lot of fake ectoplasm, which was a sticky substance that was touted as proof of contact with the spirit world. The frauds had gotten so sloppy by that time that there was even a company in Chicago that offered a catalog filled with trick "ghost" effects and equipment mediums could buy.

In time, even the public would turn against Spiritualism. They'd simply seen too much fraud and too much silliness that it had become an embarrassment. When we look back today, Spiritualism seems so old-fashioned that we forget what an impact it had on our history.

And we sometimes forget what finally brought an end to the movement. It wasn't the scientists or the stage shows – what really finished off Spiritualism was just one man.

He was no ordinary man, however. And in truth, he had no hatred for Spiritualism itself. He had always believed in the possibility of communicating with the dead, but when he tried to put that belief into action and contact the spirit of his beloved mother, he found one fraud after another -- and he went looking for revenge.

That man's name was Harry Houdini.

And this book is about what led to his destruction of Spiritualism. It's also about love, friendship, hatred, trickery, illusion, Houdini's need to become a legend, his promise to reach out from the other side after death, his fascination with the spirit world, a broken promise to reunite him with his dead mother, and the complicated life of a man who was a true American original.

And like jazz and Spiritualism, Houdini also changed the world.

Troy Taylor
Summer 2025

THE YOUNG MAGICIAN

IN THE 1962 FILM, *THE MAN WHO SHOT LIBERTY VALANCE*, the character of Maxwell Scott realizes that sometimes a true story doesn't sell as many newspapers as a legend. The character exits a scene with one of the greatest lines in movie history.

"When the legend becomes fact, print the legend."

While Harry Houdini was no western movie character, the legends that he created about himself became fact to legions of his fans in the early 1900s.

Although legend had it that he was born Erich Weiss in the small Wisconsin town of Appleton, he was, in fact, born Erik Weisz in Budapest, Hungary, on March 24, 1874. Appleton came later, when he was a little boy. Later, his father, Rabbi Mayer Samuel Weiss, moved the family to Milwaukee, where he ministered to a large Reform Jewish congregation.

Trying to help his impoverished family, Erich shined shoes and sold newspapers, then became an apprentice to a locksmith, where he learned to assemble and take apart locks with his eyes closed. This would be a skill that would serve him well later in life – if the story were true. Most likely, it's more legend than fact.

Around this time, Rabbi Weiss, leaving his wife and children in Milwaukee, went to New York, believing that a teacher of

Young Erich Weiss

religion would do better serving a city with a larger Jewish population. Erich soon followed, leaving his mother with one less mouth to feed, and worked his way east to join his father. Between the two of them, they saved enough money to bring Erich's mother and the other six children to Manhattan.

Magic was just one of Erich's many interests in those days, but that changed after he read the memoirs of the famous French illusionist, Jean Eugene Robert-Houdin. Soon, he wanted nothing more than to become a professional magician, but the idea seemed impossible for a young man working in a necktie factory on Lower Broadway.

Until it wasn't. Eventually, Erich worked up the courage to quit his job and, with assistance from his friend and fellow necktie factory employee Jacob Hyman, he managed to get himself booked to perform his magic in New York beer halls and small theaters.

Erich began working under the stage name of "Houdini," which he had borrowed from his hero Robert-Houdin, and he and Jacob began playing one-night shows wherever they could find someone to book them. Erich was just thrilled to be on stage, but Jacob became discouraged since there was little money to be made if they weren't booked for longer runs. He decided to quit and return to the necktie factory.

Luckily, Erich's younger brother, Theo, was eager to take his place. The "Brothers Houdini" continued to perform in beer halls, but they also managed to get booked into dime museums, putting on shows on stages next to snake charmers, acrobats, and human oddities.

Erich and his brother, Theo, performed magic at America's greatest fair –
The World's Columbian Exposition in Chicago in 1892.

In 1893, they managed to get booked for shows at the World's
Columbian Exposition in Chicago, the great World's Fair that was
held on the shores of Lake Michigan. The Brothers Houdini put on
20 shows each day for $18 a week on the Midway, which became
the inspiration for carnivals and sideshows in the years to come.
This section of the fair, which offered the world's first Ferris Wheel,
rides, shows, and a variety of popular attractions, drew massive
crowds, and the brothers were a hit. To add some mystery to the
show, they darkened their skin, put on white, flowing robes, and
passed themselves off as conjurers from the "Mysterious Orient" by
chanting a jumble of nonsense syllables while they performed.

Minor success continued for Erich and Theo, and while they
sometimes struggled to raise the money to travel from place to
place for shows, they couldn't imagine doing anything else. Erich
was constantly working to improve the show and to create a

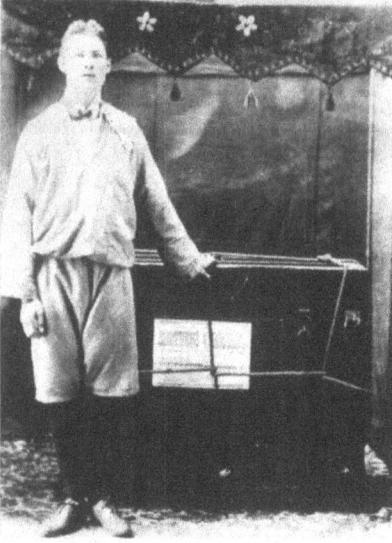

Erich's brother, Theo, affectionately known as "Dash", replaced Joe Hyman in the magic act when went on tour with his brother

persona for himself. His friends and family usually referred to him as "Ehrie," so he decided to adopt a new first name to give some alliteration to his stage name. His nickname was Americanized to "Harry," and "Harry Houdini" was born.

The performance schedule for the Brothers Houdini always brought them back to New York, and they happened to be there when Rabbi Weiss died at the age of 63. Before he passed away, he called Erich to his bedside and made him promise that he would always provide for his mother, Cecilia. It was an unnecessary request. Erich had always been very close to his mother, and not only did she encourage him to follow his dream as a magician, but she also made the costumes for his act. He loved her deeply, and the bond between mother and son only grew stronger over the years to come.

The Brothers Houdini continued to travel and perform, spending weeks in dime museums across the Midwest. While these museums didn't pay much and were considered the lowest rung of the show business ladder, they did give up-and-coming performers the chance to polish their acts. It was hard work, in any case. They were expected to perform at least six times a day, and sometimes, on weekends and holidays, they might do as many as 20 shows in two days.

Magic acts weren't the only attractions at dime museums. There were the kinds of acts mentioned earlier, as well as sword swallowers, fire eaters, contortionists, and hypnotists, like a bearded German named Dr. Josef Gregorowich, whom Houdini met in Milwaukee. In addition to hypnotism, he also dabbled in Spiritualism and séances. Houdini was fascinated by the description of his act. When Gregorowich invited him to attend a séance that he was hosting at a private home in the city, Houdini quickly accepted.

Later that night, Houdini was seated in the darkened séance room and watched as the doctor stood next to the bed of a sick woman. Gregorowich held an empty glass over his head and called for the lights to be turned out. The room faded into murky darkness, and he pleaded for healthy energy to be sent from the spirit world. When the lights came back on, Gregorowich claimed that the glass was now filled with "spirit medicine." He gave it to the sick woman so she could breathe in the healing vapors and promised her she would be well in three days.

Houdini was so intrigued by how easy it was to convince people that what they were seeing was real – no matter how fantastical it was – that his new friend offered to show him some of his other "wonders." The German wrote down his address and gave it to Houdini, who later wrote, with tongue in cheek, "I thought surely a man who lived so close to the police station must be honest."

When he arrived at the older man's home, Gregorowich gave him a guided tour. At his suggestion, Houdini inspected an upright wooden post that had been nailed to the floor in one room. A metal ring was bolted to the center of it. The German sat on a stool in front of the column as Houdini tied the man's hands behind his back with a surgical bandage and knotted it a dozen times. He tied this to the metal ring in the post. Houdini then looped the tape around the man's neck and nailed the ends of the strip he'd created to the post. Two more strips secured him to the legs of the stool. Then, each knot was sewn with a needle and thread and wrapped with adhesive tape. It seemed impossible for him to escape from the bindings without help.

Finally, a coffee cup was placed on Gregorowich's lap, and an ordinary spoon was placed in the cup. Both items were far out of reach of his hands and mouth.

Gregorowich nodded toward the curtained doorway between the sitting room and the bedroom. He told Houdini to step into the next room, close the curtain, and ask any questions that came to mind. He told him, "The spirits will answer with one clang for yes, two for no," using the spoon and coffee cup.

Houdini did as he asked, stepped through the curtain, and asked a question out loud. On the other side of the curtain, he heard the jangle of the spoon inside the cup.

Delighted, Houdini pulled aside the curtain. He found Gregorowich tied up exactly as he had been when the curtain was closed. He knew that wrists could be tied for a quick release – it was a trick he practiced himself – but he was sure the man couldn't have used this technique to free his hands.

Houdini was impressed, and for several years after seeing it, he wondered how the trick had been accomplished. He later found the secret in an old book of magic – and it was devilishly ingenious. He had been looking for a cleverly hidden release when one wasn't needed. By sliding his seated body back and to the left of the post and straining to bring his tied hands forward, the performer could reach the spoon. A series of knots were tied atop one another, and by using the correct diameter of a metal ring, it allowed the performer just enough slack for one hand to manipulate the cup and create "spirit manifestations."

It was Houdini's first encounter with a phony medium, but it certainly wouldn't be the last.

AFTER THE COLUMBIAN EXPOSITION IN CHICAGO ENDED, THE Brothers Houdini returned to New York City. They played for a week at Miner's in the Bowery over the Fourth of July 1894, while other, more popular acts were entertaining crowds at the seashore. Over the rest of the summer, they continued to be stuck playing dime museums in Manhattan and Harlem. Finally, though, they obtained a booking at Worth's Theater in Midtown, where they were held over for a three-week run.

Their success at Worth's can likely be attributed to the new feature they added to their act. Houdini was padlocked in an empty beer barrel, from which he managed to escape in less than 20 seconds. Audiences were amazed but were even more pleased with their next illusion, which they called "Metamorphosis."

The illusion involved having "Dash" – Theo was now using this nickname, given to him by his brother – placed in a locked box. A curtain was dropped and raised again seconds later, which revealed to the audience that the

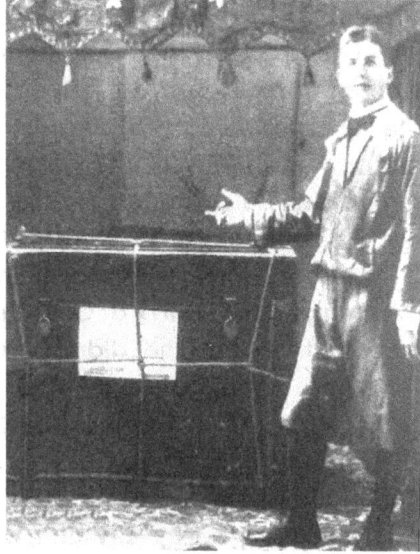

Houdini showing off the trunk used for the "Metamorphosis" act that he performed with Theo

assistant and performer had swapped places. Dash could make the switch very quickly, but not as quickly as the young woman who soon replaced him in the show. Her name was Wilhelmina Beatrice Rahner – known to friends and family as "Bess" -- and Houdini met her while performing at Coney Island. The pair fell in love and quickly married.

There are three different versions of the couple's whirlwind courtship. The first came from Bess, and she said that she was in the front row when Houdini performed in a school show in Brooklyn. He accidentally knocked a glass from his table and stained her dress. Her mother was furious and threatened to have the apologetic young magician arrested. Bess managed to whisper to Harry that she thought he was wonderful. Mrs. Rahner, sensing trouble, halted her tirade and stalked away with her daughter in tow.

In Houdini's version of the story, he first met Bess on a

streetcar. He was on his way to perform for a private party, and when he dropped the equipment he was carrying, a pretty young woman in a white dress helped him to pick it up. To his surprise, she turned out to be a guest at the birthday party where he was performing. It was at the party that he remembered ruining the girl's dress. He arranged for his mother to make a new dress for her, which he delivered to Brooklyn.

In both versions of the story, Bess snuck out of her home one evening and met Harry at Coney Island. But Bess claimed that when the night ended, she didn't want to go home, so when Harry proposed to her, she accepted. They bought the best rings they could afford and were married by midnight.

Harry recalled the proposal but said it didn't happen at Coney Island. He noted that Bess was wearing her new dress, and when they passed by City Hall, a wedding party was coming out. Bess remarked that she looked like a bride in her new white dress. Impulsively, Harry suggested that they get married, and they did.

Dash offered the third – and most likely – version of the story. He explained that Bess had been one-half of a song-and-dance act called The Floral Sisters. He introduced Bess to Harry, and the two fell in love. Two weeks later, they eloped.

Harry and Bess as a young married couple

At the time of the wedding, Harry was 20 years old, and Bess was 18. She weighed only 94 pounds and was nearly four inches shorter than Houdini, who was five feet, five inches tall.

No matter how the pair first met, though, all three versions of the story agreed on the reaction of both sets of parents. When the couple called at the Rahner home, Bess' mother, Balbina, flew into a rage and refused to see Houdini, the Jew who had stolen her Catholic daughter. She refused to speak to Bess for the next 12 years. It

Houdini with his wife and mother -- his "two sweethearts", as he wrote on the photograph. Bess knew to never come between her husband and his mother, although Cecilia loved her daughter-in-law very much.

wasn't until 1906 that she agreed to see her daughter again, and that was only because Harry and one of his brothers went to her home and refused to leave. Bess was seriously ill and wanted her mother.

Cecilia Weiss's reaction to her son's marriage was completely the opposite. She was happy and understanding and welcomed the newlyweds into her home. After their courthouse marriage, Harry and Bess, hoping to please their families, repeated their marriage vows in separate ceremonies with a rabbi and a priest. Cecilia was happy; Balbina was not. Bess, on the other hand, joked about the entire experience: "I'm the most married person I know, three times -- and to the same man."

When Houdini went back on the road, Bess went with him, hurriedly training to become his assistant. Dash kept working on his own, using another girl – dubbed "Madame Olga" – as his stage companion. Soon, Bess was able to change places with Houdini during the "Metamorphosis" illusion at a speed that Dash readily admitted was beyond his power.

In October, Harry and Bess began a two-week booking at Barton's Theater in Newport News, Virginia, and three months later, they were booked at Tony Pastor's Theater in New York City. Pastor's intimate show house was in the Tammany Building on East 14th Street and was a prime spot for a new act to be seen. But if Harry thought this was to be his entry into the big time, he was disappointed. There was no invitation for a return engagement.

Tony Pastor wrote his opinion of the show on a sheet of theater stationery dated February 4, 1895: "The Houdinis' act as performed here, I found satisfactory and interesting."

It was a single sentence that, for a sensitive performer struggling to make a name for himself, chilled the heart. He was beginning to wonder if he would ever achieve the success that he wanted so badly to find.

THE SPIRIT MEDIUM

FOR 26 WEEKS IN 1895, HARRY AND BESS TRAVELED WITH THE Welsh Brothers Circus, which was based out of Lancaster, Pennsylvania. It was not a top-tier circus by any means, but it managed to draw decent-sized crowds as it traveled around the country. They were a "mud show," which meant that they journeyed from town to town along America's roadways, not quite able to afford to move the circus by railroad.

Because it was a small troupe, everyone did what they could to pitch in and earn their keep. When not performing magic, Harry sold soap, combs, toothpaste, and other necessities to his fellow performers. During his act, he manipulated playing cards, changed the color of silk handkerchiefs, yanked knotted pieces of braid through his neck, and shot a borrowed watch to the center of a target.

Bess sang and danced, and together, they presented what was called a "second sight" act. Bess was blindfolded on stage, and Harry walked through the

Harry and Bess toured with the Welsh Brothers Circus in 1895. The Houdinis are in the front row, to the right, just to the left of the clown in the striped suit.

audience, asking her to identify various objects that audience members removed from their pockets and handbags. Thanks to a series of code words they'd worked out, Bess was always successful. They closed each show with "Metamorphosis," much to the delight of the crowds.

When Houdini wasn't performing, he was pursuing something new for the act – handcuffs. They were a device rarely used by stage magicians when Harry acquired his first pair. Despite their reputation as secure devices, he found they could be easily opened with a concealed duplicate key, a small piece of metal, or even a bent wire. A single key would open every set of the same pattern. With less than a dozen hidden keys and picks, Houdini was sure that he could escape from every kind of manacle used by various police departments in the United States. He read every piece of information that he could find on locking mechanisms and began collecting different kinds of cuffs, taking them apart, and studying their mechanisms. When he added them to his act, he quickly became known as the "Handcuff King," thanks to the ease with which he escaped any restraints.

Though Houdini sent half of his weekly $20 salary home to his mother, by the end of the tour with Welsh Brothers, he had saved enough money to buy an interest in a burlesque show called the American Gaiety Girls. His cousin, Harry Newman, was the company's advance man, traveling ahead of the production, booking theaters, and generating publicity. It was a wise investment and allowed Harry to perform on the same bill as the Gaiety Girls, working regularly.

Around this same time, Houdini devised a publicity stunt that he'd use over and over throughout his career. When the show was playing in Gloucester, Massachusetts, in November 1895, Houdini – with a reporter in tow – amazed officers at the local police station by freeing himself from every pair of handcuffs they tried to restrain him with. He repeated the stunt in every town where they played, always making news.

Houdini was starting to build a good reputation and seemed on his way to success – but not quite yet. The show abruptly closed in Rhode Island when the company manager was arrested for stealing the show's profits.

Disappointed, Houdini scrambled for another booking and managed to sign on for a tour with "Marco the Magician" in Nova Scotia, Canada. However, business was so bad in Halifax that Marco canceled his appearances and returned to Connecticut and his real job as a church organist.

But Houdini decided to stay on in Canada and managed to line up a string of shows. The first stop was in St. John, the largest city in New Brunswick, where he ran into an old friend who was a doctor.

It turned out to be a fortunate meeting.

One afternoon, Harry accompanied his friend on his rounds at a mental institution. As they walked down a corridor, Houdini stopped outside the padded cell of a patient who was frantically trying to escape from a straitjacket. He watched in fascination,

Harry began perfecting his straitjacket escape, long before it became one of the most sensational parts of his act.

playing out in his mind what he would do to escape. He was soon convinced that a straitjacket escape would be effective on stage. He obtained one from his friend and then, after a few weeks of strenuous practice, was ready to try out his escape in front of an audience.

Several eager volunteers hurried on stage to restrain him. They tightly buckled Houdini into the canvas jacket, of course, not realizing that he had created some slack by flexing his crossed arms as the sleeves' straps were fastened. They carried him to a cabinet onstage and closed the curtain.

Behind the curtain. Houdini strained his muscles and, a little at a time, he forced one sleeve, then another, over his head. He managed to open the buckles for the straps using the pressure of his fingers through the heavy canvas. He twisted, turned, and finally squirmed free of the jacket. He shoved it away from him and burst through the curtain to take a bow.

And was greeted with silence.

There was no applause, just a feeling of bored confusion. The escape had fallen flat, and suddenly, Houdini knew why – the audience hadn't witnessed his struggle. They assumed an out-of-sight assistant must've helped him to get free.

Houdini had learned how to perform remarkable escapes, but he was still working to develop the kind of showmanship that would keep his audiences enthralled.

Next time, he told himself, it would be better.

And it was, but there were few spectators to see it. Harry and Bess had the worst winter of their lives in 1896, with new bookings failing to appear until spring. Even then, they struggled for months and were so broke by August that Houdini wrote to respected magicians Harry Kellar and Hermann the Great, offering the services of Bess and himself as assistants. Kellar wrote back to say that he wasn't hiring at the time but wished Houdini good luck in the future. He received no reply from Herrmann the Great.

Difficulties and hard times continued for Harry and Bess until 1897, when they began touring with a Midwestern medicine show called Dr. Hill's California Concert Company. A regular salary of $25 a week offered the couple more security than they'd had in a while. The owner of the company, Dr. Hill, sold patent medicines to crowds that gathered in small towns to watch the free entertainment supplied by members of his troupe. He would then sell tickets to the spectators for another show that was being performed that night.

The main show was a mix of singers, dancers, comedians, and other performers, followed by the presentation of a melodrama called "Ten Nights in A Barroom," a play about the evils of alcohol. Harry and Bess were part of the nightly show, presenting their magic and escapes, while also doubling as actors in the play. Bess also sang on some nights.

In one of the towns on the circuit, Dr. Hill heard that a professional spirit medium had been attracting sizable audiences and wanted to do something that might bring the medium's customers to his show. When Houdini heard about this, he quickly offered to stage a séance as part of his performance. Eager to see his name at the top of the bill, he promised Dr. Hill he could match any professional medium he'd ever seen.

Since his first introduction to Spiritualism by Josef Gregorowich, Houdini had remained interested in not only the possibility of life after death, but in the ways that spirit mediums achieved the events that occurred at their séances. Skilled mediums could astonish the believers who came to them to speak to dead loved ones by producing knocks and raps, conjure up messages on ordinary slates, and cause spirit hands, faces, and apparitions to appear. Houdini was convinced he could imitate anything a medium could do.

He made his debut as a "Spiritualist medium" on January 8, 1898, in an opera house in Galena, Kansas. Inside a cabinet on stage, Houdini was tied to a chair by a committee of audience volunteers and pretended to enter a trance state. Almost as soon as the curtain closed, the crowd could hear music from a mandolin that had been placed in the cabinet with the restrained performer. Then the jangle of bells and tambourines joined the melody, much to the delight of the crowd. The curtains on the cabinet then flew open, showing that Houdini was still tied to his chair. The curtain closed, then opened again moments later, and Houdini emerged, "freed from his bonds by the spirits."

When the applause faded, Houdini walked to the front of the stage and began to speak to the audience about the spirit world. He said that he could sense eerie presences on the stage. He closed and opened his eyes and gasped that messages were coming through from the other side. He recited a number of names, offered the dates when loved ones had "traveled to the other side," and even spoke of family secrets that he shouldn't have known. According to local newspapers, this sent chills down the spine of those "who received communications from the dead."

Harry wasn't speaking to ghosts. He'd done a little homework instead, writing down names and dates he found on tombstones in the town cemetery, reading back issues of the local newspaper, and visiting restaurants and saloons, where he listened to local gossip. When Houdini pretended to contact the spirit of a man who had been recently murdered – and spelled out the man's name – many spectators panicked and fled from the theater.

Dr. Hill was so thrilled by the performance and the night's take that he asked Houdini to create a Sunday night séance for every town on the circuit.

In Garnett, Kansas, Houdini delivered a message to a woman

who had recently lost her son. He told her not to grieve. The boy's spirit was calling to her, he explained, trying to tell her that he was happy. Soon, she would be blessed with another child to take his place.

The woman, who was pregnant, was embarrassed, and her husband was furious. He stormed backstage and grabbed Houdini, ready to give him a sound thrashing, but Houdini talked fast, blurting out the story of an incident from the man's past. The fellow was so stunned by this that he let Harry go. The research that he'd done into the family had saved him from a beating that, he later admitted, "I richly deserved."

Houdini's time pretending to be a spirit medium in the circus would be crucial to his later career as a debunker, knowing how many of the tricks of dishonest mediums were accomplished.

Houdini quickly realized that an audience that came to see a séance was far easier to satisfy than one that came to see a magician. Believers in Spiritualism readily accepted messages from the dead. They were already convinced of the authenticity of the medium before they even arrived for the séance, making his job much simpler. However, even skeptics were confounded by the accuracy of his revelations. The ruse of getting information beforehand was so simple that otherwise rational people refused to consider that Houdini's "psychic gifts" were trickery.

The séances served a purpose other than just making money. They also helped Harry become adept at other skills he could use in his act. He'd always used his hands in his escapes, but now he'd learned to use his feet, too. He had seen armless entertainers in dime museums write, shave, and play musical instruments with their feet, but he had never tried to develop these skills himself. As part of his act, he created messages from the spirits on chalkboard slates that were placed under a table, practicing with his toes until he could pick up a piece of chalk and write with it.

He also mastered several table levitation techniques. One of the best involved pressing firmly on the top of a table and forcing it to tip until it was balanced on two of the legs. He then slipped a foot under the closest table leg and, by clamping down with his hand on the corner above it, he could make the table "float" with his foot. On the darkened stage, with three volunteers holding their fingertips lightly on the table, the "levitation" seemed uncanny. After leaving the stage, the volunteers would insist the table was lifted by psychic powers alone. How high did it lift? It seemed it was a little higher each time the volunteer re-told the story.

In St. Joseph, Missouri, Houdini was approached by several locals who asked him to expose a fraudulent spirit medium who had been taking advantage of people in town. The medium agreed to meet with Houdini and was frank and honest with him. He confessed to using trickery – he was a showman, just like Houdini was – and since the public wanted séances, he was giving them what they wanted. Contrary to what Houdini had been told, he was making very little money from the scene. In fact, he claimed to be nearly broke. He planned to give one more séance to raise some funds and then planned to leave town if Houdini agreed not to expose him.

Houdini attended the séance that night with no plans to expose the man. He'd made the medium promise to leave town, and that seemed punishment enough, but the man apparently decided to make that last séance one to remember. Houdini later wrote, "While I had the table walking, someone threw a rock on it. I am satisfied that someone brought the rock along to help the medium if he got in trouble. They [his supporters] were not taking any chances of his being unable to give a sign at the right time."

It turned out there was a downside when it came to the popularity of Houdini's spirit medium act – it was so profitable that he was now unable to get bookings as a magician. So, Harry

Bess and Harry while performing as spirit mediums with the circus. Occasionally, their "mind-reading acts" became a little spooky.

and Bess made the best of it, performing séances on stage, finetuning their mind-reading act, and using Bess as the "voice" of the spirits.

On occasion, though, the phony séances became a little spooky.

They were in Canada when a spectator named Mary Murphy asked where her long-lost brother John could be found. From offstage, a "spectral" Bess called out an address on East 72nd Street in New York. The next day, the woman returned to the theater with astonishing news. She had sent a telegram to New York and found her brother at the exact address that the "spirits" had announced the previous night.

Harry was baffled. How had Bess known the man would be there? She replied that she didn't know – she'd made it up. She explained that the name "Murphy" reminded her of Mrs. Murphy's confectionery shop, a few blocks from her family's home on East 69th Street. So, she'd used the address of the shop, never guessing the brother was the owner.

Bess insisted it had been a coincidence. However, those who later claimed the couple weren't just pretending to be mediums, but had actual psychic abilities, often pointed to this incident as proof.

Or maybe it had been just a lucky guess, as Bess always said it was. Who knows?

On another evening, Harry recognized a woman who had attended one of his earlier séances, scolding her son for being reckless on his bicycle. The spirits sent her a message through Houdini. He said he saw a vision of her son speeding down a hill on his bicycle, then losing control as he turned a corner. He then saw the boy walking with his arm hanging limply at his side.

The woman fled the show in shock, but she returned the next day – the second séance attendee to "confirm" the psychic skills of Harry and Bess. On the same evening that Houdini told the woman of his vision, her son fell from his bicycle and broke his arm. Another coincidence? A lucky guess based on seeing the woman complain about her son's recklessness? Or something else?

But the eerie predictions, which generated a lot of publicity, didn't make any extra money for Harry and Bess. They were still making barely enough to live. Of course, Harry could've made a lot more money by claiming to be a genuine medium, but he refused to do so. The messages and manifestations were just show business. He'd never use his act to steal money from people.

Unfortunately, honesty wasn't putting food on the table because after the medicine show tour ended, Houdini was unable to book his illusion and escape act. Even though the pay was terrible, he and Bess signed on for another season with the Welsh Brothers Circus. At the end of the tour, the owners offered the couple a letter of recommendation to help them find work in the off-season. One portion of the letter read:

We can cheerfully recommend Harry and Beatrice Houdini with their unique and mysterious act called 'Metamorphosis' as being the strongest drawing card of its class in America. Their act is totally unlike others and always creates a profound impression... We will be pleased to play them at any time. The Houdinis are truly great people.

Despite the glowing praise, Harry and Bess were no better off than they had been playing spirit mediums. At 24, Houdini was still on the lowest rung of the show business ladder.

He promised Bess that he would give it one more year. If he hadn't found success by then, he would give up magic and find another, more profitable, line of work.

"THE UNDISPUTED KING
OF HANDCUFFS"

On January 5, 1899, a story about an unknown dime museum performer appeared on the front page of the *Chicago Journal*. A reporter had been at police headquarters when a magician who called himself Harry Houdini arrived and boasted that he could release himself from any type of handcuffs the police might have. Officers quickly fastened him into restraints and, just as quickly, Houdini released himself.

But later that night, a police sergeant named Waldron showed up at the Kohl and Middleton's Clark Street Museum, where Houdini was playing, and locked the performer into his own personal cuffs. This time, though, one of the cuffs managed to withstand Houdini's assault. When Waldron eventually admitted that he had dropped a slug into the lock, Harry was furious and embarrassed.

Houdini was challenged again a short time later, in St. Paul, Minnesota, but with different results. A short, plump, German man approached him after the show and asked if Houdini could free himself from other handcuffs, or only from those that were props in the show. Harry bragged that the restraints that could hold him

Houdini finally began to make a name for himself with his Handcuff Challenge, daring audience members to produce a pair of cuffs from which he could not escape. Harry invented the challenge, which would soon have imitators across the country.

had yet to be invented.

The next evening, the little German returned with his own handcuffs, locked them on Houdini's wrists, and pocketed the key. When the brash young magician easily escaped from the manacles, the man introduced himself as Martin Beck. He was the acclaimed booking agent for the Orpheum vaudeville circuit, the largest in the country. He offered Houdini a trial date in Omaha if he was willing to put together a new act with dramatic escapes.

Finally, thanks to Martin Beck, Houdini left the dime museums, circuses, and small theaters behind and began taking steps toward becoming an American – then a worldwide – sensation.

In Omaha, where Harry was booked for $60 a week, he began his trial run for the Orpheum circuit. The sleight-of-hand tricks that had opened his old show were dropped at Beck's recommendation. He wanted Houdini to emphasize his ability to escape from what seemed to be impossible circumstances.

When the curtain rose on the first new show, the audience saw that the stage held six chairs and a table loaded with manacles. A trunk stood to one side, and a large cabinet, with curtains on all sides, occupied center stage. Houdini walked to the middle of the stage and addressed the crowd, explaining that he would attempt to escape from the most difficult restraints ever created. He invited a committee of audience members to the stage, promising not to embarrass any of the volunteers. If anyone had brought their own handcuffs with which to challenge Houdini, they could bring those to the stage, too.

The volunteers were invited to examine the cabinet and to see for themselves that there was nothing concealed inside it. Harry picked up a pair of handcuffs from the table. They were regulation police irons, he assured the audience, used to hold dangerous criminals. A committee member examined the cuffs and then locked them on Houdini's wrists. The man was told to place the key in his pocket and keep it in his possession.

Music began to play, building excitement, as Harry entered the cabinet. The curtains were closed, but then flung aside less than 30 seconds later, when Houdini emerged from the cabinet. The cuffs were still locked – but they were no longer on his wrists. He tossed them to the committee.

He was just getting started. Several pairs of handcuffs and leg irons were displayed for the audience. Houdini identified each by name and gave a brief history of each of them, drawing out the act to create suspense.

Volunteers tested the restraints, finding all in working order, and then placed them on Harry's hands, arms, and legs. He stretched and strained at the chains, tugging at them, and dramatically looked worried as he was placed inside the cabinet. Music, which had started slowly, increased in tempo until it finally screeched to a stop when the cabinet's curtains were pulled aside and Houdini stepped out, miraculously freed from his chains.

More escapes followed, accompanied by resounding applause, and then the act ended with "Metamorphosis," during which Harry slipped out of ropes knotted at the wrist, a sealed bag, and a locked trunk in a mere three seconds. When the trunk was opened, Bess was found in his place, tied up just as Harry had been.

Harry's performances continued all week. Drama was added to each show when challengers appeared with their own handcuffs, hoping to stump him. Since this was the highlight of each show, Houdini hired men to sit in the audience with handcuffs from his own collection. If no legitimate challengers appeared, these men came forward to make sure it was an exciting evening.

At each performance, Harry proudly proclaimed himself the originator of the handcuff challenge, which was already transforming Houdini's performance from a small-time magic show to one worthy of the Orpheum circuit. The genius of the act came from the work that Harry put into it. He spent countless hours becoming familiar with every kind of handcuff and restraint. He worked with locksmiths, learning

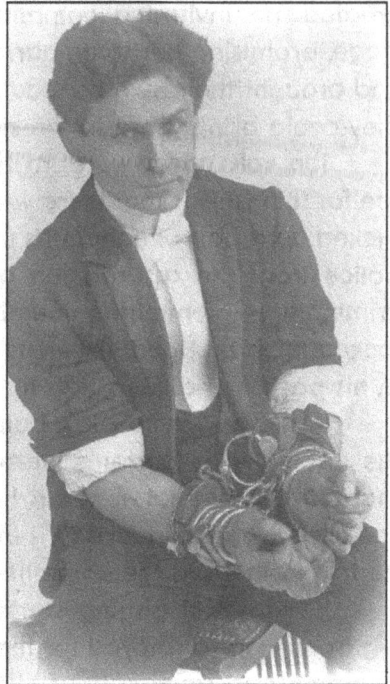

Harry's handcuff escapes took the vaudeville world by storm, but he soon upped the ante with spectacular escapes.

their trade, and read every book he could find on locks, cuffs, and manacles. He visited museums and police stations and studied both old and new restraints. He created "skeleton" keys to open any device and made his own lock picks from twisted wire and bent steel that were smaller than keys and easier to conceal. His sleight-of-hand skills, even though he wasn't using them openly during the act, became invaluable when he needed to misdirect the audience and hide his picks or keys in unlikely places.

At the end of the week, Martin Beck received an enthusiastic report from the Omaha theater manager. Impressed, he signed Houdini for the Orpheum circuit tour. By the time he reached his first engagement in California, his salary had jumped to $90 a week – the equivalent of about $3,500 today.

In San Francisco, Houdini was stripped to the skin in the office of the San Francisco detective force and examined by a police surgeon. He then proceeded to slip out of 10 pairs of handcuffs, a wide leather belt used to subdue dangerous prisoners, and a regulation straitjacket. The escapes took place behind a closed closet door, and the detectives could not explain how it was done.

Houdini began earning a reputation for escaping from jail cells in the cities he visited on tour. When he arrived, he began to be challenged by the local police to escape from one of their cells. If they didn't, he challenged them and never failed. These escapes soon became a standard publicity stunt for every town he visited.

However, the lengthy newspaper account that described this incident failed to mention that Houdini had visited the detective bureau in advance to inspect the restraints. It also didn't mention the kiss he received from Bess before being placed in the closet. Even if it had, readers wouldn't have any way of knowing that Bess had slipped a key to her husband with her tongue as they kissed.

Houdini quickly began winning over audiences, and his salary climbed to $150 per week. Soon after that, he started placing large ads about himself in the trade papers, announcing his accomplishments. Martin

Beck used the ads, as well as newspaper stories about his escapes and box office reports during the Orpheum tour, to secure a place for Houdini as the headliner on the Keith Theater tour. He publicized the new tour in Kansas City, escaping from handcuffs at the Central Police Station.

He returned to the Orpheum circuit after playing a series of dates with Keith Theaters and announced his return with another publicity stunt. Stripped naked, fastened at his wrists and ankles by five pairs of irons, he was locked in a cell from which there seemed to be no escape. But in less than eight minutes, he escaped from not only the manacles but from the cell, too.

The newspapers were wild about Harry, and he rode the wave of popularity for a string of sold-out shows. Houdini now had money in the bank and a scrapbook filled with news stories, editorials, theater advertisements, official police letters verifying his escapes, and playbills with his name at the top of the list.

His mother, Cecilia, couldn't have been happier. She was sure that with all this success, her son would be able to spend more time at home with her. But that wouldn't be the case. Harry was about to make the biggest gamble of his life, and it would be months, perhaps years, before he would see his mother again.

AN AMERICAN MAGICIAN ABROAD

AFTER FINALLY BECOMING SUCCESSFUL IN THE UNITED STATES, Harry became convinced he could achieve even greater things in Europe. Eager to travel abroad for the first time, Harry and Bess sailed for England on May 30, 1900.

Harry was so sure of himself when he arrived in London that he wasn't discouraged by the fact that not a single booking awaited them. He knew he could amaze European audiences just as he had American ones – he just needed someone to give him a chance.

But that wasn't easy to find.

He met with theater managers, who flipped through his scrapbook, read his reviews, skimmed his testimonials from police departments, watched him slip out of handcuffs, and then offered him no more than weak promises and a shrug. They told him that when he performed somewhere, they'd come and see him.

Harry continued to be frustrated until he met a young theatrical agent named Harry Day, who had just started in the business. With only a handful of other performers on his roster, Day was eager to meet with Houdini, and the two men took an instant liking to one another. Day was able to arrange for Houdini to audition at the acclaimed Alhambra Theater.

Harry and Bess in Germany

Theater manager C. Dundas Slater was impressed with Houdini's skills but was skeptical about his ability to escape from restraints that weren't used in his act. Harry Day immediately arranged for a visit to Scotland Yard for his new client. At the famous police headquarters, Superintendent Melville directed Houdini to put his arms around a sturdy pillar, and then he locked a pair of cuffs on his wrists with a laugh. He and Slater left for a cup of tea. They would return, Melville said, when the young man had exhausted himself. He knew very well that Houdini would never escape.

But before the two men could even reach the door, they heard the loud clatter of iron manacles hitting the marble floor. Melville's cuffs were lying at Houdini's feet. Houdini himself was casually leaning against the pillar he'd been briefly chained to.

Soon after, Houdini landed his first British contract.

Throughout July 1900, he performed at the Alhambra and then traveled to Germany, where he set new box-office records in Dresden and Berlin. The demand for handcuff acts on European vaudeville circuits became so great that Harry brought his brother, Dash, from New York and set him up to tour as "Hardeen." Within a year, they were the two most popular performers in Europe.

Houdini never turned down a chance to get his name in the papers. When a German police captain named Werner Graf wrote a hostile article that accused Houdini of lying when he said that he could escape from any sort of police restraint, Houdini sued

Graf for slander. It dragged through two appeals, but he eventually won the case. Houdini celebrated by issuing a new advertising lithograph picturing him in a tuxedo and manacles, standing before the highest court in Germany. The lithograph was titled "Apologize in the name of King Wilhelm II, Kaiser of Germany," and it included a few words on Graf's forced apology and the fact that he had to pay all of Houdini's court costs.

Houdini loved publicity, especially when he could get it by seeking revenge for an insult. In 1902, a Circus Sidoli escape artist named Engelberto Klepini advertised that he had defeated Houdini during a handcuff competition. He probably assumed that Houdini would never see the advertisement, but he turned out to be wrong. Not only did Harry see it, but he traveled from Holland to Dortmund, Germany, to confront Klepini in person. In disguise, he took a seat in the stands and waited through the show until Klepini announced that he had beaten Houdini in a contest. At that point, Harry leapt into the circus ring, ripped off his disguise, and challenged the startled performer with a handful of banknotes in his hand. He announced that he would give Klepini $5,000 if he could escape from a pair of Houdini's handcuffs – and he would offer another $5,000 if Houdini couldn't escape from a pair owned by Klepini.

Prodded by the circus's business manager, Klepini agreed to allow Houdini to lock him into a set of what were called French letter cuffs the next night. The handcuffs were opened by turning the letters inside a cylinder that spelled out a word that would unlock them.

Before showtime, the business manager was shown the manacles, and Houdini demonstrated how they could be opened by turning the five cylinders to spell out "c-l-e-f-s," the French word for keys. He was satisfied there was no trickery involved.

Klepini confidently entered his cabinet, but after 30 minutes, the cabinet was moved to the side of the ring so that the rest of the show could continue. More time passed, hours ticked by. The show ended, and workers moved the cabinet back to the center of the ring. Suddenly, Klepini pushed his way out from between the curtains and ran across the ring to the manager's office – still in shackles.

Finally, at almost 1:00 A.M., the manager ordered Klepini to surrender. Houdini spun the cylinder on the lock until the letters "f-r-a-u-d" fell into place. The cuffs sprang open. He had changed the combination before the manacles were placed on his competitor's wrists, just in case he had some help from the circus manager.

Klepini was forced to admit defeat publicly – and to admit that he had never beaten Houdini at all. He'd made up the story.

IF A POLICE DEPARTMENT DIDN'T CHALLENGE HOUDINI IN A CITY where he performed, Houdini issued a challenge on his own. During an engagement in Moscow in May 1903, he dared the head of the Russian secret police, Inspector Lebedoeff, to imprison him in one of the "escape-proof" jails on wheels that had been designed to transport enemies of the state to Siberia. Houdini had seen one of these strange horse-drawn vans on the street and had examined it while the horses were drinking from a water trough. Escape was impossible from the front, sides, bottom, or top, but the entrance door on the rear of the wagon was fastened with a single padlock, located just below a barred window. Harry believed that his arm could pass through it.

There were no reporters present on May 11 when he was

stripped and searched by five officers. Harry said that it was the most difficult examination he'd ever endured. Two iron bands, joined by a short metal bar, were padlocked on his wrists. A pair of manacles, linked by a chain, was enclosed around his ankles. He was then locked inside the wagon, which had been turned in the prison courtyard so that Lebedoeff and his staff couldn't observe the door.

It took Harry 28 minutes to get free.

When he emerged from the wagon, the police were furious. They marched around the wagon to the door and discovered it was still locked. Inside, lying on the metal floor, were the shackles that had been locked on Houdini's arms and legs.

Houdini was seized and searched again, even more thoroughly than before. Then they turned on Franz Kukol, the owner of the theater where Houdini was appearing, and even though he had been kept far away from the wagon, he was stripped and searched anyway. Nothing was found.

Houdini asked Lebedoeff to sign a document that verified his escape, but the chief of the secret police refused. It was bad enough that Houdini escaped. Lebedoeff was not going to publicize the fact. Despite a newspaper blackout, news of the escape spread throughout the city, and Houdini's month-long booking was extended to eight weeks. In addition, lithographs began appearing in stores that showed the American magician outwitting the Russian secret police.

A SHORT TIME LATER, HARRY AND BESS RETURNED TO AMERICA in 1904, and Houdini found himself in great demand. His European exploits had been widely reported in the press, and audiences were demanding to see his show at home.

What Houdini would call one of the "high points of his life" had nothing to do with being in demand as a performer or his death-defying stunts. While in England, he purchased an elegant dress for his mother that was said to have been made for Queen Victoria. Back in New York, he arranged a grand reception where

The brownstone that Houdini purchased on West 112ᵗʰ Street in New York City

he presented Cecilia in the dress to all their relatives. He said it was the happiest day of his life.

Houdini also purchased a new four-story brownstone at 278 West 113th Street in Harlem for $25,000. When he and Bess moved in with Cecilia, it was predominantly a German and Jewish neighborhood.

Life was finally going well for Houdini. His wife and mother were happy, he had a new home, and he was now selling out theaters all over the country. Eager audiences couldn't wait to see the show that had taken Europe by storm.

Houdini's one irritation, though, was with the scores of imitators that had appeared during the years he was abroad.

One of the most irritating was Robert Cunningham, who had shortened his name to "Cunning" for the stage. He was one of the most successful of the "escapologists" who appeared on the American vaudeville stage during the five years when Houdini was in Europe. Cunning's press material claimed that he had traveled the globe (he hadn't), gained his magical skills in exotic places (he hadn't), and now was the greatest handcuff and jail escape artist in the world (he wasn't).

Houdini and his brother, Theo – or Dash, who was still billing himself as Hardeen – were in the audience on September 11, 1095, when Cunning appeared at Hyde and Behmen's Theater in Brooklyn. Dash managed to be picked as a volunteer and was one of five men who brought manacles to the stage at Cunning's request. The cuffs offered by the others were accepted, but Cunning took one look at Theo's manacles and refused to put them on. Not only did he steal his act from Houdini, but he also stole the other magician's line when he decided not to use the cuffs: "These cuffs are not regulation."

But Dash was not deterred. He pulled a banknote from his pocket and said that it would go to charity if Cunning escaped from his cuffs. The theater manager came out of the wings and bet $100 of his own money that Cunning would succeed. Cunning shook his head and pushed the cuffs back into Dash's hands, which caused a chorus of catcalls, groans, and jeers to erupt from the audience.

Almost immediately, the curtain came down, followed by a punch being thrown at Dash. He swung back and, for a moment, it seemed that a brawl was going to break out. A policeman pushed his way through the melee, arrested Dash, and took him to the station house. He was charged with disorderly conduct. Houdini put up his bail money. The next day, a judge heard the case and dismissed it, commenting that it was obviously a publicity stunt.

But the Brothers Houdini were not finished with Cunning.

At his next show, at Hurtig and Seamon's Music Hall on 125th Street in Harlem, Cunning feared more trouble after getting a look at the volunteers who had taken the stage. He told the audience that one of the men was a rival's brother. The man in question insisted that his handcuffs be accepted for the challenge, and the audience shouted for Cunning to comply.

Against his better judgment, the wary Cunning agreed. He allowed seven pairs of manacles to be locked on his wrists and arms and then stepped into a cage-like cabinet. A cloth was draped over it, and the audience was left to wait for him to emerge.

And they waited. And waited some more. The audience grew more restless by the minute, yelling insults toward the stage. Finally, Cunning emerged from the cabinet, but only one of his wrists had been freed from the restraints.

The man whom Cunning had questioned shouted that he wanted his handcuffs back, and his remarks led to more chaos. The curtain dropped again, and the challenger tried to get behind it to find Cunning. Stagehands shoved him back, but he still managed to get through the curtain. Four men grabbed him, though, and they hustled him out to the lobby.

He waited until his irons were returned, but when he had them in his hands, he took one look at them and angrily shouted, "They're ruined! The teeth have been filed off!" He now refused to leave until he was compensated for his damaged property. The theater manager called the police, and he was arrested.

When he arrived at the station, he was ordered to reveal his identity – William Weiss. The charge was dismissed, and Houdini's older brother went free.

Cunning's reputation was ruined, but there were plenty of other imitators who were stealing Houdini's act. The whole family eventually got into the act. Harry's younger brother, Dr. Leopold Weiss, traveled all over New England harassing performers who also tried to steal Houdini's act with the "defeater handcuffs" he'd devised. Houdini regarded himself as the originator of the challenge escape act and insisted that anyone else who used it was a thief.

HARRY WAS ALWAYS TRYING TO DRUM UP PUBLICITY, AND HE devised a novel stunt to generate excitement. The New York newspapers were told that Houdini planned to compete against his student, Jacques Boudini, in an underwater escape contest. Each man had wagered $500 on the outcome, and the winner would take all. A tugboat took them out into New York Harbor on September 20. Both men were shackled hand and foot, tied with ropes, and dropped overboard.

For the next 90 seconds, reporters and photographers saw only ripples on the surface of the water. Then Houdini's head popped up, and he spat out a stream of water. He asked if Boudini was up yet and was told that he wasn't. Harry surged up out of the water, waved his hands to show they were free, and then sank out of view.

Another minute passed, and Harry bobbed up again. He gasped for breath, looked around, and then went under again. Another minute went by, and then he reappeared and asked about his competitor, who had still not appeared. Harry laughed and kicked a leg in the air to show that one of his ankles was free. He went under once more and came up again one minute later to show that he was completely free of his bonds. He swam to the side of the boat and was lifted out of the water.

After another excruciating minute, Boudini was retrieved from the water. He looked more dead than alive. His manacles were still locked on his hands and feet. He was hauled onto the deck of the tugboat and given artificial respiration. Eventually, he opened his eyes and gasped, "I swallowed some water." He closed his eyes again as the boat steamed back to the dock.

Back at the dock, all but two of the reporters who had been on the boat hurried off to file their story of the exciting underwater contest. The two that stayed behind were soon having a laugh with Houdini and the actor he'd hired to play "Boudini." It hadn't been a contest at all – merely a publicity stunt to show off Houdini's skills.

Even the newsmen who weren't fooled filed a story about the contest. It was just the sort of story that people liked to read.

WHEN HOUDINI BEGAN HIS RETURN TO AMERICA TOUR AT THE Colonial Theater in Manhattan, it was apparent that his years performing in Europe had sharpened his skills, showmanship, and timing. He had the audience eating out of his hand, and after two weeks at the Colonial and another two weeks at the Orpheum, he began his tour. Business was booming in Detroit, Cleveland, Rochester, and Buffalo, but when he reached Washington, D.C., he struck publicity gold.

It was there that he staged his most remarkable prison break so far. In March 1906, officials locked the naked performer in a cell on "Murderer's Row" that once held Charles Guiteau, the assassin of President James Garfield. Officers then locked Harry's clothing in another cell and returned to the warden's office.

In a matter of minutes, Houdini managed to free himself and then proceeded to open all the cell doors on the block and switch the prisoners around from cell to cell. He didn't run into any trouble, and in fact, the inmates were highly entertained, although surprised by the sudden appearance of a naked man.

Houdini visited police stations whenever he arrived in town on tour and used the publicity from his challenges to promote his shows

After moving all the men on the block to different cells, Harry locked all the doors, got dressed, strolled to the warden's office, and knocked on the door. The entire stunt took just 27 minutes.

Two documents were created and signed to verify the incident, one by the warden and the other by prison superintendent Major Richard Sylvester. The latter's document read, in part: "The experiment was a valuable one in that the department has been instructed as to the adoption of further security which will protect any lock from being opened or interfered with."

Houdini's security suggestions -- and the feat itself -- effectively blocked any future rival who wanted to duplicate the stunt.

Another of Houdini's highly publicized escapes was made on March 19, when he was locked up at the Tombs, New York City's infamous prison. He slipped out of cell #60, broke into cell #77, where his clothing was, and got dressed. Then, instead of going to the superintendent's office, he ran across the prison yard, climbed a brick wall, vaulted over an iron railing, and hurried through the snow to his dressing room at the theater. Once there, he telephoned the Tombs to report his escape. Startled and amused, reporters insisted that he return to the jail so that photographs of his escape could be taken for the papers.

Between shows one night in Boston, Houdini went to Cambridge and performed at the Harvard Union. He slipped out of a pair of handcuffs, a straitjacket, and a roped chair. He cut the rope into small pieces and gave them out to the students as souvenirs.

On March 25, Houdini performed at the Boston Athletic Club, and as part of the show, he lectured about his travels and displayed some of the relics he'd collected over the years. He spoke at length about Hindu fakirs, dismissing the prevalent idea that they worked miracles. Anyone could duplicate their feats, he said -- with practice. To prove it, he pushed a long steel needle into his cheek without drawing blood. There was no deception involved. Houdini learned the feat during his dime museum days. He ended his performance with his straitjacket escape, which brought the audience to its feet.

After the show, Houdini was given a head-to-toe examination by Dr. J.E. Rourke, anatomist at Massachusetts General Hospital. The doctor, who had examined numerous human oddities and circus strongmen, was eager to see how Houdini's arduous escapes and the physical punishment he inflicted on himself had affected his body. He pronounced Harry to be in excellent physical shape, capable of incredible activity, and able to harden his muscles to sustain strenuous blows.

The doctor predicted he'd live to be a very old man.

Despite his full schedule, Houdini still found time to publish a small book called *The Right Way to Do Wrong*, which revealed the methods of burglars, pickpockets, con artists, and even some of the most obvious tricks of fraudulent spirit mediums. The book sold well at Houdini's shows, but it earned criticism from some. A man named A.F. Hill wrote to Houdini about this book: "You are advertised as if you intended to expose some evil in astrology, clairvoyance, mediumship, etc. Fake mediums are not any worse than a mechanical fake magician. I have seen you perform, but what good are you to society?"

The *New York Sun* also took a shot at him around this same time, revealing the method of one of his escapes. It ran a short account of his escape from the police court jail in Yorkville. According to officers there, they'd spied on Houdini through a peephole while he was attempting to escape from one of the cells and saw him take something from between the toes of his right foot. He then reached through the bars and opened the Yale lock on the door.

Dr. Albert M. Wilson, the editor of the magicians' journal, *Sphinx*, had little use for Houdini and reprinted the *New York Sun* story in the pages of the journal. He also added that Houdini was "swelling out his chest like a pouter pigeon, protruding his abdomen like a cormorant and dropping calumny from his lips like the malodorous emanations from the glands of a Mustelidae mephitis."

The public didn't share Wilson's opinion – and also likely had no idea he was comparing him to a skunk – but Houdini was irritated by it. He sought revenge by starting his own magician's magazine, *Conjurer's Monthly*, in 1906. It remained in publication for the next two years.

Houdini's shows continued to draw enormous crowds. Five times as many people saw Houdini in Pittsburgh in October 1906 at the Grand Theater as attended Ethel Barrymore's performances at the Nixon Theater across town.

His offstage publicity kept his name in the news. During a naked jailbreak at the Allegheny Central Police Station, Houdini switched a deserter from the 11th U.S. Infantry from one cell to another. The soldier reportedly gaped at the nude intruder and asked where he had left his clothes. Harry replied, "I pawned them."

ATTEMPTING THE
IMPOSSIBLE

A DIFFICULT PERIOD FOR HOUDINI BEGAN ON NOVEMBER 26, 1906. While playing at Detroit's Temple Theater, he refused to accept a challenge to escape from handcuffs presented by a policeman named Alphonse Baker. They were not in proper working order, Harry said, and had been rigged to defeat him. The audience shouted at him to try them anyway, and Houdini agreed. As he walked, manacled, to the cabinet, he spotted a bookkeeper and part-time magician named Harrison L. Davies in an upper box. He called out to Davies and asked him if the manipulated cuffs were his work, but Davies shook his head. They were not, Davies assured him.

Houdini struggled in the cabinet for more than 90 minutes before managing to release the cuffs. Long before he was free, Bess left the stage in tears. The *Detroit Journal* reported that her tears turned into hysterics in the dressing room. After Houdini returned the handcuffs to the police officer, he asked if they were his personal manacles. No, Baker replied, another Detroit man had asked him to take them to the stage. Whoever that man was, he was never identified.

A short time later, Deputy Sheriff James V. Cunningham offered $100 to anyone who could successfully break out of the

Wayne County jail. Houdini inspected the cellblock before he took the wager. When he saw that a single sliding bar locked every cellblock in the row, he knew that escape was impossible without assistance. He could pick a lock that he could reach through the bars, but when the control lever was at the end of the corridor, he was helpless.

To avoid professional embarrassment, he announced he would make a dangerous bridge leap instead. On the morning of the stunt, Houdini and his assistant, Franz Kukol, went to the police storage barn and borrowed a coil of heavy rope. While there, he hastily wrote his will on the back of an envelope: "I give it all to Bess." Several officers added their names below his signature as witnesses. He passed the envelope to Kukol for safekeeping.

The two men traveled out to the Belle Island Bridge, and despite the chilly winter weather, scores of Detroit workers came out during lunch hour to see the spectacle. Harry stood at the bridge railing and stripped off all his clothes except for his trousers. He shivered in the raw air as two pairs of police handcuffs were fastened to his wrists, and one end of a safety rope was tied around his waist. He posed briefly for photographers before he jumped into the cold water 25 feet below.

A loud gasp came from the crowd, who were packed side-by-side on the bridge and on both shorelines, as his body sailed through the air and vanished beneath the surface of the river. There were cheers when he surfaced, waving the open cuffs in his hands, and swam to a waiting boat.

Bess hadn't known about the bridge jump until her grinning and still damp husband returned to their room at the St. Clair Hotel a short time later. And when she found out, she was furious. A bridge leap in warm weather was bad enough, but on a bitterly cold day, it was ridiculous. Harry obviously had no regard for himself, but he needed to consider his wife occasionally. After her tirade was over, she helped him undress and change into some dry, warm clothes.

That afternoon, he performed at the Temple Theater. The house was packed with those who'd already seen the front-page story of his underwater escape, which had been printed in the morning papers. They cheered loudly as Harry escaped from a packing case that had been nailed shut in just nine minutes.

Years later, the story of the escape was greatly enhanced, claiming that a hole had to be cut into the ice so that Harry could jump through it that day. This wasn't true. It was November 27, and while it was cold that day, the river was not frozen.

But stories about how he had to swim in circles underwater until he could find a place where the ice was thin enough that he could break through it were certainly a better story. Why simply be cold when imminent death was much more exciting?

IN DECEMBER, A MIDWESTERN ESCAPE ARTIST NAMED LOUIS Paul challenged Houdini with a pair of handcuffs at the Majestic Theater in Chicago. After a quick glance at the cuffs, Harry convinced the audience that the manacles had been manipulated, so he then challenged Paul to escape from a pair that had not been tampered with. Paul refused and was booed off the stage.

A man who identified himself as a special detective from the Central Police Station also offered handcuffs as a challenge. Houdini examined the irons and approved of them. He then turned so that the detective could lock them behind his back – then he worked for nearly an hour and a half before he was able to free himself. The theater, which usually closed hours earlier, stayed open that night until midnight, and the audience remained in their

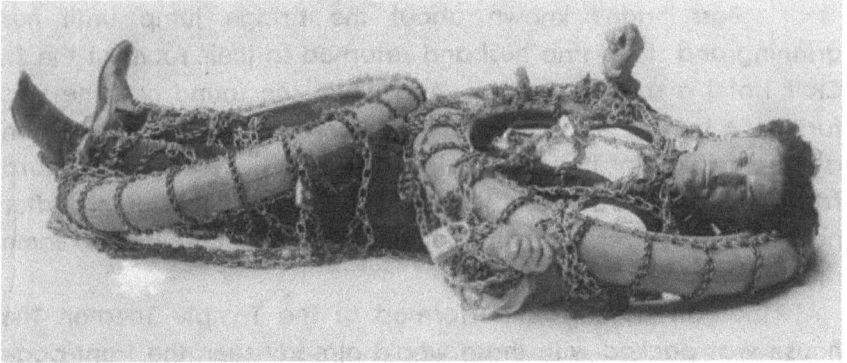

seats to watch.

Once Houdini was finally free, he examined the cuffs again. But the more closely he examined them, the angrier he became. He showed the audience how an extra rivet had been added to try to prevent his escape. He turned to the man and accused him of switching the cuffs, stating that the ones that had been locked on his wrists were not the same cuffs he'd inspected. Several audience members seized the man, who turned out not to be a Chicago police detective, and searched him. They found a second pair, which almost matched, in his pocket.

A review of the show appeared in the *Chicago Daily News*: "For years, there has not been such a sensation as Houdini. His coming into the ranks for vaudeville brings a new light which is not likely to be extinguished by the army of imitators, of apes, of envious fakers."

The reporter described Houdini's straitjacket escape: "He battled with the canvas prison, tore at its leather and writhed, squirmed, crept and twisted like a tortured thing of muscles and emotion and no bones."

On January 4, 1907, Houdini accepted a challenge from the University of Pennsylvania football team. While onstage at the Chestnut Street Theater in Philadelphia, the entire uniformed squad jogged down the aisle to the stage with a giant football. They lifted it over the footlights and up onto the stage. They manacled

Houdini, who pretended to resist, bent him double to fit into an opening on the ball, and stuffed him inside. The ball was laced with chains and padlocked. Harry escaped in 35 minutes.

Houdini returned to Keith's Theater in Boston for the last three weeks of January. He was bound to a ladder by five men who spent 15 minutes wrapping chains around him and locking him into place. He escaped in just seven minutes.

He returned to Keith's Theater in February for another unusual stunt. This time, six riveters sealed him into a galvanized iron boiler. The process used to seal the boiler, with blowtorches and spurting flames, was a show in itself. A full hour passed before Harry emerged from the boiler. His hands and face were covered with soot, his shirt collar was missing, and his hair was wildly disheveled.

On another night at Keith's, employees from the Derby Desk Company pushed a six-foot-long rolltop desk onto the stage. They removed the upper storage compartments and the blotter rack and put Houdini inside. The desk was locked at 10:08 P.M. Just before 11:00, Harry performed another successful escape.

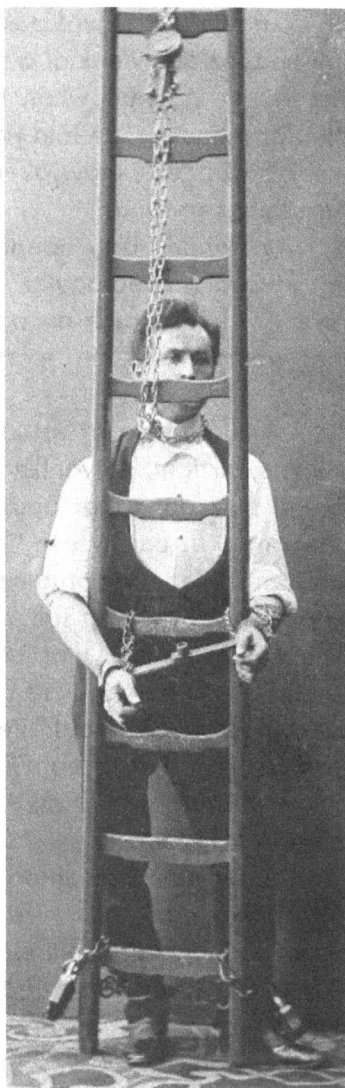

HOUDINI'S 1907 TOUR TOOK HIM ALL OVER THE COUNTRY, AND

he continued to travel during the early days of 1908. He had just finished the first week of a two-week engagement at the Columbia Theater in St. Louis when he received some bad news from the theater manager. He told Harry that box office receipts for the first week had been below average and he needed something big to turn things around.

So, when Harry opened the second week on January 27, he introduced a spectacular new escape that he'd been holding in reserve for just such an occasion. It was the first of the escapes that would make him world famous – from a padlocked water can.

A committee of volunteers was brought on stage to inspect a large, airtight, galvanized iron container. It was similar in shape to the milk cans that dairies supplied to farmers but was large enough – just barely – to hold a man. The volunteers looked on as assistants filled the container with water while Harry went offstage to put on his bathing suit.

While the can was being filled, Houdini created drama for the audience by grimly reminding them that a man could only live for a short time without "life-sustaining air." He suggested that they start holding their breath the moment that his head disappeared below the top of the tank – to see how long they might last if they were in his place.

Crew members lifted Houdini into the air so that he could enter the can feet first. He was slowly lowered until he disappeared. Water spilled out over the sides of the container, and extra bucketfuls were added to fill the can to the top. Then, a curtain was drawn around the can.

As Harry had asked them to do, most of their onlookers took a deep breath as he descended from view and held it. In less than a minute, most of them were gasping for air, but Houdini had not appeared. Two minutes passed before he triumphantly pulled the curtain aside and walked out onto the stage. A round of deafening applause greeted him – but the most thrilling part of the act was still to come.

Houdini returned to the water-filled can and prepared to climb back inside. This time, though, his wrists were handcuffed. He was helped back into the can, and more water was added until the can overflowed onto the stage. Quickly, his assistants jammed the top onto the can and secured it with six padlocks.

Escape seemed impossible.

The curtain was drawn around the can again, and time began to tick by. Audience members who had again gulped in a large breath of air as Houdini vanished into the can now gasped for air with loud, whopping coughs.

Houdini's water can escape began in 1908 and became a sensation that would eventually spawn other, even more dangerous, watery escapes

The clock ticked --- 30 seconds passed, then 60, then 90.

Franz Kukol came from backstage with an axe in his hands, prepared to break the locks to save the magician if he didn't emerge soon. He leaned toward the curtain and listened closely, but there was no sound.

Two minutes passed, then three.

Kukol raised the ax. The tension in the theater was nearly unbearable. Something must have gone terribly wrong. Audience members began shouting at the assistants on the stage, urging them to break open the locks and to free Houdini!

Finally, Kukol stepped forward with the ax and started to pull back the curtain around the milk can. Just as he did, though, Houdini, dripping wet but wearing a wide smile, ripped the curtain aside and stepped out into full view. As he took a bow, the rafters of the theater quaked from the sound of the applause.

Houdini was flushed with excitement after the success of his new escape, but his confidence took a beating when he arrived in Cleveland. When he saw the billboards outside the theater where he was scheduled to play, he was shocked. At the top of the bill was "Mr. Julius Steger," the actor who would appear in a dramatic sketch, "The Fifth Commandment." His eyes went to the bottom of the bill, where he found his name. It was printed larger than Steger's, but his day was ruined anyway.

His ego took another blow later in New York when he read a review of his act in the *New York American*. Alan Dale, a critic who had seen him performing at the Alhambra in London while abroad and who had written a scathing review of him there, went after him again. Harry pasted the horrible review in a scrapbook along with his glowing notices, to read whenever he felt he was getting too full of himself. It read:

The "famous" Houdini is a clever manipulator of handcuffs who appears to suffer in the very worst way from that terrible and baffling disease -- the swollen head. Houdini devoted the greater part of his "turn" to talking about himself in a cheap and rather pitiful way. It was as dull as ditch water. A good deal of his poor talk was "gallery play" -- what a hard time he had of it in England, how they hated to see him earning money over there, how cruelly jealous they were of him in Blackburn, but that he'd go back there and get more money. If he doesn't do a better turn in Blackburn than he did in Harlem, I don't fancy that he'll succeed in his design of "getting more money". This was all piffle and sad piffle.

Years ago, I saw this really clever young man in London and was delighted with what I saw, but now it all seems spoiled. Even the particularly effective parlor trick in which Houdini is apparently padlocked into a huge can of water, from which he successfully "emerges" in his cabinet, is marred by the offensive manners of the man.

Far from being "delighted" in London, Dale had instead written that he "preferred Houdini's literature to his turn." He also said that the handcuff escapes were "spoiled" because they were made under the cover of a cabinet. Regardless of the review, the crowds ignored it, and Houdini managed to fill the theater every night during his run.

INTO THE AIR

AFTER PERFORMING IN BOSTON, WHERE HE PLAYED SOLD-OUT shows and made an amazing escape after leaping from a bridge over the Charles River, Harry and Bess sailed for Germany in August 1908.

When Cecelia Weiss returned from seeing them off from the docks, she wound the grandfather clock in the living room of her home on West 113th Street. It remained silent and unmoving while her son was at home. Now, when she heard it chime and strike the hour, she could mark the passing minutes until he returned.

Houdini opened in Berlin in September, and the handcuff challenge was missing from his act. He would never perform it again. The army of imitators around the world had destroyed its commercial value, and that had left a bad taste in Harry's mouth. He now performed an out-in-the-open straitjacket escape, and the water-filled, padlocked milk can as his opening and closing stunts. In between, he offered several illusions, including the "East Indian Needle Trick," in which he appeared to swallow 50 to 100 needles and 20 yards of thread and cause them to reappear from his mouth with each needle threaded. This stunt was another that produced show-stopping applause.

While at the Oxford Theatre in London, Harry received one of

Before returning to England, Harry performed in Boston and made a jump from the Harvard Bridge

his most unusual challenges from five Chinese sailors. They mailed a letter to him, and when he didn't reply, they published the challenge in the *Star*. The newspaper reported that it was written in Chinese and was nearly a yard long. When translated, it dared the escape artist to release himself from the "Sanguaw," a torture device used to punish criminals in China. In its most vicious form, the victim's feet were nailed to vertical shafts of wood while leather straps held their bodies motionless, and a chain from an upper crossbar garroted their necks.

After the challenge was printed in English, Harry said that he would accept the challenge, although only if his feet didn't have to be nailed to the wood. He also requested that two doctors be allowed on stage to ensure that he didn't strangle while in the device. He said that he would have to inspect the mechanism, and if he failed in escaping in full view, he requested the opportunity to try again in a private room.

Harry went with a reporter from the *Star* to the Limehouse

district to view the torture instrument. Apparently, it met with his approval, because the next night, Friday, November 20, the five Asian men, in Western clothing but wearing long, braided hair, set up the torture device on the stage at the Oxford.

Attached to the solid base were two slanting posts that supported a crossbar considerably wider than the base. The structure resembled an inverted triangle. The sailors crossed Houdini's feet and strapped his ankles with a thick leather strap. Four chains extended outward from this strap and were pulled tight and nailed at the ends to the floor. A tangle of chains encircled Houdini's neck. They were tightened, and the ends were nailed to the extremities of the upper crossbar. Finally, his wrists were strapped together, and the ends of the chains that were attached to the strap were nailed to the tapering sides of the structure.

Houdini went to work, but five minutes of strenuous struggle only managed to yank loose a single nail, which held a chain to the upright. The nail was pounded back into the wood, and the struggle began again. Bit by bit, he managed to ease his left foot out of his shoe. The shoe fell to the stage. Then, his right shoe clattered to the stage beside it. He uncrossed his ankles in the strap that bound them and pulled his left foot up and out. Soon, his right foot was also free. The strap and chains banged down on the floor. With an agile leap, he swung his body up until he caught the top bar between his legs. He pulled himself up until he was astride the bar. Carefully perched there, he used his teeth on the buckles of the straps that bound his hands. When he managed to slip his hands out, he used them to loosen his neck from the chains, and he jumped down to the stage -- just 16 minutes after he had been tethered into place.

He made the escape seem easy, but Houdini was quick to confess to the *Star* reporter that he would never accept the "Sanguaw" torture test again.

A short time later, Harry accepted another challenge, which was to escape while in full view. He was strapped, laced, and roped into a "Crazy Crib" by three men who worked as attendants in London insane asylums.

Harry had seen his first "Crazy Crib" in 1896 in the same Canadian institution where the struggles of an inmate in a straitjacket had inspired him to attempt the escape

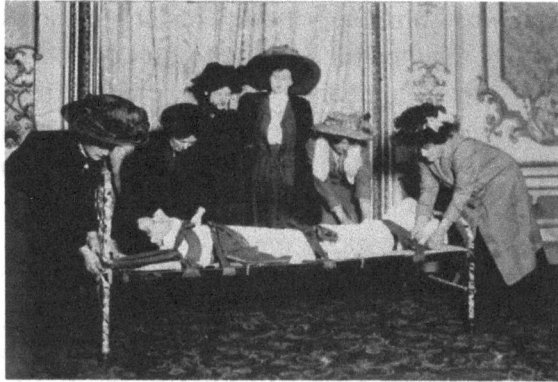

Six suffragettes bound Houdini to a "crazy crib" bed on the London stage. When one of them kissed him while he was in his restraints, it was probably the only time Harry ever blushed on stage.

on stage. At the time, he had also devised a method of escape when shackled to a bed with handcuffs and leg irons. In those days, he thought a canopy was necessary to hide his struggles from the audience. Now, his contortions caused the audience as much excitement as his out-in-the-open straitjacket feat.

Two weeks later, six suffragettes -- women dedicated to winning the right to vote -- wrapped Houdini in sheets and bound him to a mattress with bandages. Once the women were sure that he was securely tied, one of them bent down and kissed him. It was probably the only time that Harry ever blushed on stage.

Houdini's time in London broke box office records at both the Oxford and Euston Theatres. He accepted a challenge from William Jordan & Sons on December 2 and escaped from one of their milk churns rather than his usual water can.

Two nights later, he agreed to attempt an escape from a large safe. The safe was allegedly so heavy that braces had to be erected under the stage to support it, and it was large enough to hold three standing men. The release, according to one story, took Houdini 45 minutes. This report, though, was inaccurate.

In truth, the safe was a standard-sized, burglar-proof safe

that was barely big enough for one person to climb inside. It took only 14 minutes for Houdini to escape.

On December 7, Houdini jumped from the upper deck of a tugboat into the Mersey River in Liverpool. He was weighed down by 22 pounds of chains and irons. He returned to the surface of the water in 45 seconds.

The following week in Birmingham, he jumped from a houseboat, moored in the Edgbaston Reservoir during a driving rainstorm. He slipped out of his manacles in 42 seconds.

In Scotland, the Dundee police refused to permit Harry to jump from the parapet of the Tay Bridge. Hundreds of spectators had shown up to watch, and rather than disappoint them, Harry boarded a pleasure boat and, after being chained and manacled, jumped from the ship's bridge. He was free from his chains and out of the water in 30 seconds.

During his engagement at the Alhambra Theater in Paris in April 1909, Harry was frustrated because the French police refused to allow him to escape from their jails, so he decided to perform one of his stranger stunts. He sent letters to the press and to theater managers and invited them to meet him at the Pont de l'Archeveche -- the "Archbishop's Bridge" -- which crossed the Seine River.

Harry arrived by automobile just before 3:00 P.M. and brought with him a French private detective and several reporters. Houdini pulled off his coat, trousers, tie, shirt, shoes, and socks. Clad only in a swimsuit, he extended his hands, and the detective shackled them and locked a chain around his neck. His assistants erected a folding ladder, and in seconds, Harry was atop the wall of the Paris Morgue. He jumped up and down, yelled, and waved his manacled arms.

Soon, thousands of puzzled Frenchmen were pointing out the madman to their neighbors. Photographers were soon snapping photos of the spectacle and were joined by movie camera operators. Excited watchers were calling for the police when Houdini jumped off the wall and plunged into the waters of the

Seine. Once the cameramen had recorded the escape, Harry swam to the shore, slipped into an overcoat, and escaped in a waiting car.

In early June, Houdini returned to England and met Harry Rickards, Australia's leading vaudeville booker. He was in London looking for acts and saw Houdini's show at the Chelsea Music Hall. The theater was so packed that overflow seats were sold on the stage, and hundreds were turned away at the door. The show, and the audience's response to it, convinced Rickards to offer Harry a contract in Australia. It would pay him the most significant sum ever paid to a performer for a season down under. With so many other commitments already booked, Houdini's opening in Australia was set for February of the following year.

But Harry still had bookings in England to deal with, and he also had to deal with his primary irritant from the trip – a man named John Clempert, a showman who had once been a professional wrestler and then earned some fame as "The Man They Cannot Hang." Dangling by his legs from a trapeze, Clempert would attach a rope to his neck, then release his hold on the trapeze with his legs. After a breathtaking 15-foot fall, he would hang by his neck in the air. One night, however, his fall was just a little too sharp, and he seriously injured his spine. While in bed recuperating, he realized he would never be able to wrestle or do his rope trick again, so he hit upon the idea of a handcuff, chain, rope, and trunk act.

Clempert's "original" act led to him escaping from riveted boilers and packing cases and jumping off bridges. Newspapers noted that, in addition to duplicating Houdini's act as closely as he could, he was also exploiting the Water Can Escape. One writer noted, "Clempert is 'the man they could not hang.' Perhaps this is a pity..."

Since theater entertainments could be copyrighted in Great Britain, Houdini filed suit against Clempert. When his rival swore that he would discontinue stealing Houdini's feats, Harry dropped the court case, and Clempert faded away from the public eye.

Houdini continued performing in England and was too busy to return to New York for a summer holiday, so he brought his mother and Bess' mother to England for a visit. Mrs. Rahner had finally warmed up to her son-in-law during his last American tour. Better still, she and Mrs. Weiss, once they met, thoroughly enjoyed each other's company.

Everything just seemed to be getting better for the Houdini family, and soon, Harry would discover a brand-new method of escape.

He was going to be the first magician to fly.

LATER THAT SUMMER, HOUDINI RETURNED TO GERMANY FOR a series of shows, and while in Hamburg, he saw a news item about a French aviator named Grade who was going to show off his skills with a biplane.

Houdini was very interested. Aviation was one of his current obsessions, and he had once offered $5,000 for the use of the Wright brothers' airplane. He even made plans to be handcuffed and flown over London's West End. He would then parachute down, escaping from his manacles on the way, and land in Piccadilly Circus. The flight was canceled due to technical difficulties.

Houdini hired a car to take him to a local racetrack that doubled as a flying field. Fascinated, he watched the plane circle the track and then soar aloft, coming back a few minutes later for a perfect landing. He elbowed his way through the crowd and bombarded Grade with questions. Where had he learned to fly? How could Houdini learn? Where could he buy a plane? How much would it cost?

Less than a week later, in November 1909, he purchased his own Voisin biplane – even though he had no idea how to fly it.

He charmed German Army officials into permitting him to use their Hafaren parade grounds in nearby Wandsbek as a temporary airfield. Their only stipulation was that he teach the officers the mechanics of flight.

Over the course of the next several weeks, he escaped from

restraints on stage at night, and during the early daylight hours, he learned about flight from a French mechanic whom he'd hired. Cold weather, high winds, and occasional snow kept the plane on the ground, but Houdini patiently learned all there was to know about airplanes. Later,

Houdini's new Voisin plane. He learned to master it in Germany and became a skilled pilot in just a matter of weeks

he kept his promise and passed on his newly learned techniques to the cooperative German officers.

Less than a month after purchasing the plane, a confident Houdini got behind the controls of his flying machine. His mechanic spun the propeller, and the biplane smoothly lifted from the field.

Houdini made his first flight in Germany on November 26, 1909

Harry's plane was crated and shipped to Australia.

The flight, though, was a short one.

"I smashed the machine. Broke propeller all to hell," the rookie airman wrote in his diary that night. Houdini was unhurt, and the damage to the machine was slight, although it took nearly two weeks for him to get replacement parts from France. His mechanic managed to put it all back together.

Houdini made his first successful flight on November 26, 1909, over the military parade grounds. A photographer recorded the event for posterity.

Houdini with his Voisin biplane

During the rest of his engagement in Hamburg, which closed at the end of December, Harry spent all his spare time with his flying machine.

When Houdini sailed for Australia on January 7, 1910, he brought along not only his equipment for the show, but next to those crates in the ship's hold was his crated biplane, along with an extra motor and numerous spare parts. His mechanic shared a cabin with his assistant, Franz Kukol.

Houdini's first show in Australia would be at the New Opera House in Melbourne, and he publicized the show with another spectacular public stunt. On February 18, more

Houdini became the first man to fly in Australia on March 18, 1910

than 20,000 people lined the Queen's Bridge and the banks of the Yarra River to see the manacled escapologist plunge into the waters below.

A much smaller crowd was present less than a month later at Digger's Rest, a field just outside the city, when Houdini flew the first plane on the entire Australian continent.

Eager to take advantage of some good flying weather, Houdini went to the field after his show and slept in the tent that served as a hangar for his biplane. On March 16, at 5:00 A.M., Houdini's plane was wheeled out on the wooden planks that served as a take-off area. He donned a pair of goggles and a cap and climbed behind the steering wheel. He waved to Bess as the propeller started. Then, the mooring line was cast off, and the engine began to roar. The plane shot forward and up, soaring gracefully into the morning sky. Houdini circled the field and then headed back toward the runway. As the plane touched down, the assembled audience clapped and laughed with approval. Houdini came in for a perfect landing after the first sustained flight in Australian history.

Houdini made several other flights, but on April 20, the Voisin was struck by a crosswind and fell rapidly. It came in fast and low and then dipped to the ground with a heavy thud. A large rock caused one of the landing wheels to snap and break, and the plane spun sideways and stopped in a cloud of dust. Harry was unhurt, but the aircraft sustained fairly serious damage.

Bad luck continued that night at the Tivoli Theater.

During an escape stunt, three asylum attendants tied Houdini with linen bandages, rolled him like a mummy in sheets, then strapped him to an iron hospital bed frame. Buckets of water were tossed on the sheets to tighten them and make release even more difficult.

Harry began his struggle by attempting to free his feet, kicking, turning, and twisting. He then managed to slip his left hand free from the bonds. More footwork distracted the observers as he released his right hand. He squirmed an inch at a time until his head reached the railing at the end of the bed. He called Franz Kukol, who wiped the perspiration from his face with a handkerchief, then carefully tilted a glass of water for Harry to drink from.

As soon as this brief rest period was over, he started struggling again, rolling his legs from side to side. He then kicked upward until his feet were free of the sheets. A cheer went up from the audience. He now squirmed into a sitting position, and by vigorously twisting and pulling, he released his arms and then his hands.

It seemed that he was almost free, but there were still bandages tied around his knees, thighs, and chest. Finally, straining against the cloth strips, he pulled his legs out, then his midsection, then he pulled his head through the bandage around his chest. Free from the cloth strips tied to the bed, he was still wound in wet sheets. He dropped from the bed to the floor. One of the men who had challenged him to escape bent down to help him unwind from the sheets, but Harry warned him away. With a mighty effort, he suddenly rolled across the stage and jumped to his feet, completely free.

Only a man in excellent physical condition, with complete control of his muscles and careful concentration, could have beaten the challenge. It took 37 minutes of strain and tension -- with only a brief pause for a sip of water -- to do what seemed impossible.

AUSTRALIA'S FIRST AVIATOR SAILED FOR HOME ON MAY 11. A day earlier, he had supervised the loading of his repaired plane onto the ship. With the aerial triumph in Australia behind him, Harry lost the urge to pilot the plane himself. He scrapped plans to enter an air race when he returned to the United States and accepted a series of vaudeville bookings instead.

His interest in aviation continued, in any case. Houdini was in Chicago for the International Air Meet at Grant Park in August 1911. The air meet was a thrilling spectacle. Harry had the chance to meet famed flyers Orville Wright and Glenn Hammond Curtiss, who knew him only as an Australian pilot, not as a showman. They both asked him about "his country."

There were 25 planes flown in for the event. Five machines crashed on the first day, but none of the pilots were seriously injured. The tail of St. Croix Johnstone's plane was shattered, but the Chicagoan had mechanics at work on it just minutes after the crash. Lincoln Beachy, who once flew under the Suspension Bridge at Niagara Falls, was the show's star performer.

Two aviators crashed into Lake Michigan on August 14, and a biplane burned to cinders when it struck a power cable the next day. Another flyer, William Baker, crashed on the lakeshore. St. Croix Johnstone, whose plane had been repaired, nosedived 600 feet and was killed in Lake Michigan.

Flying was a perilous business in those early days.

A benefit flying show, which raised $15,000, was staged for Johnstone's widow the day after the formal air meet ended. Houdini was the star of the show. He didn't fly a plane, but he did end up in the air. With his hands and feet shackled, he jumped from a plane as it flew 50 feet above the lake, freed himself from his chains underwater, and then swam up to the beach.

If Wright and Curtiss had no idea who Houdini was before the air meet, they certainly knew who he was now.

"A SHOCK FROM WHICH I DO NOT THINK RECOVERY IS POSSIBLE."

HOUDINI RETURNED TO ENGLAND TO PERFORM THE FOLLOWING year, and while there, he hired two more assistants, James Collins and James Vickery. Both men, who stayed with him for the rest of his life, signed oaths never to reveal Houdini's secrets. Collins was an expert carpenter and metalworker, and onstage, under Franz Kukol's direction, he was an efficient aide. Offstage, though, he was put to work on Harry's most pressing problem -- the construction of a new escape to take the place of the Water Can.

Houdini was intrigued by the idea of escaping from a solid block of ice. He began trying to design it. He planned to wear a diving suit and helmet and to be lowered into a tank with a glass front. A diving helmet, he discovered, would hold about 10 minutes of air. A chemical solution that would freeze quickly would be poured into the tank, completely filling it. Once ice was formed, a curtain would surround the tank, and Harry would free himself.

It seemed simple, but it turned out to be impossible. James Collins built a tank and spent several months unsuccessfully trying to mix a solution that would freeze quickly enough for a stage show. He tried repeatedly, but it just took too long. After Houdini caught a severe cold during the tests, he abandoned the idea.

He soon devised another escape. He was sealed into an oilskin bag, which was then enclosed in a rubber bag and lowered into a water-filled tank. The top of the tank was locked in place. Behind a curtain, he freed himself and then emerged completely dry. The effect was good, but not as dramatic as Houdini hoped it would be. That escape was also scrapped.

Finally, in March, he came up with the escape that would replace the padlocked water can and become even more sensational. When completed, the new "Chinese Water Torture Cell" was crated and stored until another blockbuster attraction was needed to give a boost to his act.

While work was being done on these inventions, Houdini continued to perform all over England. In May, he attempted a double escape during a London show. He was nailed and roped into a box, which was lifted and placed into a second, larger container. This larger box was nailed and roped as securely as the first. It took him 12 minutes to slip out of both.

In Leeds, a local brewer offered to fill the Water Can with beer. Harry wasn't a drinker, but thought it would make an amusing addition to the stunt. But padlocked inside the can, Houdini was overcome by alcohol. Had it not been for quick thinking on the part of Franz Kukol, he might have drowned. He was semi-conscious when Kukol, disturbed by the silence from behind the curtain, dashed into the cabinet, broke the locks, and pulled him out.

A short time later, while in London, Houdini accepted a challenge to release himself from a "Rum Punch Hickory Barrel" at the Shepherd's Bush Empire Theater.

He made sure there was no rum in the barrel before he was locked inside.

WHEN HOUDINI RETURNED TO THE UNITED STATES IN THE FALL of 1911, he agreed to several unusual escapes. He freed himself after

being tied to the plank by three sea captains. He also escaped from a deep-sea diving suit, even after the headpiece had been bolted to the shoulders. He escaped from boxes, trunks, pianos, barrels, jails, and prisons.

In October, he accepted his strangest challenge. A "sea monster" had been found on a beach near Boston and resembled something like a cross between a whale and a giant squid. It was widely reported in the newspapers and was never identified by scientists. Taking advantage of the publicity, the Lieutenant Governor of Massachusetts dared Houdini to "play Jonah."

Harry was locked into several pairs of manacles and was forced through a slit in the semi-embalmed carcass on the stage of a theater. Assistants "sewed" the opening closed with a metal chain, wrapped more chain around the carcass, and then padlocked it. Working behind a curtain, Houdini freed himself in 15 minutes.

Afterward, he said that he would never try anything like it again. He had almost been overcome by the fumes of the embalming fluid that taxidermists had used inside the creature.

In early November, Harry was at the Temple Theater in Detroit and accepted a challenge to escape from a large bag. After he climbed in, the bag was wrapped with leather straps, but one of the straps was buckled too tightly, and it caused a blood vessel in his kidney to burst. He was unaware of the injury when it occurred – he assumed his pain was just the cost of doing his job – and bled internally for almost two weeks before he saw a doctor in Pittsburgh. The Mercy Hospital physician was shocked that Houdini had been able to continue performing without treatment.

At the doctor's insistence, Houdini grudgingly canceled his shows for the next few weeks and returned to New York, where he endured his forced respite. He had been told that he needed to rest until the injury healed, and Bess and his mother tried to keep him in bed, without much luck.

When he was forced to stay in his bedroom, Harry dictated replies to his piles of letters and correspondence, jotted down ideas for new escapes, leafed through old programs and posters in his ever-growing collection, and read scores of books that he had put aside for future study.

By December, he was back on the road. One of his first escapes was from a tank of beer in Columbus, Ohio. Since he'd nearly drowned in beer in England, Houdini had learned that he could put a coating of oil on his body to prevent the alcohol from penetrating his skin.

He did it again in January 1912 while in Philadelphia. The Bergdoll Brewing Company sent over eight gallons of lager to fill the specially designed water can. Later that month, in New York, Harry invited the owner of the Knickerbocker Brewery to send over "eight to 100 gallons" of beer. The stagehands at the theater made good use of the surplus.

In the summer of 1912, Harry came up with a new publicity stunt for his run at New York City's Hammerstein's Roof Theater. A handbill was printed announcing that on Sunday, July 7, 1912, at 11:00 A.M., Houdini would be nailed in a box and thrown into the river. He would attempt to free himself while the box was submerged.

The New York police, unlike those in other American cities, were uncooperative. They told Harry and the reporters and photographers who had assembled on Pier 6 on the East River that the stunt was canceled. So, Harry moved the act to Governors Island, outside of the jurisdiction of the NYPD. There, he was placed in manacles and leg irons and put into a heavy packing case. His

In New York, Houdini made one of his spectacular escapes from a sealed wooden box that was lowered into the water off Governors Island.

brother, Leopold, informed reporters that the box was 24 inches wide, 36 inches high, and 34 inches long.

After the lid was nailed into place, the box was tied with ropes and encircled with steel bands. Then, 200 pounds of iron were lashed to the sides of the case. The box, with Harry inside, was shoved off the side of the boat and into the water. It lurched to one side, righted itself, and then sank, leaving nothing but ripples on the surface.

Suddenly, less than a minute later, Houdini's head appeared in the water about 15 feet from where the box went down. He waved and swam to the boat. Two of his assistants and a longshoreman hauled him up. *Scientific American* magazine called it "One of the most remarkable tricks ever performed."

The stunt was so widely publicized that

Harry had a huge, 5,000-gallon tank built and installed on the stage of Hammerstein's theater. Houdini repeated the escape every night.

Two weeks later, he dreamed up an even more spectacular stunt. He was roped to the tower at the highest point of the Heidelberg Building at 42nd and Broadway at noon. Thousands watched from the street as he worked to free himself more than 300 feet above their heads.

For Harry, though, the most memorable event of the two-month run at Hammerstein's was not one of his escapes, but an event that he staged solely for his mother. He had arranged to be paid for his first week's salary in gold coins. Back home on West 113th Street, Harry told his mother to hold open her apron in her hands. He asked her if she remembered his promise to his father to look after her. She smiled and nodded her head. With a dramatic flourish, Houdini made the coins appear, and they rained down into the apron.

There was little he wouldn't do to make Cecilia Weiss happy.

BY THIS TIME, HOUDINI WAS, AT AGE 38, THE BEST-KNOWN mystery performer in the world. He soon earned even more acclaim with the introduction of his "Chinese Water Torture Cell," which he was finally ready to take out of storage. It was first shown publicly during his engagement in Germany with the Circus Busch. The heavy metal-lined mahogany tank with a thick glass front could withstand the most rigid examination. It was filled with water while the escapologist changed into his bathing suit.

A committee of volunteers had been chosen prior to the show, and they examined the tank, along with the cage that was to be lowered into the water-filled chamber. After they snapped the cuffs on Houdini's wrists, they also examined the heavy enclosures on his ankles and the massive frame that was fitted over them.

Houdini was then hauled upward, turned upside down, and lowered into the water. Assistants locked the top of the tank and

Harry introduced the Chinese Water Torture Cell into his act in 1912, and it remained a staple until the end of his career.

moved a steel frame over it with curtains attached. Houdini – upside down and submerged in the tank -- was visible through the glass on the front of the tank until the curtains around it were closed. Two assistants stood by with axes in hand, ready to break the glass in case of emergency.

Suspenseful minutes passed, and then Houdini parted the curtains to show-stopping applause. He would perform the Chinese Water Torture escape for the rest of his career.

Houdini returned home to the United States that summer because he wanted to spend time with his mother. Cecilia, who was now 72, had become frail over the last few years, and her health was failing. Harry played a single, month-long engagement at Hammerstein's Roof Theater so that he could be close to her. She sat in the front row of the theater during the American debut of the new Chinese Water Torture Cell and led the applause for her beloved son.

Confident that she was feeling better, Harry made plans to return to Europe for another series of shows. He had initially planned to postpone them, but Cecilia urged him to go. She even helped plan a bon voyage party for him, held on the day before his ship was scheduled to sail. Harry asked her what he should bring her home from Europe, but she couldn't think of anything that she wanted or needed. But to make him feel better, she said that she wanted a pair of woolen slippers.

When she returned home after his ship departed, Cecilia followed the familiar ritual of winding the clock, which she never touched while Erich was home.

Harry's brother, Theo, was scheduled to perform as Hardeen in Asbury Park, New Jersey, on July 14, so he took Cecilia with him to enjoy some time on the shore. When they arrived, he publicized that night's performance by jumping from the end of the fishing pier and escaping from manacles and chains. Billed as the "brother of Houdini," Theo accepted challenges to escape from handcuffs and slipped out of a straitjacket and a water can, all with his brother's blessing.

But that night, after the show had ended and Cecilia returned to the Imperial Hotel, she suffered a massive stroke. Stricken by paralysis and unable to speak, doctors were quickly summoned to her suite. Dr. James Ackerman was the first to examine her and pronounced her condition serious. Theo immediately telephoned his sister, Gladys, in New York, and she arrived early the next morning. Dr. Ackerman examined Cecilia again after Gladys arrived, and he put her on the critical list.

Theo continued his obligations at the Lyric Theater, rushing back to the hotel at the end of the night. On Wednesday, July 16, he was at his mother's bedside when she tried to tell him something about Harry but couldn't get the words out. She fell asleep a few moments later, and she never woke up.

Cecilia Weiss died a few minutes before midnight.

ACROSS THE ATLANTIC, HOUDINI OPENED AT THE CIRKUS Beketow in Copenhagen on the night that his mother died. Two members of the Danish royal family, Princes Aage and Axel, were in the audience. Harry delivered his stage patter in Danish and received a standing ovation.

At noon the following day, Thursday, July 17, Harry was being

Houdini with his mother, who he adored. Erich was always Cecilia's favorite son, and she missed him desperately when he was traveling abroad. After her death, Houdini did everything he could to try and get in touch with her again, which would eventually lead to his exposure of fraudulent spirit mediums.

interviewed by newspapermen in the theater vestibule when a telegram arrived for him. Houdini ripped open the envelope and discovered that his beloved mother had died.

He fell unconscious to the floor.

The hotel doctor was quickly summoned and prescribed immediate hospitalization. Houdini objected, so he ordered him to at least get some rest, which Harry also refused to do. Instead, he began making arrangements to return to New York. The Cirkus Beketow sympathetically released Harry from his Copenhagen contract, and he canceled the rest of his European bookings.

But performing was not on Harry's mind. There was only one thing he needed to do – to get home. He desperately needed to see his mother's face one last time before she was laid to rest. He cabled Theo and ordered him to delay the funeral until he could return. Houdini booked immediate passage on a ship sailing for New York. He was under a doctor's care during the entire voyage.

When the ship arrived in New York, Houdini went straight to Cecilia's home. All the furniture on the first floor had been rearranged for the funeral, shocking Harry again with the strangeness of his mother's rooms. Cecilia's body had been laid out in a

casket in the parlor. His legs shook as he walked over to her. He looked down at the familiar lines of Cecilia's face, then leaned down and pressed his ear to her chest. The heartbeat that had always reassured him as a small boy was now silent.

On his way to the ship that brought him home, Harry had recalled his mother's wish for woolen slippers, size 6, and he had purchased a pair. He took those slippers from his pocket and tearfully placed them in the casket next to Cecilia's body.

At some point later that night, Harry stopped the grandfather clock that his mother always wound when he was away. It would never make a sound again.

After the funeral, Harry visited the cemetery each day. Occasionally, in the darkest hours of the night, Bess would hear him call his mother's name. During the day, he read and re-read the letters that Cecilia had written to him over the years. Later, he had them translated into English so that he could read them more effortlessly. It was the only way that he had to keep a little part of her alive.

Cecilia's death was the greatest blow that Harry ever suffered. He often said that the death of his mother had been "a shock from which I do not think recovery is possible."

MONTHS PASSED WITH HOUDINI BURIED IN HIS GRIEF.

It was not until September that he was able to force himself back to work. He opened at the Apollo Theater while still in mourning. A black armband was added to his clothing for every show, and when he sent letters, he only used stationery that was surrounded by a heavy black border. For the first several weeks, he went through the motions during his performances, adding little to the show that wasn't scripted. This went on for weeks as he struggled to recover from his devastating loss. Eventually, though, his old desire to produce a big magic show slowly returned.

But the reminders were always there. A supper was held in his honor at the Magician's Club, and during a short speech, Houdini spoke about his mother:

My mother was everything to me. It seemed like the end of the world when she was taken from me. Not until she lay dying did I realize how inexpressibly futile is a man's intelligence and determination when face-to-face with death. When her last hour came, I thought mine would soon follow. Everything seemed to turn to dust and ashes for me. All desire for fame and fortune had gone from me. I was alone with my bitter agony. But time, the great healer, has brought me some measure of solace.

In mid-April 1914, the "king of escapologists" gave himself a new title. He also made a deal with many of the theater managers who booked his Water Cell escape act to offer a special all-magic performance during the week. For these special occasions, handbills were printed that read:

The World-Famous Self-Liberator
HOUDINI
The Supreme Ruler of Magic will present a
GRAND MAGICAL REVUE
*In which he will prove himself to be the Greatest Mystifier that
History Chronicles, introducing a number of problems from his
inexhaustible repertoire.*
WHICH WILL BE SEEN FOR THE FIRST TIME ON ANY STAGE!

Despite the bombastic wording, there was little that was new or amazing in the Houdini magical revue. He offered a vanishing assistant, coins that disappeared from his fingers and appeared in a glass box, standard illusions, and a revival of the old "Metamorphosis" stunt. Bess, who hadn't appeared with Harry on stage since he had dropped it from the act, was happy to return to working with him on this and other illusions.

In May, Houdini purchased a brilliant trick, "Walking through a Steel Wall," from London magician Sidney Josolyne. He decided to delay its initial presentation until his summer engagement at Hammerstein's in New York.

He also purchased the "Expanding Cube," a small square that grew to reveal a girl beneath it. He obtained that one from Leah Goldston, wife of Will Goldston, a British magician and magic dealer. The cube was the final creation of Buatier De Kolta, an American magician who was a contemporary of Robert-Houdin. Houdini presented this illusion in the last showing of his magic revue at the Empire Theater in Nottingham.

Despite the money and effort that went into it, the all-magic program was not a resounding success. Houdini was an adequate conjurer, but his real skills were in performing his spectacular escapes. Bookers who saw the all-magic show urged Harry to concentrate on the Water Cell act and his other escapes, which always managed to get him top dollar from theater owners.

Houdini tended to bristle whenever he was offered unsolicited advice about how to perform his shows, but he grudgingly agreed that the bookers were probably right. His escapes were what his audiences wanted, not sleight-of-hand tricks.

He didn't know then that his shows would soon gain a new element that would thrill some spectators, while angering many others.

WHEN HOUDINI ARRANGED FOR PASSAGE BACK TO AMERICA at the end of his latest European tour, he was told in confidence that former president Theodore Roosevelt would be on the same ship.

Houdini with former president Theodore Roosevelt, for whom he performed a "seance"

Though both men were from very different worlds, they had discovered the similarities in their personalities when they'd met previously. Each man was curious, had the impulsive energy of a much younger man, and each pursued his goals with relentless energy.

Houdini wanted to give Roosevelt a thrill on the voyage. Initially, he wanted to leap handcuffed into the North Atlantic and free himself, but the ship's captain forbade the stunt. So, Harry came up with another clever idea – he'd hold a séance on board the ship.

Roosevelt had always had a mild interest in the supernatural, although the miracles in the Bible seemed more real to him. Even so, he had become increasingly aware of his own mortality. His recent, ill-conceived expedition to South America and the River of

Doubt had been too much for him. Two members of his party had died in the jungle, and he, delirious from a fever caused by an infection, came close to being buried there as the third. His health never recovered from this adventure.

Harry hadn't performed a séance in years, but he was excited to do it for his friend. President Roosevelt was the guest of honor at the shipboard show. Harry asked the audience to write down questions on slips of paper. As Roosevelt wrote, he was advised to turn his back so that Harry couldn't decipher the words by watching the motion of the top of his pencil. Roosevelt then folded the paper and dropped it between two blank slates, which Houdini tied together. As instructed, Roosevelt then announced what his question had been: "Where was I last Christmas?"

Immediately, Harry parted the two slates to reveal a copy of a map, colorfully drawn with chalk, of the River of Doubt, the remote Brazilian waterway that Roosevelt had been navigating over the holiday.

Roosevelt roared in amazement. He had only just thought of the question, so there had been no time for an elaborate ruse. Then another wave of excitement came over him when he discovered that the map had been signed by the late British journalist W.T. Stead and that he had been the spirit responsible for the reply. Stead, a Spiritualist medium, had sailed to America at the behest of the spirits but had unfortunately booked passage on the *Titanic* and was lost in the frigid waters of the Atlantic.

News of the séance was transmitted to New York and Washington, and no one could figure out how Houdini had done it. The morning after the séance, Roosevelt put his arm around Houdini and asked him, man-to-man, if the phenomena of the previous evening had been "genuine Spiritualism."

With a smile and a wink, Houdini replied., "It was hocus-pocus, Colonel."

That ended Roosevelt's brief fascination with Spiritualism, even if Houdini never confessed how the trick had been accomplished.

What Houdini didn't tell the former president was that when he'd learned he'd be traveling with the former president – and his idea of jumping from the ship was rejected – he'd taken a taxi to the offices of the city's newspaper. The paper was publishing a series written by Roosevelt about his South American expedition. Thanks to a reporter friend at the paper, Harry soon had a copy of a Roosevelt map that hadn't been published yet, as well as information about the expedition that was still unknown to the public.

He knew that Roosevelt couldn't resist asking a question about the recent expedition, so Houdini was prepared with the map and his "spirit slates."

IN JULY 1914, HOUDINI OPENED HIS THIRD SUMMER SEASON IN a row at Hammerstein's Roof Theater. He used two escapes from submerged boxes in the East River to announce to New Yorkers that he was back in town.

At the start of his third week at the theater, he introduced a new stunt -- "Walking Through a Brick Wall." It had started as the steel wall illusion he'd bought in England, but Houdini felt it would be more effective if audiences could see a brick wall being built right on stage. Twice daily, bricklayers constructed a nine-foot brick wall inside a steel frame that was mounted on a wheeled base. To prevent accusations that a trapdoor could be used for the stunt, a rug was unrolled on the stage, and then a large square of muslin was placed on top of it.

A committee of audience members inspected the wall before it was rolled into position at the center of the muslin. One end of it was turned toward the crowd. Houdini, in a long white coat, stood to the left of the wall. A six-foot-high, three-fold screen blocked the view of the audience, but they could see the bricks above and to the sides of the screen. Another screen was placed on the opposite side of the wall.

As he prepared to walk forward, Harry raised his hands above the screen and waved them about. He shouted, "Here I am!"

The hands vanished from view, and he called out, "Now I'm gone."

The screen behind which he had been standing was pulled away, and Houdini was nowhere to be seen. When the screen on the other side of the wall was opened, though, the audience saw Harry standing there, smiling enigmatically.

The crowd roared. The applause and cheers were deafening. No one could figure out how the stunt had been performed.

He baffled the audience that first night, and he continued to thrill every crowd that saw it on the nights that followed. Once, he performed it with 30 spectators surrounding the structure, leaving only the front unobstructed so that the audience could have a clear view. The *Sunday World* Magazine devoted a full page to the puzzling feat -- which still amazes audiences to this day.

HOUDINI REMAINED IN AMERICA DURING THE NEXT FEW years. The Great War began in Europe in 1914, and theaters were closed there for the duration of the conflict.

With time on his hands, Houdini perfected a new publicity stunt to bring crowds into theaters – a straitjacket escape performed while dangling high in the air, upside

down, and suspended from the top of a building. More than 20,000 people turned out to watch him slip out of his bindings in Providence, Rhode Island. Another 50,000 turned out in Baltimore, and twice that many gathered in the nation's capital to watch him defy death. Houdini ended the stunt each time by letting the straitjacket fall a dozen stories or more to the street below. Then, he extended his arms and took a bow while still hanging in mid-air.

In August 1914, before going back on the road, Houdini entertained the prisoners at Sing Sing, the first major magician to perform behind the penitentiary's walls since Alexander Herrmann in 1896. Houdini kept the convicts' attention for three solid hours. Films were shown of his miraculous escapes, playing cards rose from an isolated pack at his command, a rabbit appeared from an empty box, and there was an unexpected reaction when Harry borrowed a watch and conjured it into the center of a load of bread. Houdini later wrote, "When I broke the loaf in half, two convicts grabbed the bread and ate it. It was white bread, and I think they only get gray or black... Next time I'll produce it in the midst of a pound cake."

He later said that he'd never had an audience that was so completely enthralled. Every motion of his hands, every slip out of a handcuff, and every escape from a straitjacket, water can, or wooden crate was carefully watched.

But the rapt attention paid to his escapes by one prisoner ended in a way no one expected – it inspired the man, sentenced to life behind bars, to make a successful prison break a few weeks later.

ON JUNE 12, 1917, TWO MONTHS AFTER THE UNITED STATES entered the Great War, Houdini registered for the draft.

At the age of 43, he likely knew that he would not be inducted, but he used the opportunity to offer his services performing at training camps and in Red Cross shows. He also staged a straitjacket escape high above Broadway as members of the Society of American Magicians and their wives sold war bonds in the street. Houdini had recently been elected president of the prestigious society, and, under his leadership, new affiliates were formed all over the country.

He had tried, when he played the Palace Theater a year earlier, to get permission from Police Inspector Thomas V. Underhill to stage his straitjacket escape over Broadway. The request had been refused, but now Elsa Maxwell, the gossip columnist, author, songwriter, and soon-to-be-known-as-America's most famous hostess, secured a permit for him. The Society of American Magicians gave her a gold medal in appreciation. Handbills for the fundraising event were passed out to the thousands of people who lined the streets to see Houdini's traffic-stopping stunt.

Houdini's persuasive powers managed to bring Harry Kellar, the dean of American magicians, out of retirement in Los Angeles to make a "farewell appearance" at the benefit show. The evening began with seven magicians working side by side on the stage. To finish their act, they produced a red banner with S.A.M. (the initials for the Society of American Magicians) on it in gold letters. They strung it from man to man and departed from the stage.

Raymond Hitchcock, a musical comedian, offered a burlesque conjuring act. Other magicians rolled up their sleeves before they worked their tricks. Hitchcock rolled up his trouser legs. Arnold de Biere, a noted magician, acted as his assistant. Julius Zancig and his wife, Agnes, sent and received thoughts. Takasi produced his Asian assistant from an empty sedan chair, linked and unlinked steel rings, and tore and restored tissue paper.

Then, Houdini took the spotlight. He was there, he said, to introduce America's greatest illusionist, who had made the trip from California to aid in a cause that was close to his heart. It was a moment of great humility for Harry, who was used to promoting his own name rather than that of someone else.

The crowd called out a deafening welcome to the tall, bald, sun-tanned Kellar. A table floated in the air when the aging magician touched it with his fingertips. He was tied inside a

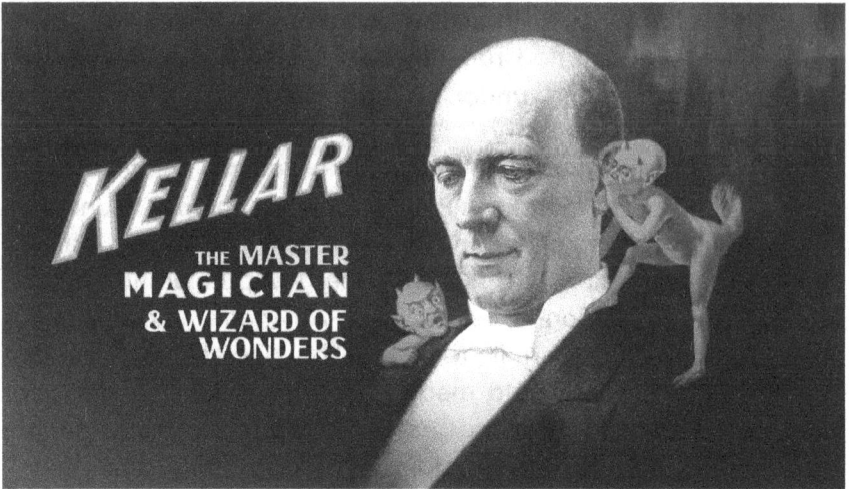

KELLAR

THE MASTER
MAGICIAN
& WIZARD OF
WONDERS

Houdini with Harry Kellar, who he often referred to as "America's Greatest Magician"

cabinet, from which he produced "spirit" phenomena. The great artist conjured up an amazing night of magical memories from days gone by.

After his final illusion, Kellar took a deep bow and turned to leave the stage. The applause literally shook the theater, and Houdini stopped him from leaving. He signaled the crowd to be silent. He could not allow Kellar to simply walk off the stage after his final performance.

Members of the society emerged from the wings with a sedan chair, and Kellar sat down on the cushioned seat. The chair was shouldered by magicians and paraded around the stage as he was showered with flowers. The audience stood, joined hands, and sang "Auld Lang Syne" as Kellar, with a final wave of his hand, was taken off into the shadows of backstage.

But there was still more show to come. Houdini performed his trunk illusion and the Water Cell escape. Louise Homer sang "The Star-Spangled Banner." A detachment of French sailors drilled with the red, white, and blue flags of the two nations, but the evening finally reached its peak when Kellar returned to the stage one last time to take a final bow.

Charles Dillingham, the producer at the Hippodrome, was so impressed by Houdini's staging of the affair that he asked him to create something spectacular at the theater in the months ahead. He had no idea at the time that Houdini would be creating what was perhaps the greatest illusion of his career.

On January 7, 1918, Houdini introduced the biggest illusion ever staged at the New York Hippodrome -- or perhaps anywhere else. He called it the "Vanishing Elephant," and for this trick, he obtained the services of Jennie, a 10,000-pound elephant, who was placed inside a wooden box that was roughly the size of a small garage.

Other magicians vanished doves and rabbits and sometimes even horses and donkeys, but no one

Harry with Jennie the Elephant, whom he made disappear at the Hippodrome. This feat has never been duplicated.

before Houdini dared to attempt the disappearance of an elephant. Harry's friend, Charles Morritt, baffled audiences in England with a "Disappearing Donkey," and he was the one who originally conceived the idea that Houdini would turn the Hippodrome stunt. When he described it to Houdini, Harry immediately bought the exclusive worldwide performing rights.

Once Jennie was inside the box with her trainer, Harry fired a pistol. His assistants opened the front curtains and removed a circular section at the back of the box to allow the audience to see through the stage curtains at the rear --- the elephant was gone! Curiously, no one seemed to notice that the trainer vanished along with the elephant.

"With this baffling mystery," wrote Sime Silverman, the editor of *Variety*, "Houdini puts his title of escape artist behind him and becomes the Master Magician."

Hippodrome patrons knew the animal could not have gone through a trapdoor. Beneath the stage was the famous Hippodrome pool. Later in the show, Houdini escaped from a box that was lowered into the water. A critic from the *Brooklyn Eagle* noted, "The program says that the elephant vanished into thin air. The trick is performed fifteen feet from the backdrop, and the cabinet is slightly elevated. That explanation is as good as any."

Some magicians said that vanishing an elephant wasn't much of a trick, but when pressed to explain it, none of them could. Three illusionists announced that they would have their own disappearing elephants the following season. One, Harry Blackstone, claimed that he had invented the illusion but could not offer a shred of evidence to prove it.

Houdini had been booked for six weeks at the theater with this illusion, but the impact of the stunt prolonged the engagement to 19 weeks, the longest theater engagement of his career.

If there had been any doubts about it before this, they had vanished like Jennie the elephant – Houdini had finally made it to the top.

HOUDINI AT THE MOVIES

BY THIS TIME, HOUDINI'S CAREER HAD FINALLY REACHED THE heights he had always dreamed about, but he was as troubled as he was famous. His grief over his mother's death had never gone away, and, in some ways, it had become worse, bordering on obsession. He visited the cemetery where she'd been buried on a regular basis and had been observed lying down on her grave several times, having long conversations with her.

But, of course, those conversations were all one-sided. He wanted nothing more than to speak to his mother again and have her answer. That was when he returned to Spiritualism, the still thriving movement that promised communication with the loved ones who had been lost.

Houdini knew fraudulent mediums existed – he had conducted fake séances of his own years earlier – but he also knew many serious, upstanding, and honest people claimed to be mediums or spoke of their contacts with the spirit world. Surely, if the entire Spiritualist movement were a fraud, those people would not continue to support it.

Hoping for the best, Harry began seeking out the most acclaimed mediums in New York City – only to be disappointed over and over again. The mediums that he visited tried to pass off cheap magic tricks as the work of the spirits. He only found chicanery that he could – and had – duplicate on the stage. Soon, his efforts to speak with his mother became secondary to his need to expose the frauds.

His hope turned to bitterness. Fake mediums had taken his love for his mother and trampled all over it. They had lured him in with false promises and given him trickery in return. He was angry, wounded, and missing Cecilia more than when he had started his quest.

And soon, Harry Houdini went looking for revenge.

AT THE SAME TIME, HOUDINI'S CAREER REMAINED ON THE rise. Before he closed at the Hippodrome, he signed a contract with B.F. Rolfe of Octagon Films to star in a movie serial called *The Master Mystery.* Houdini played Quentin Locke, an undercover agent for the Justice Department, who used his expertise as an escape artist to thwart the efforts of the villain of the serial. In various installments of the series, Houdini's character was buried alive in a gravel pit, tied in the bottom of an elevator shaft as the car was

lowered to crush him, suspended upside down over boiling acid, and even strapped into an electric chair. Somehow, though, he always survived.

Houdini didn't fare as well as Quentin Locke, though. He broke three bones in his left wrist while filming one of the early scenes, but production continued. In those days, actors usually did their own stunts, and Houdini was performing even more hazardous escapes than he did on stage – without the safety measures that his assistants arranged. When he

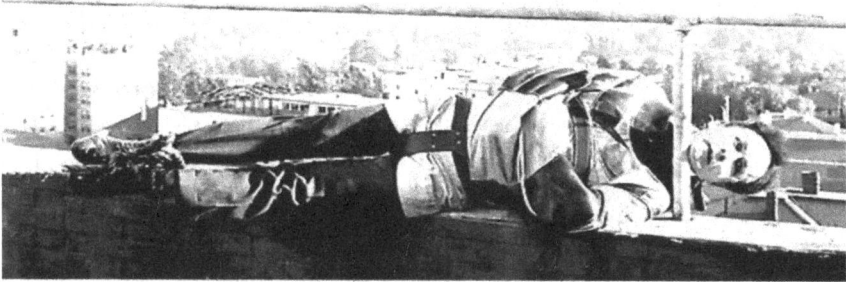

returned to the Hippodrome in August, he had to wear a leather wrist support as his bones healed, but he managed all his stage escapes and illusions without fail.

In the spring of 1919, Houdini made his first Hollywood feature film, *The Grim Game*, for Paramount Pictures. The plot of the film was designed to present the escape artist at his daredevil best. He broke out of a jail cell, climbed the exterior of a building to reach a dangling rope, and then used it to slide to the street. Captured after a fight, Houdini was taken to a rooftop, strapped in a straitjacket, and suspended upside down over the side. He released himself, fell into an awning, and dropped to the ground. Moments later, he rolled under the wheels of a moving truck, grasped the underside, and rode away beneath it. Later, he was caught in a rope-sling bear trap and tossed into a well.

If you're reading this and wondering what the story was behind this plot, well, there really wasn't one. It was really just one stunt and escape after another, loosely following some sort of secret agent storyline.

One of the escapes in the film called for Harry to make a plane-to-plane transfer in mid-air, but things didn't go exactly according to plan. As the two aircraft maneuvered into position, they collided, became locked together, and spiraled to the earth. Director Irvin Willat, following in a third plane, kept his camera running. The two flying machines managed to separate before they crashed into a bean field. Miraculously, no one was seriously

JESSE L. LASKY presents,

HOUDINI

IN

"The GRIM GAME"

By Arthur B Reeve and John W Grey Directed by Irvin Willat

A Paramount-Artcraft Picture

injured.

The footage was used in the film. Luckily, there was no need to rewrite the script to include the accident footage, so it had no story to start with.

But there was more to the crash than most people knew. One of Houdini's best-kept secrets was that he was not on the plane when it went down. His left arm was in a sling at the time. He had fallen a mere three feet during the jail escape sequence and fractured his wrist again. A double was used for the plane-to-plane switch, and other doubles were used for some of the more hazardous feats in the movie.

None of the other doubles lived to reveal that Houdini didn't do his own stunts. They weren't killed during filming – they were dummies dressed in the same costumes Harry wore in the film. They were filmed in long shots so that no one could see their painted faces, and then studio close-ups of the star were inserted to create the illusion that he performed breathtaking escapes that even Houdini himself would

Houdini and Charlie Chaplin

not risk.

After *The Grim Game* was completed, Harry returned to New York to take over the management of Martinka's magic shop, which had been purchased by Houdini's friend Charles J. Carter in 1917. Two years later, Carter had fallen into poor health and was broke, so Houdini formed a company to purchase it from his friend.

While he was in New York, *The Grim Game* opened at the Broadway Theater. The publicity campaign featured the plane accident in mid-air. Houdini offered $1,000 to anyone who could prove the collision had been faked. Like all Houdini challenges, it was a safe bet to make.

Harry barely had time to go through the stock of Martinka's and put aside choice pieces for his personal collection before returning to Hollywood to star in another Paramount film. The filming of *Terror Island* began in September, and while a new film, it followed the old formula of fast action, wild escapes, and spectacular stunts.

Motion pictures had become, as aviation had been a few years before, Houdini's major obsession. He sold his share of the magic shop and started a film-developing corporation, which lost massive amounts of money. Houdini

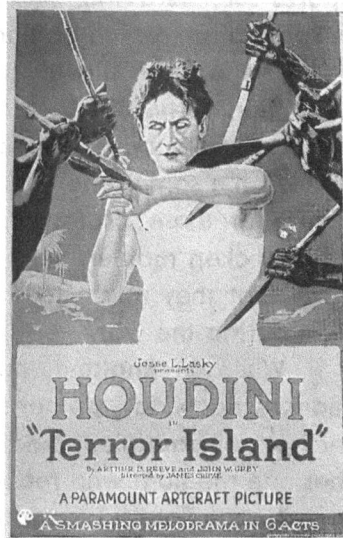

persuaded his brother Theo to leave the road and manage it, but this was not enough to turn things around. Harry Kellar, an investor in the company, advised Houdini to give it up, but he wouldn't listen. He used a good portion of his income to try to keep the business afloat.

He was spending more money, so he needed to make more to replace what he was losing, which meant it was time to go back on tour. It had been six years since Houdini had performed in England, and theater managers there were asking him to honor contracts that the war had postponed. *The Master Mystery* had been a success in Britain, and demand for his act had risen, thanks to the film. He would return to England, and this time, he wouldn't be just a vaudeville headliner; he'd be an American movie star, too. He sailed for England in late December 1919.

While working in England, Harry's friend, Will Goldston, suggested that he put together an outline for a book, *Magical Ties and Escapes*. Another project that took up more of his time was research for a book about the history of Spiritualism.

In the aftermath of the Great War, fascination with the movement had exploded. The British press reported that noted figures such as author Sir Arthur Conan Doyle were firm believers in Spiritualism, which baffled Houdini. He couldn't understand how Doyle, who had shown such keen powers of reasoning and deduction in his Sherlock Holmes stories, could be deceived by simple tricks in dark séance rooms.

At the same time, Houdini was appalled by the cold-hearted nature of those professional mediums who took advantage of grief-stricken mothers and widows who flocked to séances in the hope that they might talk with the sons and husbands who had died during the war.

While in England, he began attending as many as two séances each day, gathering material for his book, studying the methods of fraudulent mediums --- and perhaps still hoping to find that one medium who really could make contact with the dead.

Houdini visited more than 100 mediums during his 1920 British tour. Despite his self-proclaimed open mind, he found no evidence that communication with the dead was anything other than self-deception or purposeful trickery.

"The more I investigate," Houdini wrote, "the less I can make myself believe."

In March, Harry injured his right ankle while escaping from the Water Torture Cell. During his doctor-ordered week of recuperation, he put his Spiritualism notes in order. He felt there was a pressing need for a debunking book on spirit phenomena, and he planned to use his trip home to America to begin working on it.

As Houdini gathered those notes, he had no idea how his research into the supernatural would not only change his life and career but would also end a friendship that was only just beginning at that point.

During that tour, Houdini met a man with whom he would have a strange friendship that lasted for just two years. That man was the famous author Sir Arthur Conan Doyle, and their meeting began a friendly but often contentious relationship.

Doyle believed that Spiritualism was of great importance to the world, while Houdini actively campaigned against it and its "mediumistic parlor tricks." The two men, both of whom possessed a vast knowledge of the supernatural. They argued long and inconclusively about the reality of Spiritualism but remained friends despite their differences, each continually trying to convince the other of his point of view.

The friendship only ended because of what Houdini considered a terrible betrayal, and the rift that developed between them was never repaired. It resulted in both public and private battles that lasted until Houdini's death in 1926.

A HAUNTED FRIENDSHIP

WHEN THE GREAT WAR HAD BEEN DECLARED, SIR ARTHUR Conan Doyle had been one of the first Englishmen to enlist. Though he was 55 years old, he was a brave man of great energy. He still played a respectable game of cricket, was skilled at billiards, skied the Alpine slopes, raced motorcars, and was a crack shot with both an Enfield rifle and a sidearm. Respectfully, though, the War Board turned him down, and he resigned himself to training the boys and old men in the Home Guard.

There were a few civilians, though, who were as informed about the progress of British troops as he was because, even though he was officially a mere deputy lieutenant in the Civilian Reserve, Sir Arthur performed many duties for the Crown. That included propaganda writing for the military and his urgent promotion to the young men of England to take up arms in the country's defense. He urged them to fight, and to the trenches they went.

From the beginning, it had been a ghostly war. Otherworldly beings had been reported in the sky over Mon in Belgium, where, in their first action, the British Expeditionary Force was overwhelmed by German forces. Clouds in the shape of spectral warriors were rumored to have protected the small army during its retreat. Firsthand reports of these spirits were hard to come by, and yet it became widely accepted in England that a miracle had occurred.

But Sir Arthur was not so sure about that. The Germans had met the best riflemen in Europe, firing 15 rounds a minute. Had they really needed ghostly archers that day?

The battle affected Sir Arthur in a more personal way. His brother-in-law and close friend, Malcolm Leckie, had served bravely as a medical officer at Mons and had died there.

When a soldier died at the front, the soldiers would say that he'd "gone west." Sir Arthur was fond of that expression. It suggested to him that a young man had taken a distant journey but was not lost to his comrades

Sir Arthur Conan Doyle

or his family. He might be reached by some unusual mode of long-distance communication, such as through automatic writing or through a spirit medium.

As it happened, there was a young woman in Sir Arthur's home at Crowborough in East Sussex who claimed that she was a channel to the place where the dead waited to speak to the living.

The clairvoyant was his wife's best friend, and her name was Lily Loder-Symonds. She had originally served the Doyles as a nanny. Unfortunately, she developed a chest ailment that caused her to give up her childcare duties. Her condition worsened after three of her brothers were killed at the Battle of Ypres, but, by that time, the Doyles had practically adopted her as a member of the family, and she never left. On warm days, Sir Arthur often read to her in the garden, where they could hear the dull rumble of great guns across the English Channel.

Later, in the evenings, in a room that smelled of flowers and medicine, Lily often took up a pen and practiced spirit communication.

Sir Arthur later confessed that he was dubious about Lily's powers. But one night, as he and his wife, Lady Jean, sat at a small table in Lily's bedroom, something occurred that changed his mind about Lily and about the reality of Spiritualism itself.

In a trance, Lily claimed that she saw a soldier waving a gold coin and asking to speak to Sir Arthur. It was Malcolm Leckie – and that night became the first time he communicated with a dead man.

There was no way that Lily could have known that the two men had long shared a private joke about the gold coin the dead man was holding. He had given it to Sir Arthur as his first "fee" when he became a doctor. Doyle had cherished the small token and wore it on his watch chain. And now, after his death, Malcolm was reminding his friend of that coin so he could convince Sir Arthur of the reality of Spiritualism.

A single gold coin, it seemed, was a small price to pay for a miracle.

ARTHUR CONAN DOYLE WAS BORN IN EDINBURGH, SCOTLAND, on May 22, 1859. He was the eldest son of Charles Doyle, an assistant surveyor in the Scottish Office of Works, and Mary Foley, an Irish Catholic woman whose mother was Charles Doyle's landlady. Charles Doyle supplemented his earnings from his civil service job with money he made from painting and illustrating books. He was a dreamy, artistic figure who suffered from alcoholism and epilepsy, and after leaving his job while he was in his forties, he spent most of the remainder of his life in mental asylums.

As a boy, Doyle attended a Jesuit preparatory school and was then sent to Stonyhurst, another Catholic institution, at age 11. He hated it – the Spartan conditions, the corporal punishment, the bad food – and while he had initially considered dedicating his life to the church, he became disenchanted with Catholicism. He decided to pursue a medical career instead. He endured school while excelling in sports and passed his graduate exam with honors at age 16. Since his family could not afford to send him to college, he worked and attended medical school at the same time. He graduated in 1881 with a degree in biology.

Doyle began his career as a young doctor with an interest in writing stories and going on adventures.

Doyle was eager to own a medical practice but had also developed a love for writing. He hoped to supplement his practice by selling short stories to the magazines of the day. He sold a story or two and then, looking for adventure before settling into a practice, he signed on as a ship's surgeon for a whaler that was making a seven-month voyage to the Arctic.

But even a trip to the Arctic didn't quench his thirst for action. He signed on to another ship after his return. This time, he served as a ship's doctor on a voyage taking cargo down the west coast of Africa. This adventure turned out to be far less enjoyable. He became extremely ill, likely with malaria. This finally cured his wanderlust, and he used the money he'd earned to start a medical practice in the small town of Southsea.

He spent the next eight years as a village doctor, making little money, but supplementing what little he was earning by selling stories to literary magazines. He wrote historical stories, action tales, horror thrillers, and more – anything that caught his fancy.

Then, in 1886, he penned his first mystery about a detective named Sherlock Holmes but found it impossible to sell it. He eventually received a small sum for it, but the publisher told him

Doyle wrote many stories and several novels, including his first Sherlock Holmes stories, before he decided to give up medicine and write full-time.

that it wouldn't be printed for at least a year. The market, they said, was already flooded with cheap fiction."

The story, called "A Study in Scarlet," appeared in *Beeton's Christmas Annual* for 1887 and met with success, but Doyle had no interest in being merely a writer of short detective stories. Instead, he wrote a lengthy historical novel called *Micah Clarke*. The book appeared in 1889 and was another immediate success. Six more stories about Sherlock Holmes followed in the new *Strand Magazine*, and an American publisher requested a Holmes novel, spurring Doyle to write *The Sign of the Four*. Doyle meant to write only those stories about Sherlock Holmes and no more. He thought of himself as a serious novelist, and the Holmes stories were merely a distraction to him. However, when the publishers offered huge sums for additional tales, Doyle surrendered, and more Sherlock Holmes stories followed.

Even with all his success, though, he still saw himself as a doctor first. Writing was still only a way to make extra money for him, even after he became so busy meeting the demands of his literary work that his brother, Innes, had to move to Southsea to assist with the medical practice.

In 1885, Doyle married Louise Hawkins, a sweet and docile woman who remained in the background, often overshadowed by her larger-than-life husband. In 1889, their daughter Mary was born. Tragically, though, Louise was diagnosed with tuberculosis in 1893 and was given only a few months to live.

In the depths of his despair over his wife's impending death, Doyle moved his family and medical practice to London. He rented space in Devonshire Place, at the top of Wimpole Street. It was a quiet and ideal location -- for writing. Rarely did a patient darken his doorstep. He spent most of his time writing, and it was here that he created his next set of Sherlock Holmes stories.

The immediate success of those stories, the lack of patients, and a severe bout with influenza that nearly killed him made his next decision an easy one -- he would

Doyle's first wife, Louise Hawkins, whose life was tragically cut short by tuberculosis

give up his medical work and turn all his attention to writing.

Doyle was in his early thirties by this time, and over the next decade, he became increasingly more successful and one of the country's most visible public figures. He was someone that most men aspired to be like. He looked more like a sportsman than a man of letters, was a robust outdoorsman and an avid boxer, adept at rugby and cricket.

He was also, like many men and women of his generation, concerned about religion. He gave up his Catholic faith while still a young man and, for a time, was an agnostic. While living in Southsea, he became interested in psychical research and began reading heavily on the subject. He also had the opportunity to visit séances and attend experiments in telepathy and thought transference. His search for answers led to a meeting with Sir Oliver Lodge, one of the leading paranormal investigators of the time, and in 1893, he joined the Society for Psychical Research. He watched with interest the public's fascination with Spiritualism but did not understand how what he knew about the movement could inspire the kind of belief that people seemed to have in it.

It was interesting, but he was skeptical – for now.

Tragically, his personal life had not fared as well as his professional one. After Louise had lived longer than doctors had originally predicted, Doyle refused to accept the subsequent advice given by doctors. He became determined to find his own cure for her illness, sure that he could prolong her life. He set aside his career and began taking Louise to various places that had been recommended as being helpful to patients suffering from consumption. They traveled first to Switzerland and then were told by a friend and fellow writer, Grant Allen, who also suffered from tuberculosis, that he had found the climate in the English county of Sussex, south of London, to be of great benefit. Doyle purchased an imposing red brick home there called Undershaw in the village of Hindhead. The house was one of the first in the region to have electric lighting. It became Louise's home until she died in 1906.

The strain of caring for Louise took its toll not only on Doyle's mental state but also on his relationship with his children. A son, Kingsley, had been born in 1892, and for the boy and his sister, Mary, their father was a lovable but slightly fearsome character. He could be reckless and boyish with them, but then, when tired or worried, could be sharp and irritable. Doyle did all he could to make sure that his children were loved and happy, but his constant worry often overshadowed his best intentions.

Doyle's stress undoubtedly worsened in 1897 when he met a young woman named Jean Leckie. They became close, but their relationship remained strictly platonic until after Louise's death. They married a year after Louise passed away and together had three more children.

Doyle's grief over Louise's condition – as well as his mixed emotions about Jean – led him to escape into his writing and into public life. He attended dinners, joined literary societies, went on trips, and took his brother, Innes, who was about to enlist in the military, to America for a book tour, which included readings and lectures.

He became very popular with Americans, who loved his bluff manner, his cheerfulness, his Scottish accent, and his unpretentious and straightforward ways. Doyle found the wide-open spaces and outdoor life of the United States to be invigorating and felt very much at home. Since Americans loved the stories of Sherlock Holmes as much as the British did, Conan Doyle was probably the best-known Englishman in the U.S. for many years.

Doyle married his second wife, Jean Leckie, more than a year after Louise's death. They would remain together for the rest of his life.

During the Boer War in South Africa, Doyle achieved even greater fame. The war began in October 1899, and the British military suffered three staggering defeats at the hands of an army of farmers. There was great alarm in Britain, along with a surge in patriotism, and Doyle decided to volunteer for South Africa. His mother, Mary, was angry and distressed, believing that his life was of more value to his country at home. There were thousands who could fight, she told him, but only one who could have created Sherlock Holmes.

As a sidenote, Sir Arthur's mother never understood her son's apathy toward the great detective. She was very angry with him when he killed Holmes off by having him plummet over Reichenbach Falls during a fight with his archenemy, Professor Moriarty. The Queen shared her anger, and it was those two women who led Doyle to bring Sherlock back from the grave.

Mary also believed that Doyle's sympathies should be with the

Boers rather than with the wealthy companies that were using the military to protect their interests in the African nation.

Many in England shared her feelings about the Boers. The discovery of gold in the Witwatersrand region of South Africa in the 1880s led many seeking a quick fortune to descend on Johannesburg. Cecil Rhodes was the operator of many commercial endeavors who used the British "Imperial ideals" as an excuse to run roughshod over the people of the area.

Doyle himself admired and respected the Boers, but his loyalty to Britain and the Empire was unquestioning. He decided to enlist, but the army had little use for a 40-year-old recruit and placed him on a waiting list. When the chance came for him to join a hospital unit -- at his own expense -- that had been put together by his friend John Langman, he jumped at the chance. As a doctor and unofficial supervisor, he shipped out to South Africa.

Doyle remained in South Africa for a little more than three months. After the capture of the Boer capital of Pretoria, he believed the war was over. He found the time he spent in the country to be profoundly satisfying, and after obtaining many first-hand accounts of the fighting, he wrote a book called *The Great Boer War* when he returned to England. The book became very popular, although it quickly became outdated because what seemed to be the end of the war was not. It continued as a guerrilla conflict for nearly two years.

This didn't hurt the success of the book, though, and many paid attention to its last chapter, in which Doyle suggested what he believed were some badly needed military reforms. They included the abandonment of cavalry swords and lances, the development of a highly trained infantry that volunteer militia units could supplement, and the concealment of large guns. This was particularly important after Doyle had witnessed two batteries lost during one battle when a commander foolishly pushed them ahead of the infantry with no cover for them. These recommendations seem sensible today, but they shocked the military establishment at the time.

To his dismay, Doyle also became mixed up in the controversy that surrounded the final months of the war. The continued guerrilla fighting brought a severe response from the British army. The Boers were highly mobile, living off the land and moving around constantly, striking at British forces and then vanishing. The military established a series of blockhouses to try to contain the guerrillas. They burned their farms and built concentration camps for the women and children. The camps were dirty and badly run, and various epidemics like measles and typhoid killed many of the prisoners.

Numerous articles and pamphlets were printed that accurately described the horrible conditions of the camps, but they also made false claims about the conduct of British soldiers. The articles inflamed other European countries, as well as many in Britain, and the military was harshly criticized.

In response, Doyle wrote a small booklet called "The War in South Africa: Its Causes and Conduct," in less than a week, made up of eyewitness accounts that denied the claims in other writings about British soldiers raping Boer women and using dum-dum bullets that expanded on impact. While he admitted the camps had problems, he said they were a necessary alternative to allowing women and children to starve. The booklet served to counter the anti-British sentiment, and while certainly propaganda, it supported a cause that Doyle sincerely believed in.

But that was not Doyle's first brush with politics. In 1900, he stood for Parliament in the general election. He was a Conservative candidate and, while not in a position to support the Liberal policy of social reform at home, he'd run with little chance of winning in a mostly Liberal area. His campaign was very effective, however. He spoke to workers, gave informal speeches in the street, and rented out an opera house for formal speeches in the evening. He ended up making 14 appearances in less than three days, genially acknowledging the hecklers who called him "Sherlock Holmes" and focusing on the importance of military reforms and national defense. Things looked well for him until, on election day, a fanatical Protestant hung posters throughout the district that proclaimed Conan Doyle to be a Jesuit-educated, Catholic agent -- a lie that must have galled a man who had long ago abandoned the Catholic faith. He lost the election, but not by much, and certainly had a better showing than any Conservative candidate in the area had managed in years.

Later, he confessed that he was glad to have lost the election and stayed out of politics. He said he would have been a poor party man, and he disliked campaigning. He never had much interest in politics, but he was a fighter by nature, and fighters never liked to lose.

Doyle was now a famous author and one of the most famous men in England, and soon after his work on behalf of the country during the South African War, he was offered a knighthood. He immediately refused, though, saying that a knighthood was a discredited title. His mother was furious with him and harassed him until he reconsidered. She eventually got her way, and in 1902, he became Sir Arthur.

But in a way, he had the last laugh. A few years later, in one of the last Sherlock Holmes stories, "The Adventure of the Three Garridebs," Dr. Watson mentions in passing that Holmes had refused a knighthood for his service. In what year? 1902, of course.

During the last decade of the nineteenth century, Sir Arthur had published five collections of short stories and 11 novels. There were many more to come, including *The Lost World, The Hound of the Baskervilles,* and others. In 1903, he purchased his first automobile and began entering auto races in England and on the Continent. He also began to watch the buildup of the military in Germany closely and feared war was on the horizon.

He began preparing for possible war in the best way he knew how – with his pen. He told his brother, Innes, that he had deep concerns that England was not ready for a fight. He was convinced that dirigible airships would prove to be more important than they turned out to be but was almost uncannily accurate about the threat posed by airplanes and submarines. He wrote a lengthy story called "Danger," in which Britain's enemy had a fleet of submarines that carried out merciless attacks on merchant shipping, causing famine and forcing England to surrender. His warning about the submarine threat was mocked when it was written. However, three years later, the German naval secretary would write that Conan Doyle had been "the only prophet of the present form of economic warfare" as the Germans began preying on merchant vessels.

And while Conan Doyle was always an agent of reform and change when it came to politics and the military, he was not always so forward-thinking with some of his other ideas. In many ways, he was old-fashioned and set in his ways, and while he embraced movements like Spiritualism in his later years, he was steadfastly opposed to others. He detested the women's suffrage movement and often spoke out against the actions of its radical members, calling them "wild women."

The suffragettes responded by pouring sulfuric acid through the letterbox of Windlesham Manor, the home to which Doyle and his family had moved in the East Sussex village of Crowborough in 1909. His opposition to the suffragettes' cause was based on the belief that it was not only pointless for women to have the vote, but that it was unwomanly.

On the other hand, he was sympathetic to the reform of the Divorce Law, which at that time stated that a man would get a divorce on the grounds of his wife's adultery. However, a woman could only divorce by proving adultery, brutality, and desertion, too. He campaigned hard to get the law changed, but this all was placed on the back burner when war was declared in August 1914.

Doyle was rejected for service, and the only action he saw was training Home Guard volunteers. Regardless, he did all he could to support the military and the government during the war. He sent an almost continuous stream of ideas – many of them practical, even ingenious – to the War Office.

One of his best was a call for the invention of life jackets. Since most military ships had few, if any, lifeboats, the sailors on them had little hope of survival if the ship went down. Sir Arthur suggested the inflatable rafts for the vessels, but when this idea was rejected, he pushed for the development of inflatable rubber collars that seamen could carry in their pockets. Soon, they became standard on warships.

He also suggested that soldiers be fitted with body armor to withstand enemy bullets. This was also rejected. Many of the men who worked in the War Office agreed with his innovations, but there was nothing they could do without official approval. When Doyle went to the Ministry of Munitions to argue on behalf of body armor, he was told: "Sir Arthur, there is no use arguing here, for there is no one in this building who does not know that you are right!"

He also worked hard to rally Britain's spirits during the war, writing articles and booklets, and made plans for a history of the British campaign in France. He maintained contact with many British commanders and even visited the front on several occasions, although his hosts kept him far away from the fighting.

The end of the Great War likely caused mixed feelings for Sir Arthur. He was thrilled by the Allied victory, but his greatest – and likely his final – adventure was over. The marching and the drilling, the war correspondence, the dangerous journeys that took him to the battlefields of the conflict had indulged his boyish love of action, and, at his age, he knew he'd never see anything like it again.

The war had given Sir Arthur great purpose, but the battles and their aftermaths also brought him some of the most profound grief he'd experienced since the death of his first wife. His brother-in-law and dear friend, Malcolm Leckie, had been killed, along with two nephews and several other friends and relatives.

And then Kingsley, the only son of his first marriage, and Doyle's beloved brother, Innes, had both died within a few weeks of one another. Kingsley had been badly wounded on the Somme and had died of pneumonia in October 1918. Not long after, Innes, now a brigadier general, also contracted pneumonia and died.

Conan Doyle spoke very little about these deaths, but they must have been devastating, especially combined with the death of his mother a short time later.

These deaths occurred before Sir Arthur's embrace of Spiritualism, but it's not hard to imagine that they played a part in his search for something spiritual. He had a longtime interest in the occult, and while sympathetic to the Spiritualist movement before the war, he was skeptical of it. But the death and suffering he saw during and immediately after the conflict – especially those of his close friends and loved ones – likely raised some hope in him that spirits could live on.

It was almost impossible for Sir Arthur to avoid being exposed to Spiritualism once again. The movement saw a massive resurgence after the war and was entering into its modern heyday.

Malcolm Leckie, Doyle's brother-in-law, that he believed he'd received a message from during a seance. This was one of the main events that led to his embrace of Spiritualism

Spiritualism was one of the many interests that Sir Arthur was passionate about, beginning when he was a young doctor in Southsea. He followed the research and writings, attended some séances, and kept notes about what he witnessed. He warily considered the idea that some of the things he saw were real – the knocks, raps, and messages from the dead – but remained cautiously skeptical until the evening when he believed Lily Loder-Symonds brought him proof that the spirit of Malcom Leckie reached out to him.

It was at this point that his cautious skepticism became complete acceptance. He soon began his full-fledged support for the movement, although he kept his newfound beliefs private for

Doyle became an unshakable believer in Spiritualism, often failing to use the reasoning that he'd given to his fictional detective when it came to Spiritualist fakes and frauds

a time, believing it wasn't proper to distract the public from British war efforts.

But once the war ended, he proudly announced his embrace of Spiritualism in a magazine called *The Light*. While Spiritualists around the world applauded him, the critics immediately attacked. None of them could understand how the creator of the logical detective, Sherlock Holmes, could be so gullible that he'd accept the so-called "wonders" of Spiritualism. However, Conan Doyle's convictions came from a place of supreme self-confidence, and whether the public shared his beliefs or not, he never doubted that he had found the true path.

Doyle plunged headfirst into Spiritualism with all the enthusiasm he showed to everything else. Even after several setbacks and the exposure of frauds he'd believed were authentic, Doyle could not be shaken from his beliefs. He was firmly convinced of life after death and the possibility of making contact with the spirit world.

In October 1917, he began his first lectures in support of the Spiritualist cause, appearing in Bradford and London. In the years that followed, he visited almost every town in Britain, finding what he described as critical but attentive audiences. It's possible -- perhaps even likely -- that most people came primarily to see the creator of Sherlock Holmes, but if this was the case, he didn't care.

After numerous appearances in London and throughout

England, Doyle and his family also visited Australia and the United States, all on behalf of Spiritualism. He also lectured throughout Europe and in South Africa, Kenya, and Rhodesia, which were then far-flung corners of the British Empire.

In 1926, he published a spiritual adventure story called "The Land of the Mist," which featured the popular Professor Challenger character from his earlier book, *The Lost World*. He also wrote a massive, two-volume book called *The History of Spiritualism* and, throughout the 1920s, spent more than £250,000 advancing the Spiritualist cause.

Not to be outdone by her famous husband, Lady Jean began to develop the skills of a medium during this time. This was in sharp contrast to her earlier feelings about the movement. She had disapproved of her husband's interest in the occult and disliked his concerns with Spiritualism, which she called "uncanny and dangerous." However, the death of her brother Malcolm during the war changed her feelings, and she also wholeheartedly accepted Spiritualism as genuine. In 1921, she was suddenly given what her husband called the "gift of inspired writing." She began to receive communications from the other side and became known among family and friends for the uncanny messages she produced through automatic writing.

In his writings and at his personal appearances, Doyle recounted dozens of bizarre and seemingly unexplained occurrences, but whether such occurrences were supernatural or were the result of his desperate willingness to believe remains open to debate.

Regardless, he often claimed to have touched phantom hands, had seen objects move by their own power, and to have witnessed the wondrous works of talented mediums. He also said that he possessed notebooks filled with information that had been given to his wife from spirits -- information that Doyle believed was "utterly beyond her ken."

He also came face-to-face with at least one ghost and investigated a haunted house in Dorset. He chronicled this

Sir Arthur, Lady Jean, and their children while on tour in support of Spiritualism

adventure in his book *On The Edge of the Unknown*, which makes for compelling reading whether you share the author's belief in Spiritualism or not. After Doyle's investigation, the house burned down, and a child's body was found buried in the garden. This discovery brought an end to the haunting, and Doyle believed the child's spirit had been responsible, trying to draw attention to the burial.

Doyle also collected a massive number of so-called "spirit photographs," which were alleged to be spirits of the dead captured on film. He believed that most of the photos were genuine and even wrote a book in support of using cameras to obtain evidence of the spirit world called *The Case for Spirit Photography*.

Unfortunately, most of the photos that Doyle championed appear blatantly fake today, the obvious results of fraud and double exposure. He became particularly involved with a spirit photographer named William Hope, who produced several hundred alleged spirit photographs during his heyday. Doyle posed for many of them, and – not surprisingly – every developed plate contained a spirit or two that was looking over his shoulder. The credulous author believed all of them to be authentic.

Then, in 1920, Doyle met a man whom he instantly liked and yet who challenged every belief that he had in Spiritualism and the supernatural.

DOYLE MET HOUDINI FOR THE FIRST TIME DURING THE magician's 1920 tour of England. It's no surprise that they met, and even less surprising that they became friends. They were two of the most famous men in the world at the time, leaders in their chosen fields. They were both widely read and shared many interests, including in the occult and the supernatural.

The friendship thrived despite their opposing views on something important to each of them – Spiritualism. Houdini was delighted to learn that there was at least

Doyle and Houdini

one intelligent person who believed in Spiritualism. He admired the fact that Doyle was so convinced of the value of the movement that he had given up most of his lucrative writing career to lecture about Spiritualism – even if Houdini had come to regard the mechanics of Spiritualism with skepticism.

Doyle was delighted that Houdini's knowledge of the spirit world was as vast as his own, even if some of their ideas were

very different. However, Doyle did agree with some of Houdini's work in exposing fraudulent mediums because he believed their existence damaged the legitimacy of the movement.

The problem was that, since he lacked his friend's magical training, Doyle was usually unable to see how fraud was accomplished. Houdini tried to show him the ways by which fraudulent mediums took advantage of people, but Doyle insisted that the mediums he knew were good and honest people who would never trick or cheat their followers. Besides that, Doyle stated, just because the feats of the spirits could be duplicated did not mean that they were not real.

In other words, just because Houdini could prove fraud existed, that was not enough to convince Doyle that it was occurring.

The two men argued good-naturedly, and while the conversations never became contentious, neither man converted the other to his point of view. However, the interests of both men were stirred by their shared interests and the lengthy correspondence about those interests that followed.

Thanks to the passionate nature of both men, though, it was a friendship that could never last.

Their relationship began fraying at the edges when Doyle began publicly taking the side of a faction of Spiritualists who believed that Houdini accomplished some of his greatest escapes using supernatural powers.

Houdini had spent several years exposing fraudulent mediums in private, in print, and during his stage shows, and this had made him a maligned figure in Spiritualist circles. Many among them were baffled by Houdini's refusal to accept the possibility of spirit communication because he publicly stated that he was open-minded and often spoke of a pact that he'd entered into between himself and several friends that whichever of them died first, they'd try to contact the others. If Houdini was willing to publicize this, why was he spending so much effort damaging the reputation of Spiritualism?

Some believed they could solve this mystery -- Houdini's exposure of mediums was simply to cover the fact that he was a medium himself. They claimed that many of his extraordinary escapes were achieved by Houdini "dematerializing" from the traps into which he had placed himself.

"This ability", Doyle stated, "to unbolt locked doors is undoubtedly due to Houdini's mediumistic powers and not to any normal operation of the lock. The effort necessary to shoot a bolt from within a lock is drawn from Houdini, the medium, but it must not be thought that this is the only means by which he can escape from his prison. For at times, his body can be dematerialized and withdrawn."

Houdini was stunned by this announcement, which was patently ridiculous, but he found himself stuck in the class magician's "catch" position. This meant he could only go so far in denying the Spiritualist's claims. By doing anything other than denying the allegations, he would have to expose how his escapes were accomplished, which he could never do.

He could only reply to questions that were asked by explaining that all his escapes were managed by purely physical means. It was all, as he told Theodore Roosevelt, "hocus pocus." He told reporters that his battle against Spiritualist fraud was simply an effort to protect the public from charlatans. He admitted that he was skeptical, but he tried to make it clear that he did not assume that all mediums were frauds. He was willing to give any medium an opportunity to prove they were genuine. It was just that, in his experience, he shrugged, they had all failed so far.

THE MAN
FROM BEYOND

AFTER HOUDINI RETURNED TO AMERICA FROM BRITAIN, HE began a new show business venture, only after turning down offers from both the Keith and Orpheum entertainment companies for tours during the fall and winter of 1920. Harry had decided to step away from vaudeville and stage performance and to start producing his own films. He formed the Houdini Picture Corporation, with himself as president.

Harry took just 10 days to write a script for his first production. The script called for the lead character, played by Houdini, of course, to be chopped out of a block of ice, where he had been frozen a century before. He was thawed out and then was forced to cope with the complexities of twentieth-century life.

Much of the footage for what was titled *The Man from Beyond* was shot in Fort Lee, New Jersey. The arctic scenes were filmed in Lake Placid, New York, and in May 1921, the company traveled to Niagara Falls for a big rescue sequence.

Burton King, who had directed Houdini's serial, *The Master Mystery*, artfully blended shots of the thundering falls with Houdini's dramatic rescue of the film's heroine just before her boat plunged over the edge. It was later said that dummies were used for some shots and that the 48-year-old escape artist had a safety line tied around his waist, but no trickery like this can be seen in the finished film. The reels for *The Man from Beyond* were processed at Houdini's film developing plant, and he edited the movie himself, supervising the cuts and splices.

The film company stressed Harry's bank account over the next three years. The production costs for the film far exceeded estimates, and to raise money to cover the expenses, he took the film on tour, taking advantage of box-office battles between the Keith and Shubert theater companies to get the best salary. He ended up signing on with the Keith chain for a considerable sum, and he showed the film, along with performing escape stunts and illusions.

The world premiere of *The Man from Beyond* was held in April at the Times Square Theater. The film had its flaws, but critics agreed that the Niagara Falls scene alone was worth the price of admission. "It has a whale of a punch," Variety said. "Houdini does a sensational rescue of the heroine in the Niagara rapids on the verge of the cataract, and I almost cheered when they made the crawl to safety."

A writer for the *Tribune* stated, "There is no fake about this; Houdini actually does it."

Harry, always the showman, was taking no chances with the opening of his first film, which explored themes of reincarnation

and suspended animation. His personal appearances at the Times Square Theater featured the "Vanishing Elephant," which had not been seen since its lengthy run at the Hippodrome. He borrowed an elephant for the illusion from the Ringling Brothers Circus – and when it disappeared, the audience once again found the vanishing impossible to explain.

Houdini's combined live show and screening for *The Man From Beyond* ran for three weeks, and when he moved on to the next city, Harry had no reason not to think that his future as a movie producer, director, and star wouldn't continue for many years to come.

"MENE MENE TEKEL UPHARSIN"

WHILE HOUDINI WAS MAKING HIS FIRST ATTEMPT TO BECOME a film producer, his friendship with Sir Arthur Conan Doyle continued. Although the two men had spent little time together in person during the passing months, they had written many letters back and forth, debating the merits of Spiritualism and discussing various aspects of the supernatural.

Doyle's connections with the Spiritualists who badgered Houdini about his escapes strained the relationship between them, but Houdini's admiration for Doyle overcame his irritation.

While in England, Doyle encouraged him to seek out mediums on his own, convinced Houdini would find the person who could convince him that Spiritualism was real. Harry followed his advice, and his cautious investigation of the spirit world monopolized his time when he wasn't on stage. He later estimated that he averaged at least one séance a day for months. And yet, even the mediums that Doyle recommended could only conjure up strange whispers that relayed meaningless information from the other side.

Houdini noted in his diary: "This is ridiculous stuff."

Doyle attributed his friend's inability to make contact with his beloved mother to his own turbulent vibrations, which he was sure intimidated the sensitive mediums that he visited. Even so, Doyle was convinced he was making progress in his search.

Doyle suggested that Houdini sit with amateur mediums, avoiding the frauds who, according to Sir Arthur, were less prevalent in England than in the United States, but just as devious. He told Houdini that sooner or later he would find a good clairvoyant, but he advised that in his efforts to find her, Harry should "persevere and get it out of your mind that you should follow it as a terrier follows a rat."

Houdini apparently heeded the advice. Though a few mediums had warned that he was out to make trouble, most of the psychics he visited reported that he was well-behaved and a perfect sitter.

At Doyle's suggestion, Houdini attended seances with a medium known as "Eva C."

In fact, one medium was pleased to perform for him. Before returning to America, Houdini participated in a Society of Psychical Research investigation of the French medium known as Eva C., who specialized in producing ectoplasm. The phenomena that she created were purely physical, so she was not the kind of medium that Sir Arthur supported. She brought no uplifting messages from the next world – spirit communication was not in her repertoire. Instead, she was known for manifesting clouds of ectoplasm that took the form of spectral hands, limbs, and faces.

Few mediums in Europe were as thoroughly and intimately tested as Eva. Researchers were known even to probe her vagina to ensure that no fake ectoplasm was stashed there. Houdini could relate – he was often searched as invasively before his jail escapes, proving he had no key or lock pick inside his body.

Regardless, Houdini wasn't convinced that Eva had been searched as carefully as she should've been.

The phenomena that Eva produced came over several evenings with Houdini and the SPR investigators gathered in the séance room. There was a glowing mass that emerged from her nostrils, an ectoplasmic rod projected from above her eye, a filmy object emanated from her mouth and then vanished, and once, the misty face of a spirit.

Houdini was both skeptical and captivated. He noted that female members of the committee had searched Eva in an adjoining room, and her orifices had not been checked in a way that Harry felt was essential.

He told some researchers that, as amazing as it all seemed, it wouldn't be difficult to duplicate. Back in his dime museum days, he explained, he'd been taught by a Japanese acrobat how to swallow and regurgitate a billiard ball. He had known sideshow performers who did the same with frogs, snakes, and other creatures. He suspected that Eva swallowed a slimy piece of ghost-white plaster, concealed it in her gullet, then expelled it later. He was not yet convinced there was any such thing as ectoplasm. He reported to Doyle: "Well, we had success at the séance last night, as far as productions were concerned, but I am not prepared to say that they were supernormal."

Aware of the kind of trickery he used in his own performances, Houdini was not ready to pronounce that any medium was genuine. He was still as skeptical about what Doyle believed was the "truth of Spiritualism" as he was before attending all those séances.

He knew that the Doyles didn't share his hesitation. Sir Arthur and Lady Jean made no major decisions without consulting their dead loved ones. But he also knew the Doyles were utterly sincere in their beliefs. He knew that Sir Arthur had not gone soft in the mind, as so many critics claimed.

Harry was delighted to hear that Doyle was returning to the United States soon for a lecture tour, and the two men made plans to meet while the author was on the East Coast. Little did they know when they made those plans that Doyle's visit to America was going to shatter their friendship beyond repair.

DOYLE'S MAY 1922 TOUR GOT OFF TO A ROCKY START.

After arriving in New York, he gave a press conference that was derided and harshly criticized in the *New York Times* the following day. He tried not to let this bother him. Instead, he dined with his family, became acquainted with his tour manager, Lee Keedick, and caught up with old friends.

Doyle and his family while on their 1922 American tour

New York was suffering under a heat wave, which turned his first lecture at Carnegie Hall into a struggle. The humidity and stagnant air in the packed lecture hall were intense, but it didn't keep people away. A record-breaking crowd filled the building, and they listened attentively as he spoke for more than an hour about the mysteries of the spirit world. The following day, a much more tolerant article appeared in the *New York World*. It read, in part:

Sir Arthur Conan Doyle made an extraordinary impression last night at Carnegie Hall, in his attempt to prove the existence of life after death and the possibility of communication with the dead. The effectiveness of his talk depended on the fact that, in spite of the imagination of his writings, he seems to be a downright person. He does not look like a man who could be easily stampeded. His audience was profoundly attentive. Evidently, it was a crowd which had its dead.

Doyle gave seven lectures in New York, all of which were well attended and well received. He later told Houdini that his lecture tour had raised $125,000, all of which was earmarked for the Spiritualist cause.

On stage, Doyle spoke of his own experiences with mediums and at séances and showed lantern slides of spirit photographs, mediums exuding ectoplasm, and more.

Some of the events at the lectures were unsettling, however. Women fainted when strange, spectral faces glowed on the screen, accompanied by eerie strains of music from a Victrola. Others called out, begging for words from their dead loved ones. Every new slide brought a chorus of screams, moans, and fainting spells. Distracted people wandered up and down the aisles, some sobbing uncontrollably. When each lecture ended, Doyle's dressing room became packed with well-wishers, while the hallway outside the room was lined by desperate people who believed that he could help them make contact with their dead loved ones.

Reports of those lectures described them as "weird" and "chilling," but what was happening around them was even stranger than anything Sir Arthur said or did onstage.

Newspaper reports of the lectures were blamed for an extraordinary series of suicides by people who wanted to see the "next world" immediately. Several of them made front-page news.

One woman, Maude Fancher, heard Doyle giving a speech on the radio and then murdered her infant son and consumed the contents of a bottle of Lysol cleaner. Before she swallowed the poison -- which took a week to kill her -- she wrote a letter to Doyle and told him that Spiritualism inspired her to the act. Then, she left a detailed letter for her husband explaining that she wanted her baby nestled in her arms when she was placed in the tomb.

A Brooklyn man named Frank Alexi stabbed his wife in the

head with an ice pick, claiming that he had been followed home by an evil spirit from Carnegie Hall who had attached itself to his wife. He'd killed her to free her from the spirit.

Another young man had killed himself and his roommate because, he explained in the letter he left behind, "there were no gas bills in the afterlife."

When confronted with these and several other peculiar incidents, Doyle stated without hesitation that they were the result of "a misunderstanding of what Spiritualism is meant to be." He did not, in any way, condone such behavior.

The bad press about the aftermath of his lectures encouraged Sir Arthur to retreat to the safety of the séance room. He attended sittings with several mediums that he knew, but even those séances went badly.

During one séance, a "spirit" continually referred to him as "Sir Sherlock Holmes." At another, an apparition appeared from a spirit cabinet with the face of Doyle's late mother. When he grasped the spirit to embrace her, he was stunned to find the muscular shoulders of a man beneath the "spirit robes." Rather than expose the fraud on the spot, Doyle waited to do it privately. Unfortunately, before he could do so, the medium was exposed for his part in another hoax a few days later. When Doyle was accused of helping the medium cheat his clients, he related the story of the séance and his plan to confront the man – but reporters greeted his claims with skepticism, and he was savaged in the newspapers.

It must have seemed like a relief to be able to get away from the pressure of the tour and spend time with his friend, Houdini. The two men had dinner together and then went to Harry's New York apartment.

While there, Houdini demonstrated how "spirit hands," which were typical elements in séances, could be made from wax casts. Fraudulent mediums often used them to fool sitters into believing the hands of the dead were touching them.

Houdini filled a rubber glove with air, packed the wrist with wood, then dipped the glove in melted paraffin wax – and a "spirit hand" was created.

If a hand needed to be more detailed and fingerprints were needed, he explained, a mold of a hand could be created using dental wax or plaster. An impression was then made of both sides of the hand, and the two sides were fitted together. Next, the entire hand was duplicated in rubber, and the fingerprints were preserved. Once it was dipped in wax, the process was complete.

Doyle was uncharacteristically silent after Houdini's demonstration. When he spoke, he admitted that it was all very interesting, but he couldn't accept that this was the only explanation for the ghostly hands that appeared at séances. He maintained -- as he usually did when Houdini tried to expose the tricks of phony mediums – that just because ordinary methods could duplicate something didn't mean that a supernatural explanation wasn't also possible.

We can only imagine the frustration that Houdini must have felt when his friend once again denied the possibility that so-called supernatural events could be duplicated by simple trickery.

He was now determined to prove to Sir Arthur once and for all that simple stage magic could be just as baffling as the events that occurred in the séance room – and could be just as phony.

THE DIM LIGHT CAST EERIE SHADOWS ON THE FACES OF THE three men in the drawing room. One of them was the owner of the house, Bernard Ernst, the esteemed president of the American Society of Magicians. In his hand was a decanter of brandy, and he poured a healthy amount of amber liquid into three crystal glasses.

Bernard Ernst

He handed one of the glasses to the taller man who stood on his right – Sir Artur Conan Doyle, the famous author turned Spiritualism proponent. Though older than the other men, he had the robust appearance of a man of much younger years. He accepted Ernst's offer of a glass of brandy and raised it to his lips, which were barely visible under his luxuriant white mustache.

Ernst knew why the three of them had gathered that night. Doyle was one of the most famous authors in the world, but he had turned his back on his creative work and now devoted his time to lecturing and writing about Spiritualism, a movement that had become a sticking point in the friendship between Doyle and the other man in the room.

That man – a small, wiry fellow with dark, unruly hair – was Harry Houdini and, like his friend, was one of the most famous men in the world. He declined his own glass of brandy, intent on the task that was before him. In a few moments, he planned to prove to Sir Arthur that he could easily recreate the same things that Doyle had witnessed in séance rooms – and would recreate them by natural means.

Ernst had eagerly agreed to host the demonstration in his own home. It was neutral ground, after all, and somewhere that

Houdini couldn't have prepared anything in advance. The three men had dinner together earlier and then adjourned to the drawing room, where Houdini began preparing for his illusion. He opened a wooden case and removed the items that he planned to use.

Houdini used a wire to suspend an ordinary chalk slate from a light fixture in the center of the room. He invited Sir Arthur to examine the slate, and then Houdini handed him five balls that were made of cork. He asked him to choose one of the balls. Doyle rolled all five of them around in his hand and looked at them closely. He juggled them back and forth in his hands, weighing each of them and trying to see if one might be heavier than the others. Finally, satisfied that each of the balls was exactly alike, he chose one of them at random.

At Houdini's direction, he dropped it into a small container of white paint. With a forefinger, he pushed it down into the paint, allowing the cork to soak up the thick liquid.

Then, Houdini handed him a piece of paper and a pencil. "Please write down any words or any phrase that you would like, Sir Arthur, but please do not let me see what you have written," Houdini instructed him. "You are welcome to leave the room, or even the house if you like, to ensure that your message remains a secret."

Paper in hand, Doyle walked out of the drawing room. He exited the house, walked three blocks, and turned a corner. He shielded the paper with his hand, looked all around him to make sure that no one could see him, and wrote down a short message. When he finished writing, Doyle folded the paper carefully and placed it in his pocket. He looked around once more and, satisfied that the nearby streets were empty, he returned to the Ernst home.

While Doyle had been away, Ernst stayed in the drawing room with Houdini, making sure that the magician had remained in the room the entire time. Houdini sat silently in a chair, with his eyes closed and his fingers folded together. He appeared to be completely at peace. He only stirred when Doyle walked back into the room.

As Sir Arthur waited with anticipation, Houdini asked him to carefully remove the paint-soaked cork ball from the can of paint and stick it to the face of the slate, which was still suspended in the air. Doyle plucked the ball out of the paint and gently pressed it to the slate. It stuck to the surface as if it were affixed with adhesive. Ernst handed him a handkerchief, and he wiped the residue of paint from his fingers.

As he stood there watching, Houdini made a few theatrical flourishes, and the cork ball inexplicably began to roll over the surface of the slate. As it rolled, words began to form. They spelled out the biblical phrase, *Mene Mene Tekel Upharsin*. The words, from the Book of Daniel, are often referred to as "the writing on the wall." They were interpreted as a divine judgment against King Belshazzar – a clear sign of impending doom.

Doyle was visibly startled by this turn of events -- they were the exact words that he had written on the piece of paper. How could such an amazing feat have been accomplished? Houdini could only have done it by supernatural means!

But Houdini insisted this was not the case. It was a trick, but he couldn't reveal how he'd done it. It was a cardinal rule among practitioners of magic that the secrets of illusions could never be revealed. But he assured Doyle that it was only a trick, nothing more. He had certainly not used any occult powers to make the cork ball move or to spell out the phrase that Doyle had secretly written on the paper.

But Sir Arthur refused to believe it. He demanded to know -- if he hadn't used mysterious powers, then how had Houdini done it? It seemed the Spiritualists who insisted that Houdini was a powerful medium were correct.

But they weren't correct, Houdini told him again, it was simply an illusion. But he also repeated that he was unable to reveal how it was done.

Bernard Ernst, a magician himself, understood Doyle's confusion. He was just as baffled by the trick. He also pleaded with

Houdini – he begged him to explain how the illusion was done. He promised that he and Sir Arthur would keep the secret in the strictest confidence. But again, Houdini refused.

So, how was the illusion accomplished?

To this day, no one knows. Houdini always maintained that it was nothing more than trickery, but this explanation didn't satisfy Sir Arthur. Houdini's plan had backfired. He had been trying to convince Doyle that a good stage magician could duplicate anything supernatural, but instead, he'd managed to convince his friend of the opposite.

Of course, it would have been much easier for Houdini to demonstrate for Ernst and Doyle how the illusion was created, whether it violated the magician's code of ethics or not. He could have ended the speculation about his paranormal powers once and for all, but he didn't.

Why? I'm sure that Houdini would say that it was because it was disreputable to reveal how tricks were done, but perhaps there was more to it than that.

The fact is, Houdini never performed that illusion in any of his shows – before or after this night – and no one has ever been able to reproduce it. Bernard Ernst later admitted that Houdini's own reaction to the illusion reminded him of a particular mind-reading stunt that Houdini had stopped using because, as he told Ernst, it was "too spooky."

Houdini certainly didn't achieve his goal with the illusion, which was to convince Sir Arthur that stage magic could duplicate any séance stunt. But I have to wonder if he managed to do something else when he performed it – and that was accidentally spooking himself with a bit of magic that turned out to be a little too real.

ATLANTIC CITY

SIR ARTHUR WAS STUNNED BY THE EVENTS AT THE HOME OF Bernard Ernst. While Houdini insisted that nothing his friend had seen was real, Doyle managed to turn the tables on Houdini on June 2, when he was the guest of honor at a banquet given by the Society of American Magicians at the Hotel McAlpin on Broadway.

He was among his toughest critics at the dinner, but he laughed heartily as the magicians performed a tribute to Spiritualist vaudeville. He gave every impression of a man who was enjoying himself immensely.

When Harry called on him to speak, the audience expected to hear an impassioned call for communication with the dead. However, instead, he told the group that he was going to show them something that was "psychic" and "preternatural" but only in the sense that it was "not nature as we can now observe it."

After building up an atmosphere of excitement and expectation, Doyle ordered the lights to be put out. Suddenly, the audience was astonished to see an actual film of prehistoric creatures, including an iguanodon, a tyrannosaur, and a brontosaurus, clawing and biting in a primeval swamp. No one had ever seen anything like this on a movie screen, and many of the magicians believed they were watching actual psychic images of beasts from another dimension.

Before the lights were turned out, Doyle had told the audience that what they were about to see would speak for itself, and he planned to answer no questions. He ducked out of the hotel ballroom while the audience was enthralled by what they were seeing onscreen.

"How did you do it?" Houdini asked him as he made his escape, but Sir Arthur only smiled.

The next morning, the *New York Times* printed a breathless story that was headlined "Dinosaurs Cavort on Film for Doyle." The writer pondered whether "these pictures were intended by the famous author as a joke on the magicians or were genuine pictures. If fakes, they were masterpieces."

Later that day, Houdini received an amused letter from Doyle, who revealed that the creatures had been constructed by "pure cinema of the highest kind" and were a sequence from the motion picture version of his book, *The Lost World*, which was being produced in Chicago. Willis O'Brien, who would later go on to make the acclaimed original version of *King Kong*, had animated the creatures using stop-motion photography.

He revealed that his purpose in exhibiting the film without any explanation "was simply to provide a little mystification to those who have so often and so successfully mystified others."

That was Sir Arthur's official explanation -- but I have a feeling that shocking a room filled with magicians who had just spent more than an hour duplicating the works of the spirits on stage tasted a little bit like sweet revenge.

AFTER FINISHING HIS LECTURES IN NEW YORK, THE DOYLE family went to Atlantic City to enjoy a short vacation on the shore. Sir Arthur sent a telegram to Houdini with an invitation to join them at the Hotel Ambassador for a few days. Harry enthusiastically accepted and was soon floating in the hotel swimming pool, where he taught the Doyles' two sons to dive and swim.

Later in the afternoon, the group moved to the beach, and

Houdini and the Doyles in Atlantic City in 1922

while Lady Jean and the children swam and played with a beach ball, Doyle and Houdini sat in deck chairs and enjoyed a breezy conversation.

As it often did, their discussion turned to Spiritualism. As Doyle described the work of a London spirit photographer named Ada Deane, Houdini maintained a stoic silence, knowing that Mrs. Deane had been caught substituting a photographic plate from her purse for one exposed at a séance. He only offered a few careful comments and conversations, being careful not to upset his friend and ruin the peaceful and enjoyable holiday.

The following day, Bess joined the group. Sir Arthur was pleased to see her, as was Harry, who had been having a pleasant time playing with the Doyle children. He entertained them with small magic tricks, delighted by their laughter.

He and Bess were sitting on the beach in the afternoon when Sir Arthur approached them and told them that Lady Jean, who was blessed with the type of mediumship called automatic writing, wanted to invite Houdini to a private séance in their suite. She told her husband that she felt strongly that Houdini's mother would come through that day. Houdini quickly accepted.

Harry was excited for more than one reason. He liked Jean very much and knew what a decent and sincere woman she was, but his excitement was also high because that day was his mother's birthday, something the Doyles had no way of knowing.

For the past two years, Houdini had believed that the history of Spiritualism was nothing more than one long tale of charlatanism. But Sir Arthur had an answer for that. "I see that you know a great deal about the negative side of Spiritualism. I hope more on the positive side will come your way."

Could a private séance with Lady Jean be the positive event that Sir Arthur had wanted him to experience? While catching rogues and frauds was a sport that Houdini relished, he never wanted to appear eager to entrap or intimidate the sincere mediums that Sir Arthur admired. He professed to be an open-minded investigator who hoped, with Doyle's help, to gain access to any clairvoyant who might bring him even a single authentic word from his mother, who had been silent in death for seven long years.

Houdini walked to the hotel, filled with hope. Perhaps his chance to speak with his mother again had finally arrived. He was finally sitting down with a medium that he knew he could trust.

Sir Arthur apologized to Bess for she would not be able to attend, fearing that another presence might influence the results. But she was happy to leave her husband in the Doyles' care. She planned to take a nap. Lady Jean had once told her that the living and the dead could comingle in sleep. On many nights, Bess had heard Harry wake up, asking, "Mama, are you here?"

Perhaps on this day she would be.

Inside the suite, Jean was ready to begin. She asked Houdini to sit down while her husband pulled the curtains. She was sitting at a large table, where a pile of paper and a pencil lay ready. Doyle sat next to his wife, and Houdini sat on the opposite side of the table. Doyle then offered a solemn prayer and then asked his wife if she was ready. Her hand struck the table three times (a Spiritualistic code for "yes") and then she sank into a deep trance.

Houdini closed his eyes and listened to the roar of the sea. Without having to be vigilant for trickery, he had never felt more relaxed at a séance. Quieting his doubts, he tried to accept the beliefs of the Doyles.

Houdini wrote later: "I had made up my mind that I would be as religious as it was in my power to be, and not at any time did I scoff during the ceremony. I excluded all earthly thoughts and gave my whole soul to the séance. I was willing to believe, even wanted to believe. It was weird to me, and with a beating heart I waited, hoping that I might feel once more the presence of my beloved mother."

Before long, Jean sensed someone in the room with them. She began to breathe deeply, and her eyes fluttered. Her hand, as though moving on its own, dashed with astonishing speed across sheets of paper. Doyle handed them one by one across the table to his friend.

Houdini turned pale and began to tremble. The message began:

Oh, my darling, thank God, thank God, at last I'm through. I've tried, oh so often -- now I am happy. Why, of course, I want to talk to my boy -- my own beloved boy -- friends, thank you, with all my heart for this.

The message continued with an expression of joy about Cecilia's new life and the beauty of the next world. She concluded with, "I wanted, oh so much -- now I can rest in peace."

Doyle then asked Houdini if he wanted to ask his mother a question, for "her reply will prove that she is at your side."

Houdini looked upset and could not speak. Conan Doyle suggested a question: "Can my mother read my mind?"

Houdini silently nodded his agreement, and Lady Jean's hand began to move again. "I always wanted to read my beloved son's mind," the message continued, "there is so much that I want to say to him." The message then went on for several hundred words, mostly expressing joy at communicating with her son and her appreciation of the Doyles.

At the end of the séance, Houdini sank back in his chair, utterly drained and exhausted. The Doyles, too, were emotional. They knew how much this reunion meant to their friend.

Jean had channeled 15 pages of automatic writing, and

Houdini seemed to accept every word to be as genuine as the letters that Cecilia had once written to him when he was on tour.

Yet Houdini seemed to want the spirits to perform an encore. Just when Sir Arthur thought the séance was over, Houdini picked up a pencil and tried automatic writing for himself.

The word "Powell" immediately came through.

He had been thinking of his friend Frederick Eugene Powell, a fellow magician who was about to go on the road with one of Houdini's touring companies to promote the film *The Man From Beyond.*

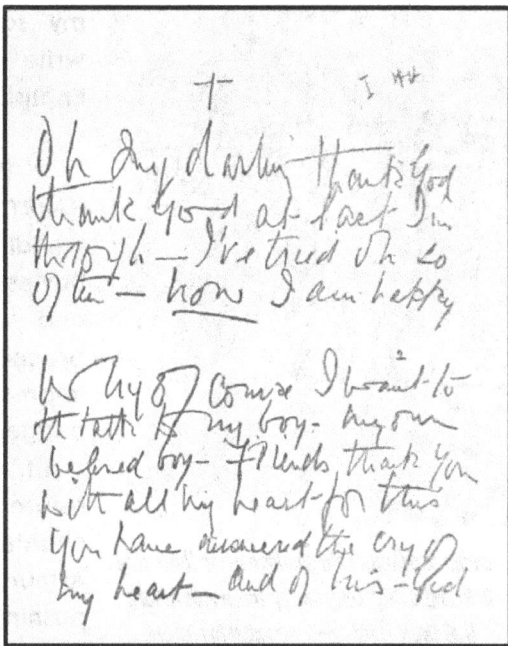

The first page of the "automatic message" produced by Lady Jean at the seance she performed for Houdini

But Doyle misunderstood the message completely, and he stood up from his chair in shock. A good friend of Doyle's, Ellis Powell, editor of the *London Financial News*, had died just three days earlier. He was convinced that Houdini, with the gift of a medium, was trying to say that Powell was in the room.

He wasn't. He knew Sir Arthur's friend wasn't in the room.

And neither, he was convinced, was his mother.

Houdini gathered up the pages on which Lady Jean had written. Before he left, unseen by the Doyles, he scribbled a note on the first page of the message: "Message written by Lady Doyle claiming the spirit of my dear mother had control of her hand ---

Houdini and Doyle said goodbye after their stay in Atlantic City. Only one of them was aware that their friendship was nearing its end

my sainted mother could not write English and spoke broken English."

THAT EVENING, BESS AND HARRY CELEBRATED THEIR 28TH wedding anniversary with the Doyles. The four attended a show and were surprised when the proceedings came to a halt. The impresario, Raymond Hitchcock, begged Houdini to "do a little stunt." He good-naturedly refused, even as the audience chanted his name, but then Sir Arthur settled the matter by pushing him onto the stage. With the show stopped, the actors, crew, and chorus gathered around the stage to watch as Houdini swallowed five packages of needles and then brought them back up in a flourish, all tied together. There was thunderous applause, and Harry bowed deferentially to Doyle.

The following day – their American adventure at an end – the Doyles gathered on the deck of the ship that would carry them home to bid farewell to the throngs of well-wishers and reporters on the pier.

As the whistle sounded and the ship cast off, Sir Arthur couldn't help but feel satisfied about his mission. He took pride in the fact that so many had responded to his lectures, garnering respect from newsmen and others he'd believed would mock his work. There had been those who scoffed, and embarrassments and mishaps had occurred, but overall, he considered the tour a success. He had set lecture hall records in New York, spread the Spiritualist message from the East Coast to the Midwest, tested American mediums, and won over many new adherents to the cause.

But, most important of all, he had helped his friend Houdini to find some peace by helping him make contact with his beloved mother.

Sir Arthur truly believed that he had finally convinced Harry about the truth of Spiritualism and helped him find answers to the mysteries that had plagued him for so long.

BUT DOYLE'S BELIEF COULD NOT HAVE BEEN MORE WRONG.

Houdini's stunned reaction to the automatic writing session wasn't because he believed his mother had finally made contact with him. He was in shock because he realized that even though he considered the Doyles to be truthful, sincere people, he now knew they were deluded in their beliefs about Spiritualism.

His mother had not come through during the séance. If she had, she would have mentioned her birthday, which the Doyles knew nothing about. Cecilia would have known that Houdini considered her birthday to be very important, but the message made no mention of it. He had not felt her presence in the room, hadn't smelled the scent of her favorite perfume, and when the message ended, he'd felt as lost and alone as he had when she died.

A war was waged within Houdini. Should he disclose the truth about the séance? If he did, he knew the Doyles would be hurt, perhaps even ruined. But if he kept quiet, he would allow the Spiritualists a false history.

He had no idea what he planned to do, but out of decency, he decided to withhold any statements about the incident until after the Doyles returned home from America.

But even then, he hesitated. Days passed, weeks, and months. He made no statement until December 19, 1922, when he released the news that his mother had not made contact at the séance with Lady Jean. In fact, all evidence pointed to that. His mother could not read or write and could barely speak English, and in addition to that, Lady Jean had started her automatic writing by scrawling a cross on the top of the paper. His mother had been Jewish and would never have done this. The headline that appeared concerning his disillusionment with the Doyles and Spiritualism read: "DISAPPOINTED INVESTIGATOR SAYS SPIRITUALISM IS BASED ON TRICKERY AND THAT ALL MEDIUMS CHEAT AT TIMES – BELIEVERS SELF-DELUDED."

Doyle was stunned by what he saw as Houdini's betrayal. He protested the claims, stating that language and earthly dates meant nothing to the spirits and that Lady Jean's drawing of a cross on the paper was merely a sign of protection against lower entities. It wasn't meant to be interpreted as a message from a spirit.

But Houdini refused to be convinced. He didn't think the Doyles had deliberately tried to trick him but had deceived themselves by their own gullibility.

As for the Doyles, they weathered Houdini's criticisms, although his statement badly damaged the warm and friendly relationship they once had. Doyle tried to remain loyal to the magician and convinced himself that Houdini was too nervous about the encounter with his mother's spirit to admit that it was genuine. Sir Arthur and Lady Jean also maintained in some reports that another message had also come through that day, claiming that Houdini would die soon, and this was the reason he denied the authenticity of the communication. If this were true, the message would never have been made public.

For a short time, the two men tried to pretend that their friendship had not been ruined, but it was too late to salvage it. The hurt was just too deep on both sides. To the Doyles, Houdini was willfully blind and appallingly ungrateful, but to Houdini, the Doyles had made a terrible mockery of the deep feelings that he had for his mother.

What little remained of their friendship was destroyed in 1923 when Houdini became a member of a *Scientific American* magazine panel that announced plans to investigate mediums and psychics. Doyle was disgusted by his presence on the panel.

"The commission is, in my opinion, a farce," he wrote, "and has already killed itself."

When the panel became embroiled in a particularly controversial investigation, the friendship between the two men came to a bitter end. Doyle wrote to Houdini: "You force me to speak, and I have no wish to offend you, but you cannot have it both ways. You cannot bitterly and offensively, often also unruly, attack a subject and yet expect courtesy from those who honor that subject. It is not reasonable."

Within a few years, in 1926, Bess Houdini would be shattered by her husband's premature death. While sorting through his papers and vast library, she uncovered many books on Spiritualism and the supernatural and thought they would make a nice gift for Doyle, whom she still considered one of the best friends that Houdini had in life.

She wrote to him and offered the books, but Doyle was reluctant to take them, believing that Houdini had harbored bad feelings about him at the time of his death. Bess quickly replied that this was not the case and blamed most of the problems between the two men on the press.

Houdini had never given up on the possibility of contacting his mother and told Bess so while on his deathbed. She added to her letter: "If, as you believe, he had psychic powers, I give you my word that he never knew it.... He was deeply hurt whenever any journalistic arguments arose between you and would have been the happiest man in the world had he been able to agree with your views on spiritism. He admired and respected you... two remarkable men with different views --- it is usually the third party that distorts the word or the meaning."

Sir Arthur accepted the books and cherished them until the end of his life, always wondering how things might have turned out differently between him and Harry if they had been able to put their differences aside and put their friendship ahead of their diverse beliefs.

EXPLAINING THE UNEXPLAINED

HOUDINI'S FILM, *THE MAN FROM BEYOND*, OPENED AT THE Rialto Theater in Washington, D.C. in August 1922. Instead of promoting the film with his usual escape stunts, Harry used the attention to launch an all-out attack on psychic fraud. Making personal appearances to promote the film, he projected slides of famous mediums and denounced the deceptions they performed during their séances. In newspaper columns that appeared throughout the country, he answered questions about the methods used by false mediums.

Though he continued to perform in vaudeville, most of Houdini's offstage hours were spent tracking down and exposing what he called "vultures who preyed on the bereaved." Often, he attended séances wearing a false beard, mustache, or other disguise, behind which he could observe the happenings without being detected. When he had gathered enough evidence to make an exposure, he would leap up, tear off his disguise, and shout something like, "I am Houdini! And you are a fraud!"

His activities received extensive press coverage, but he claimed he was not doing it for the publicity. Yet even if he was, deep down, he still held a small hope that one day, he would meet a genuine psychic – and one who could connect him with his mother again.

Until then, he continued to expose fakes and frauds, and he didn't always do it alone. He had several undercover assistants who worked with him in his crusade. He called them "my own secret service," and they attended séances and reported back to him about what they saw. His most effective operative, though, was the woman dubbed his "secret weapon," Rose Mackenberg.

Houdini's 'secret weapon" Rose Mackenberg

Rose was born in 1892, the daughter of Russian immigrants in Brooklyn. As a young woman, she worked as a stenographer in a law office but later became a private detective. When a wealthy banker asked her to investigate a medium who had advised him to invest in stock that turned out to be worthless, Rose consulted with Houdini. He taught her how to uncover fraud, and then he recruited her to join his ranks of investigators.

By her count, she investigated more than 300 mediums in the two years that she worked for Houdini and many more after that. In a career that lasted for decades and even included her testifying before Congress, she proved to be sharp-witted, skilled at disguises, and never taken advantage of. In 1949, she told a reporter, "I smell a rat before I smell the incense."

For example, in 1925, Rose visited an Indianapolis medium named Charles Gunsolas, who had, in an irate letter to Houdini, called himself "one of the leaders of Spiritualism." Pretending to

A newspaper feature about Rose and her attempts to expose fraudulent spirit mediums

be a mother who had recently lost a child, Rose told Gunsolas that she wanted to check on her baby in the afterlife.

As part of his "act," Gunsolas claimed to contact an 800-year-old Hindu guide in the spirit world and received information from what he called his "spirit wife," whose name was Ella. He told Rose that he could teach her how to access the afterlife by staring into a bowl of water for just $25. He explained that it would be easier for her to contact the Hindu guide if Rose took off all her clothes. She declined.

Rose maintained her cover and reported what happened to Houdini, who came to Indianapolis six weeks later to give a performance. He made sure that Gunsolas was in attendance. Houdini called him out from the stage, telling the audience about Rose's experience. Gunsolas, his face pale with shock, muttered that he also hated fraud and fled the theater to jeers and catcalls from the audience.

Rose wore a variety of disguises for the séances, including what she called the "rustic schoolteacher," the "credulous servant girl," and the "tipsy consultant." She usually posed as a grieving mother or a mourning widow, although, as she told a St. Louis reporter in 1929, "I never married, but I have received messages from 1,000 husbands and twice as many children in the world to come. Invariably, they told me they were happy where they were, which was not entirely flattering to me."

Rose was also frequently groped and propositioned by the so-called mediums she visited, but she always resisted Houdini's suggestion that she carry a gun.

Rose's most newsworthy case occurred in 1926 when Congress was considering a bill to make fortune-telling illegal. Public hearings became chaotic as competing claims were heard about the validity of psychic abilities. Houdini was a star witness and shared the results of his investigations into fraudulent mediums, cross-examining many psychics himself.

Rose appeared during the hearings to testify about her recent undercover experiences visiting Jane Coates, a notable Washington, D.C. medium. Her statements created fireworks in the meeting room.

Why?

She said that Coates had confided in her that the proposed ban on fortune tellers would never be passed because her regular customers included at least four senators and because "table tipping séances are held at the White House with President Coolidge and his family."

Coates denied the allegation, but according to newspaper reports, the day's session was "unusually disorderly and came near winding up in a free-for-all fist fight."

After Houdini died unexpectedly in 1926, Rose continued their work, taking on clients who hired her to investigate fraud, including police departments and insurance companies. She gave lectures on how to expose phony psychics and revealed tricks that she had seen performed by fake mediums in dark séance rooms. She also wrote scores of newspaper and magazine articles on the subject, along with an autobiography that was (sadly) never published, called "So, You Want to Attend a Séance?"

In 1949, a Hearst syndicate article described her as "perhaps the only woman 'ghost-buster' in the world."

Despite a lifetime exposing frauds, Rose – like Houdini – insisted that she wasn't a non-believer in Spiritualism. She was willing to be convinced of the existence of an afterlife; she just said that she'd never seen any proof of it.

Before she died in 1968 at age 75, Rose lived for decades in an apartment in Manhattan. She always kept the place well-lit, she said, because after years of attending seances, "I get tired of dark rooms."

Houdini in a disguise he used to infiltrate a seance. He always revealed himself after he discovered the tricks

IN ADDITION TO ATTENDING SÉANCES IN DISGUISE AND directing undercover operations, Houdini also began to re-enact séances and spirit manifestations during his stage shows. He showed how so-called "spirit forms" and "ectoplasm" could be created by a stage magician.

And while his shows were undoubtedly the most dramatic, he was not the first magician to expose the tricks of mediums on stage.

From the earliest days of Spiritualism, there had been a battle waged between mediums and magicians. In 1853, just five years after the Fox Sisters gained fame in rural Hydesville, New York, a magician named J.H. Anderson issued the first challenge. He offered a monetary award to "any poverty-stricken medium" who could produce spirited raps in the public hall where he gave his regular performances. The Fox Sisters were among those who accepted Anderson's challenge, but the magician backed out, amid catcalls and hisses from the audience, and refused to allow the mediums on the stage.

Despite Anderson's failure, magicians caused more people to question the authenticity of spirit mediums than any scientist did. Magicians were adept at recreating the "miraculous" phenomena of the mediums. On stage, they duplicated and then exposed their effects. The methods practiced by the mediums were simple, the conjurers claimed, and were merely stage illusions just like the ones being created before audiences in vaudeville theaters across the country. "If I can only get your attention intently," one magician claimed, "an elephant could pass behind me and you would not see it."

Before Houdini's war on Spiritualism, one of the greatest rivalries between mediums and magicians involved the Davenport brothers.

Ira and William Davenport were professional mediums who were the first to popularize the "spirit cabinet" in their performances. Their special cabinet was a large wooden box that had three doors at the front and a bench running lengthwise inside. It was large enough that both mediums could fit inside. The center door had a small diamond-shaped opening covered by a curtain, through which various phenomena would manifest. Before each performance, members of the audience were allowed to inspect the cabinet and to make sure that the Davenports, who sat astride the bench, facing one another, were securely tied and unable to move about. Within seconds after the doors were closed, the brothers were able to produce raps, musical sounds, and a variety of other effects.

Although the phenomenon they produced was typical of the Spiritualist séances of the day, the Davenports were ambiguous about their powers. They never presented themselves as Spiritualists but, on the other hand, insisted the manifestations they created were genuine.

While in England, they became the subject of controversy. They held séances every night for more than two months in a hall

The Davenport Brothers inside of their famous "spirit cabinet" from which they produced their manifestations

in London. Various committees studied these demonstrations without finding any evidence of fraud; nevertheless, the brothers were met with widespread public opposition and even hostility as they began their tour of the rest of England.

For the most part, their performances in early 1865 did well, but they ran into problems in some communities. In Liverpool, in February, two members of an inspection committee selected by the audience used a complicated knot to secure the brothers. The Davenports protested that the knots were too tight and cut off their circulation, but a doctor who examined them disagreed. They refused to perform and asked one of their assistants to cut the ropes. The crowd became angry, and the ruckus turned into a riot, and the Davenports quickly left Liverpool.

Finally, in March 1865, the Davenports played at the Cheltenham Town Hall and encountered John Nevil Maskelyne -- the only investigator who would ever uncover their manifestations as fraud.

Maskelyne was one of the most popular of the early British stage magicians. The son of a saddle maker, he was born in Cheltenham in December 1839. Intrigued as a boy by an entertainer's "dancing dinner plates," he practiced until he was able to keep several dishes whirling about at the same time on a table. At 19, he began working as a clockmaker's apprentice and constructed his first piece of conjuring equipment -- a small chest with a secret panel. He could lock a borrowed ring inside, bind the chest with tape, and then secretly extract the ring as he gave the box to a spectator. The box was so well constructed that it managed to withstand even the most rigorous examinations.

On March 7, 1865, Maskelyne attended a séance given by the Davenport brothers at Cheltenham Town Hall. Although it was the middle of the afternoon, heavy curtains were fastened over the windows to darken the hall. Lamps were used to illuminate the stage, where trestles had been erected to support the large three-door

British magician John Nevil Maskelyne

wooden cabinet. The doors were standing open when Maskelyne entered the hall. A plank seat ran down the middle of the cabinet, and a guitar, violin, and bow, two hand bells, a tambourine, and a trumpet were placed inside.

A lecturer introduced the Davenport brothers and then called for volunteers. Maskelyne and several other men rushed to the front of the theater to inspect the equipment and to lash the mediums' wrists behind their backs and bind their ankles as they sat facing each other in the cabinet. The doors were closed, a signal was made to put out the lights, and the room plunged into murky darkness.

Almost immediately, bells rang and flew out onto the floor of the stage. Pale, ghostly hands waved through the apertures in the center of the cabinet. A tambourine jangled, a guitar strummed, and a violin played eerie music. Yet, when the lamps were lit and the doors opened, the brothers were found to still be tightly bound, exactly as they had been when the séance had started.

England was sharply divided over whether the Davenports were genuine mediums or clever tricksters, but, purely by chance, Maskelyne discovered they were frauds. A ray of sunlight from a poorly draped window had flashed briefly on the spirit cabinet during the performance, and from his vantage point on the side of the stage, Maskelyne had been able to see into the cabinet through a crack in the door. He saw Ira Davenport vigorously ringing the bell. He had slipped out of the ropes, and Maskelyne knew that if one brother could free himself, then the other one could, too.

Maskelyne told several people what he had seen, but a clergyman who had been watching from the other side of the stage scoffed at this explanation. Determined to prove his point, Maskelyne persuaded a friend to help him build a cabinet so that they could work together and duplicate what the Davenports were doing.

Once they learned the technique of slipping their hands out of and back into tightly knotted ropes, producing "spirit music" was easy for the two men. After three months of practice, Maskelyne appeared at Jessop's Gardens on June 19. Trick by trick --- and they stressed they were tricks --- he and his friend duplicated the entire Davenport séance.

Five days later, the *Birmingham Gazette* offered a long account of the performance and showed that Maskelyne had proven that spirits were not necessary for a "spirited" séance. Of course, by then, the Davenports had moved on to the rest of Europe and were being wined and dined by royalty. Most of their audiences had no idea that their clever act had been exposed as just that -- an act.

Maskelyne went on to become one of England's most famous magicians. In later years, he continued to offer "spirit shows" and duplicated the methods of mediums in his performances.

One of the most flamboyant magicians of the early twentieth century was William S. Marriott, who wrote a series of articles about fraudulent mediums for *Pearson's Magazine*, starting in 1910. Unfortunately, little is known about Marriott's early years, how he got started in the magic field, or what led him to pursue the truth behind Spiritualist mediums. What we do know is that he was described as a likable man with "a pair of well-waxed mustaches" and that he was a professional magician who performed under the name of Dr. Wilmar.

Magician William S. Marriott with some of the fake ghosts that he purchased from a catalog that supplied tricks to dubious spirit mediums

At some point, in the early 1900s, he became interested in exposing the hoaxes that were being carried out by fraudulent mediums, and one of his first – and most valuable -- exposures came when he located and publicized a copy of a catalog called "Gambols with Ghosts: Mind Reading, Spiritualistic Effects, Mental and Psychical Phenomena and Horoscopy."

"Gambols with Ghosts" was a secret catalog that was circulated among mediums and was filled with tricks, apparatus, and paraphernalia that could be used to dupe the public. The catalog was published in 1901 by Ralph E. Sylvestre of Chicago. It was designed for private circulation among mediums, on the understanding that it would be returned to Sylvestre when tricks had been selected from it. It was never meant to be seen by the public.

The catalog had an introduction that read:

Our experience during the past 30 years in supplying mediums and others with the peculiar effects in this line enable us to place before you only those which are practical and of use, nothing that you have to experiment with. We wish you to thoroughly appreciate that, while we do not, for obvious reasons, mention the names of our clients and their work (they being kept in strict confidence, the same as a physician treats his patients), we can furnish you with the explanation and, where necessary, the material for the production of any known public 'tests' or 'phenomena' not mentioned in this, our latest list. You are aware that our effects are being used by nearly all prominent mediums of the entire world.

The notorious "Gambols with Ghosts" catalog

This notorious catalog included equipment for slate-writing, stuffed ghosts, self-playing guitars, self-rapping tables, materializations, and a "Complete Spiritualistic Séance." Marriott obtained many of these illusions from the catalog and had himself photographed posing with them.

He had, like so many others in the business, become disenchanted with the deceptions being carried out by dishonest mediums. Spiritualism was riddled with cases of outright fraud. Many deceptive mediums would do whatever they could to bilk unsuspecting clients and sitters out of money to "contact their deceased loved ones." And while not every medium was dishonest, there were enough of them to color the entire movement -- and to give Spiritualism a bad name.

One of the most thrilling aspects of any séance was the materialization of the spirits. Some mediums, like Florence Cook, built an entire career on such materializations. Because this was such an essential part of a good séance, fraudulent mediums would do just about anything to cause it to happen -- from smoke to mirrors to even more dishonest shenanigans.

As the heyday of the Spiritualist movement began to wind down, the fraudulent mediums became increasingly sloppy with their tricks and manipulations. Gone were the days of elaborate stage shows. Cheap displays and shoddy hoaxes had replaced them. A case that illustrates this point was reported in newspapers in 1906. As it turned out, though, two ardent and legitimate Spiritualists were responsible for exposing the fraud.

These men went to an apartment where a séance was to be conducted and became suspicious of the chair and the cabinet used by the medium. They managed to examine the chair and found a secret compartment in the rear, and a keyhole, which was carefully concealed beneath the chair's upholstery. The investigators had a skeleton key made, which would open the lock, and found another secret compartment that was 15 inches deep.

At the next séance, the men noticed that the back of the chair seemed to be thicker than it should be and suspected that "ghostly" materials had been placed there before the sitters arrived. During the séance, the men were not surprised to see all kinds of "ghosts" materializing.

When it was over, they exposed the medium as a fraud. They opened the secret compartment on the chair with their own key and began removing the items contained inside. They found a collapsible dummy head made of pink material, a flesh colored mask, six pieces of silk, two pieces of black cloth, three beards and two wigs of various color and length, a telescoping rod from which drapery could be hung to represent a second ghost, a small flashlight with four yards of wire and a switch, which would be useful to make "spirit lights," and various other contraptions.

Exposures like this one prompted Marriott to begin his own

The series that Marriott wrote for Pearson's including photographs that demonstrated how many spirit medium effects were created, including "table tipping" with his foot

investigations, and he soon made a name for himself --- and many enemies among the frauds of the Spiritualist movement.

In 1909, *Pearson's Magazine* approached Marriott and asked him to conduct, on the magazine's behalf, a series of investigations of spirit mediums. The results were published afterward in four issues of the magazine. In the first installment, he delved into Spiritualist séances and wrote of several hilarious incidents that occurred.

At one séance, the medium entered the spirit cabinet as the lights were being turned out, and after a time, the curtain parted, and a form emerged from the cabinet. The "spirit" was partially luminous and carried a shimmering globe in his hand, which he held near his face to make it more visible. The figure graciously inclined his head, gestured as if to bless the sitters, and then retired back into the cabinet. Marriott wrote more of what happened next:

This should have closed the séance. Tonight, an unrehearsed effect was in store for the believers. As the form entered the cabinet, he sat down on what he thought was the settee. It happened to be my knees. I had quickly slipped into the curtained enclosure and was sitting, waiting for him to come back. As my arms went around him, he gave a yell followed by language which I will not repeat. My friend had the light up in a moment. And there, for the faithful, was the edifying sight of the medium, clothed in flimsy white draperies, struggling in the arms of myself!

Marriott's reputation as an investigator became widely known. He was well respected on "both sides of the aisle" because he was not just offering money to anyone who could perform a paranormal feat he couldn't duplicate. Rather, he was simply showing that alternative explanations to apparent miracles existed, and he invited open-minded observers to decide for themselves what they wanted to believe.

"If I am one of the 'scoffers'," wrote Marriott, "it is not because of any original bias, but because of the arrant humbug, cheap trickery, and pathetic self-delusion that I have encountered at every point of my investigations of Spiritualism..."

OTHER MAGICIANS – LIKE HARRY KELLAR, HOWARD THURSTON, and many others also debunked the antics of fraudulent mediums onstage, but none of them did so as successfully as Houdini.

This is likely because he wasn't just performing recreations of séances during his shows. He was also out searching for evidence, uncovering fraud, and chasing after any supernatural phenomena that purported to be genuine.

But not everything he witnessed during his psychic investigations was easily explained away. He kept vast files and records of his investigations, and when he died, Bess turned those files over to Joseph Dunninger, a friend, fellow magician, and researcher of the supernatural. Dunninger played a significant role in creating Houdini's posthumous legend – and in investigating the many attempts to contact Houdini after his death.

He also wrote a few books and numerous articles about Houdini's investigations. One article was about an incident that baffled Houdini. Dunninger found a handwritten account of the incident in his friend's files, dated April 11, 1923.

Harry was approached about Mrs. Mary Fairfield McVickers, who had, before she died, requested that photographs be taken of her body at 5:00 P.M. on the afternoon of her funeral. If possible, she planned to appear in spirit form at that time. She had announced this unusual news in July 1922, on her 73rd birthday. She explained to her friends at the First Spiritualist Temple of Los Angeles -- where she was a member -- that she had experienced a vision of her approaching death. She told those gathered at her birthday gathering, "I feel that if a picture is taken over my body about 5:00 P.M. on the day of my funeral, I will appear in spirit form."

Mary died the following April, and one of her friends, Albert H. Hetzel, contacted Houdini and told him about the unusual request the woman had made for a photograph to be taken of her body. Houdini was intrigued, and so he got in touch with a friend and movie producer named Larry Semon about borrowing a cameraman.

On the afternoon of the funeral, Nathan B. Moss, who worked for Keystone Press Illustration Service in Hollywood, arrived with a professional camera and a plate holder loaded with 14 negatives. Houdini had not told the man what they would be photographing, and he and Moss went to a place called Howland and Dewey, who were Kodak representatives in Los Angeles.

Houdini wrote that Moss "had no idea what I wanted but was under the impression that I was going to do a stunt and wanted a stunt picture. I told him that I wanted him to reload his plate holder with brand-new plates, which I would buy. He, not knowing the importance of the test, derided the fact of my not wanting to use his plates, but I told him that I might have to take an oath that I bought the plates and that, therefore, it was important."

When they arrived at the camera store, they asked for a dozen 5X7 plates, and the clerk, Frank Hale, pulled out four packages that contained 12 plates in each one.

Mat Korn, a customer in the store and a stranger to Houdini, was standing nearby, and he was asked to choose one of the packets. He picked one up and handed it to him, but Houdini noticed that one end of the package wasn't tightly sealed. He refused the package and all the others that had been chosen with it.

He asked for five more packages, and he asked another customer, a photographer named Wheeler, who worked for the *Los Angeles Record*, to choose one for him. Houdini purchased that package of plates, and he and Moss entered the darkroom on the premises and removed the plates that Moss had already placed in the camera, substituting them with the brand-new plates. When they were finished, they left for the church so that they could arrive just before 5:00 P.M.

At the front of the church, the body of Mary McVickers had been placed in a white, open casket to the right side of the pulpit. Flowers surrounded it. Moss took 10 photographs of the scene, each of them taken under the same exposure time of three minutes. In addition to Houdini and Moss, the witnesses at the scene included Albert Hetzel, J.M. Hall, Virgil Vlasek, and Stanley Bruce of the *Los Angeles Examiner*.

After the photos were taken, the group left the church and went immediately to the Keystone Press Illustration office. The plates were developed in Houdini's presence, and on one of them, they noticed a peculiar streak.

Houdini wrote:

Mr. Moss made a print from this plate, which caused a great deal of talk. Not one photographer could explain how this could be tricked. Mr. Moss offered $100 to anyone who could produce it under the same conditions, whereas no one could duplicate it.

Houdini was bothered enough by this incident that he made a note of it in his personal diary: "Took pictures at church. A peculiar test," he wrote.

Dunninger published Houdini's narrative in a small book titled *Houdini's Spirit Exposés* in 1928 and stated that Houdini offered

The mysterious photo from the McVicker's funeral that Houdini was unable to explain. His friend, Joseph Dunninger, found notes about the photograph in Houdini's files after his death

$1,000 to any magician who could duplicate the photo. No one accepted the challenge.

The photograph with the mysterious light was the second plate used. The streak was a heavy band of light that started a few inches from the floor and then extended up to about two feet above a five-foot-high black screen. This screen had been placed between the open casket and the auditorium. At the upper end of the streak, the light became a diffused, glowing mass of a larger shape. Looking closely at the streak, one can see that it has an interesting formation, starting as a sharply defined, broad band and then shifting to make two parallel lines. Just before it turns into a glowing mass, a third line starts to appear. Several photographic experts studied the plate but stated that, because of the nature of the image, it would have been practically impossible for it to have been caused by a defective plate, a damaged plate holder, or a camera.

A hoax was out of the question. Creating a fake "spirit photograph" would not have helped Houdini's campaign against fraudulent Spiritualists. Instead, he ended up with something that he couldn't explain – and had the integrity to admit that the photograph was something he couldn't dismiss.

Dunninger wrote that Houdini did not attempt to debunk or explain the photograph: "He did not see the light. It made itself only evident in the photograph. This report shows that Houdini was willing to believe if the proof was brought before him -- and was willing to give credit whenever credit was due."

As Houdini had always maintained: "I am willing to be convinced. My mind is open, but the proof must be such as to leave no vestige of doubt that what is claimed to be done is accomplished only through or by supernatural power."

Dunninger knew this as he was one of seven friends with whom Harry had made a pact that stated if he should, he would make contact, if possible, with the rest from the other side.

To prove that it was really him, he devised a secret code word with the one person he trusted most – his wife, Bess. If a message should arrive, she would be able to tell if it was authentic or if it really was Harry making contact.

Some have suggested that Houdini came up with the idea of the "death pact" because he already had some foreboding of his death, but this is not the case. He merely wanted to demonstrate that he believed in the possibility of the other side.

And while Houdini may have been willing to believe in the unexplainable, he was still unwilling to suffer those he considered to be fools and frauds.

In 1923, he took time off from his vaudeville engagements to travel across the country on a lecture crusade against fraudulent mediums. He published a book, *A Magician Among the Spirits*, the following year, which was a scathing look at the fraud being perpetrated by fraudulent American Spiritualists.

If the Spiritualist community didn't hate him before the book, they certainly despised him after it was released.

IN ADDITION TO PERFORMING, INVESTIGATING SPIRIT mediums, and writing books, Houdini's fascination with the movie business continued. But now, as a producer, he found himself in a quandary. He had to choose between three scripts for his next film -- *Il Mistero*

di Osiris or The Mystery of the Jewel, a story of Ancient Egypt; Yar, the Primeval Man -- the adventures of a caveman; and Mr. Yu or Haldane of the Secret Service.

It was a difficult decision because he had great faith in the screenwriter -- Houdini had written all the scripts himself. Finally, Mr. Yu was chosen, but he shortened the name to Haldane of the Secret Service.

In the film, Heath Haldane (played by Houdini) fights a gang of counterfeiters that had been chasing Adele Ormsby (played by Gladys Leslie). The gangsters throw the Secret Service man into the Hudson River, and he is rescued by a passing boat. Reviving quickly, Haldane swims out to a passing ocean liner and is taken on board after climbing hand over hand up a rope. Haldane goes on to track down phony banknotes in Hull and London (using footage shot in England), then he visits the Apache Café in Paris, where he learns the counterfeit bills are being produced in an old French monastery. The "monks" trap him and lash him to a large wheel. With his hands and feet manacled and rushing torrents of water engulfing him, he manages to escape, round up the criminal gang, and unmask their "Chinese" leader as the heroine's father. The picture ends with the girl safely in Haldane's arms.

Honestly, it's as bad as it sounds, and it received only lukewarm reviews. Houdini was no Rudy Valentino. His shy, restrained love scenes hardly had women swooning in theaters. The film was promoted for its sensational value alone. Unfortunately, there was nothing in the new film to match the Niagara Falls rescue in The Man from Beyond or, really, any of the fantastic escapes of the earlier films. Harry read the reviews with dismay and compared his cost sheets with his income statements – he was losing too much money to continue.

He made the sad decision to cancel the films he'd been planning to make, and his career as a producer, screenwriter, and movie star came to an end. He never made another film.

Houdini with the cast and crew of Haldane of the Secret Service. It would be the last film project of his career

But he still had *Haldane of the Secret Service* on his hands and was determined to make the best of it. He wanted to recoup as many of his expenses as he could, so he mounted an extensive advertising campaign for the film. Giant cutout figures of Houdini, manacled in a diving position, were made available for display in front of theaters. Thousands of small slips of paper were printed with a message that read, "This lock is not HOUDINI-proof. He could pick it as easily as you pick a daisy. See the Master-Man of Mystery HOUDINI in *'Haldane of the Secret Service'*, a picture that will thrill you to your marrows." The notes were inserted in the keyholes of doors in cities where the movie was shown.

He then devised a novel stunt for publicizing the film. Two men carrying identical black satchels met on a busy downtown street. One man shouted that the other had taken his bag. After the dispute drew a crowd, one of the satchels was opened, and the two men whipped out a large cloth banner and held it up for all to see. The banner was printed with the name of the film and the theater where it was showing.

Houdini also spread rumors like the ones that had helped draw attention to *The Grim Game.* Reporters were told that the giant waterwheel in the film had broken as it whirled him around. He claimed that he had almost drowned before he could free himself from the wreckage.

It generated some publicity, but it wasn't enough. *Haldane of the Secret Service* was a financial disaster – but the promotion behind it served one purpose. All the advertising and publicity stunts managed to keep Houdini in the news and made tickets for his upcoming performances even more desirable.

He was now making more money than he'd ever made at any point in his career.

... AND THEY NEVER SPOKE AGAIN

IN 1923, HOUDINI'S EXPLORATION OF THE PARANORMAL continued when he joined a committee assembled by *Scientific American* magazine. It had been assembled for one purpose – to find a genuine spirit medium. To encourage mediums to perform for the committee, the magazine offered the sizable reward of $2,500 for an authentic exhibition.

The members of the committee included Dr. William McDougall, professor of psychology at Harvard; Dr. Daniel Fisk Comstock, from the Massachusetts Institute of Technology; Dr. Walter Franklin Prince, research officer for the American Society for Psychical Research; Hereward Carrington, a prolific writer on the occult; and Harry Houdini.

The committee had been Houdini's idea. The magazine had approached him to write a series of articles on Spiritualism, but, because of his vaudeville commitments, he could not accept the offer. He suggested instead that *Scientific American* form an investigative committee, on which he would serve for no fee -- if he were granted the right to select or reject its other members.

Harry did not exercise his power of approval to limit the committee membership to only people he knew would agree with

him. The committee would eventually have several members with whom Houdini could not get along. Even the original membership was problematic. Houdini's opinion of Hereward Carrington, for example, was that the writer was an opportunist who professed to believe in Spiritualism because it was a good way to sell his books about ghosts and the occult.

Before Houdini began a new cross-country vaudeville tour, he promised to cancel his bookings whenever he was called for an investigation.

The tour was soon underway, taking Houdini from city to city across the country. The Water Torture Cell was still the main feature of his act, and the straitjacket escapes that occurred high above city streets continued to tie up traffic and to draw capacity crowds for his performances.

In Denver, Houdini crossed paths with his estranged friend, Sir Arthur Conan Doyle. During Doyle's previous lecture tour of America, Houdini, with difficulty, had avoided a public controversy with his friend. Now, as newspaper headlines spoke of Sir Arthur's "spirit truths," Houdini's skeptical arguments against those "truths" also started to appear with the wire services. The controversy that had been avoided before was now turning up daily in the newspapers.

The Doyles and their children were Houdini's guests at the Orpheum Theater in Denver. Harry sent a box of candy to their young daughter and a bouquet of violets for Lady Jean. The family graciously came to see Harry in his dressing room after the show, but a friendly discussion about spirit photographs turned somewhat heated. Both men were simply too stubborn to stay quiet about what they truly believed, but neither left angry.

Harry and Sir Arthur met again the following day, and this time, Doyle insisted that Houdini allow him to introduce him to Julius and Agnes Zancig, who he claimed were genuine mediums.

But Houdini knew otherwise. Back in 1906, the couple had toured with him, and Julius was a member of the Society of American Magicians. Houdini had once bought a mind-reading act from him, with all the silent and spoken cues. Julius and Agnes had their own impressive mind-reading act – they were billed as "Two Minds with a Single Thought" – but he knew they were no more psychic mediums than he was.

Then on May 9, 1923, the *Denver Express* newspaper ran the following story:

DOYLE IN DENVER DEFIES HOUDINI AND
OFFERS TO BRING DEAD BACK AGAIN
Sir Arthur Conan Doyle, here to preach the gospel of spiritism, is going to back his psychic forces with $5,000 against the skepticism of Harry Houdini, the magician, who recently asserted that all séance manifestations were fakes. The famous writer asserted his arrival from Colorado Springs late yesterday when informed Houdini was also in Denver.

"Houdini and I have discussed spiritism before," said Sir

Arthur. *"I have invited him to attend a sitting with me, each of us backing our beliefs with $5,000. I have even offered to bring his dead mother before him in physical form and to talk to her. But we have never got together on it."*

The Doyles met Harry and Bess that evening in the lobby of the Brown Palace Hotel. Sir Arthur was apologetic, explaining to Harry that the newspaper had put words in his mouth. Houdini was very understanding. He had not seen the article, but he knew that reporters often misquoted people. He told Sir Arthur not to worry about it and then apologized for having to miss Doyle's lecture at the Ogden Theater that night because of his own performance. However, Bess was going to accept the Doyles' invitation to attend, and she would tell Harry all about it later.

The following day, Houdini decided to follow another recommendation made by Sir Arthur to see Alexander Martin, a Denver photographer whose pictures of the living also showed "spirit extras," or the faces of the dead. He took his assistant, Jim Collins, with him to Martin's studio.

When they arrived, Martin directed Houdini into a straight-backed chair and posed Collins standing behind him. The equipment was arranged, and the photograph was taken. When the plate was developed, the print showed four ghostly faces in the background -- two bearded men, a Native American, and a shrouded woman.

The next day, Harry returned for another sitting, and this time, he posed alone. Five "spirit extras" appeared on the print this time -- four bearded men and one who wore a mustache. Three of the "spirits" wore glasses. Houdini almost burst out laughing when he saw that the man with the mustache was the late Theodore Roosevelt.

Harry may have been amused, but he was not impressed. He believed that Martin was using a simple double-exposure technique. Before his arrival, he surmised that Martin had snipped the heads from other photographs, put them on a black background, and exposed the plate, masking the area in the center. With this prepared plate, ghostly extras would "materialize" when Martin photographed his subject.

Houdini later created his own spirit photographs using this same technique. In one of them, he held his own "spirit self" in his arms, and in another, Abraham Lincoln appeared with him.

Harry assured his friends that the spirit of Abraham Lincoln had not dropped in for a visit that day.

MEANWHILE, THE RUSH OF APPLICANTS FOR THE *SCIENTIFIC American* prize had failed to materialize, even after a lesser prize was added for anyone who could produce an authentic spirit photograph.

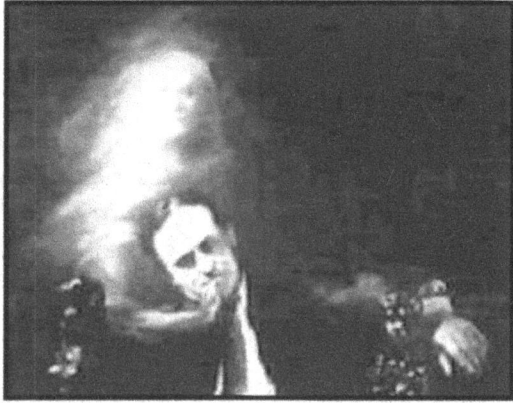

To prove the ease in which fraudulent spirit photographs could be created, Houdini experimented with many of his own at his home in New York.

Above, Houdini causes "ectoplasm" to appear from his mouth and take the shape of a woman's features and below, Houdini appears with the ghost of Abraham Lincoln.

It wasn't hard to explain the shortage of candidates. It was easy for a photographer to produce mysterious photos on his own

Medium Elizabeth Allen Thomson during one of her seances. She was caught cheating before she even got the chance to perform for the Scientific American panel.

plates, in his own studio, or for a medium to conjure up phenomena when surrounded by hymn-singing believers, but why risk their reputations being tested by observers who were well versed in psychology, physics, and trickery?

A few mediums did come forward. The first to announce that she was ready to try for the prize was Elizabeth Allen Thomson. However, she was never formally tested, since before she ever entered the séance room, she was searched and caught with 20 yards of gauze taped to her groin, flowers tucked under her breasts, and a live snake concealed in her armpit.

One contestant who looked more promising was George Valiantine. He performed two séances for *Scientific American* while Houdini was on the road. The first had been unimpressive. During the second, though, a trumpet had floated in the dark, lifted by a Native American spirit -- according to the medium, at least. The trumpet tapped various sitters, whacked a spectator's head, and then crashed to the floor just as Fred Keating, a young magician friend of Hereward Carrington, tried to grab it.

Houdini showed up to attend the third séance, and this time, science was introduced to the séance room. Unknown to the medium, men in an adjoining chamber were following his movements with light signals, a Dictaphone, and a stopwatch. Valiantine's chair had been wired. Whenever he left his seat, a light flashed in the control room, and a note was made of the time. By comparing the times that Valiantine got out of his chair with the times when phenomena occurred in the séance room, it was obvious that it was the medium, not the spirits, who had been raising a ruckus in the dark. The *New York Times* quoted Houdini when the medium was exposed.

J. Malcolm Bird, an associate editor of the magazine and the secretary for the investigative committee, was annoyed by the newspaper story. The *Times* reporter should not have written the story until he, Bird, had written an article in *Scientific American*. He resented being scooped.

Houdini helped to expose another fraudulent medium: George Valiantine

When the *Times* followed up with an interview with Houdini, Bird was enraged. The medium-trapping system used during the séance had been devised before Houdini, who was busy with his vaudeville tour, came on the scene. Yet to the public, it appeared that the magician had exposed Valiantine. Bird disliked Houdini immensely.

This would be the first time the two men clashed, but it would not be the last.

In California, Conan Doyle was upset by another newspaper story. Quotes from Houdini in the *Oakland Tribune* were "full of errors." He wrote to Houdini saying that he had to "utterly contradict" them. Perhaps Sir Arthur had forgotten he had been misquoted in Denver. Harry replied that he had given the Oakland reporter material for a single article, which had been expanded into a series. He couldn't help the fact that his statements had been misconstrued. By this time, the friendship between the two men had reached a point that it was almost beyond repair.

Houdini spent more time attacking fraudulent mediums than arranging spectacular escapes during his fall vaudeville tour. In late September, he spoke to a psychology class at the University of Illinois on "The Psychology of Audiences" and "The Negative Side of Spiritualism." The latter topic took up most of the class time. In October, he gave an illustrated lecture on mediums and their methods at Marquette University.

Meanwhile, medium Nino Pecoraro had applied for the *Scientific American* prize money while Houdini was still on the road with his lecture tour.

Doyle, during his first American lecture tour, had attended a séance held by Pecoraro and had been tremendously impressed by him. He noted that the medium, while bound with wire, caused a bell to ring, a tambourine to spin in the air, and a toy piano to play. Hereward Carrington, a committee member, had arranged the séance for Doyle. There was reason to think that the committee might give Pecoraro a sympathetic test.

Doubtlessly believing that Pecoraro would have too easy a time of it, *Scientific American* publisher Orson Munn urgently requested Houdini, then playing in Little Rock, Arkansas, to return to New York and attend a séance. Fellow committee members, he explained, planned to tie the Italian medium with a 60-foot-long rope, which caused Houdini to laugh. Even amateur escapologists could free their hands when trussed up in such a manner, he said. When Houdini arrived, he slashed the rope into short lengths and secured the medium himself. Not surprisingly, the medium produced no manifestations.

Houdini caught up with his theater tour in the Midwest. He spoke at several more colleges, which became rehearsals for a lecture tour that was booked for him around the country. His anti-Spiritualism campaign had been only for his spare time during his Orpheum tour. Now he was free -- at least for 20 one-night shows -- to devote his full energy to counteracting the propaganda that people like Sir Arthur Conan Doyle were spreading.

Houdini's lectures were a huge success. The people who attended the shows came more to see him perform than to hear about his exposure of Spiritualists. But he found that by mixing entertainment with his message, he could appeal to the crowds. To say that a medium employed a trick spirit slate was not enough. He had to show how the slate was used. The actual demonstration drove his point home and delighted the audience at the same time. To make sure that he had full auditoriums to educate, he broke out the challenge of packing boxes at every stop along his route to generate publicity.

Then, in 1924, Houdini hammered the last nail in the coffin that was the doom of his friendship with Sir Arthur Conan Doyle.

The publication of his book *A Magician Among the Spirits* that year brought violent attacks from believers, cheers from the skeptics, and the inevitable end of his friendship with Sir Arthur.

Houdini wrote that he treasured Doyle as a friend. Sir Arthur was a "brilliant man," and he had a "great mind" except where Spiritualism was concerned. Houdini respected Doyle's beliefs and was convinced that he was sincere, but the eminent author refused to accept the fact that many of the mediums he endorsed were frauds. Houdini listed numerous examples of times when Sir Arthur trusted spirit mediums who others proved to be frauds.

He also quoted the written message that Lady Jean claimed had come from his mother in Atlantic City --- then revealed why it could not have been from her spirit.

Doyle was angered and saddened by the book. He had been fascinated with Houdini the man, but when his friend attempted to destroy his beliefs and held him up to ridicule, any further friendship between them was impossible.

Houdini and Conan Doyle never wrote or spoke to one another again.

THE "MARGERY" AFFAIR

HOUDINI RETURNED TO HIS LECTURE TOUR AFTER THE Pecararo fiasco, only to hear three months later that the *Scientific American* investigative panel had deadlocked over a Boston medium named Mina Crandon, who used the stage name of "Margery."

The panel stated that it believed her to be genuine and was prepared to give her the $2,500 reward. Houdini's antagonist, J. Malcolm Bird, was one of Crandon's supporters and was eager to give her the magazine's endorsement. He allowed word of the panel's favorable findings to reach the press. "Boston Medium Baffles Experts," one headline announced. "Houdini the Magician Stumped," trumpeted another.

Houdini, who had not even been present during Crandon's séances, much less stumped by them, was stunned to think the magazine would even consider approving a medium that he had never seen. Harry immediately contacted publisher Orson Munn, and newspapers soon trumpeted what he'd told Munn – if Houdini failed to expose Margery as a fraud, he would add $1,000 of his own money to the *Scientific American* prize.

When Sir Arthur Conan Doyle heard the news that Houdini was going to be joining the investigation of Margery – a medium he, of course, strongly supported – he was outraged. He called including such an outspoken enemy of Spiritualism in a fair and unbiased examination a "capital error." He wrote: "The Commission is, in my opinion, a farce."

Scientific American editor (and Houdini nemesis) J. Malcolm Bird with Sir Arthur Conan Doyle

Mina Crandon, however, seemed to welcome the opportunity to test her mettle against Houdini. The prize money meant nothing to her since her husband was a wealthy doctor. However, the opportunity to win the approval of such a prestigious committee -- at the expense of Houdini -- proved too great a temptation for her to resist.

Houdini traveled by train to Boston with Orson Munn, and on the way, he reviewed the findings of his colleagues on the investigative panel. In his way of thinking, the investigation was poorly handled from the start. Margery did not perform under the same test conditions as those forced on other mediums. She was allowed to hold her test séances at her home in Boston, which opened things up widely for the possibility of fraud.

Most of the committee members had availed themselves of the Crandons' generous hospitality during the proceedings, staying in their home, eating their food, and socializing with them. Houdini believed that this had badly compromised their objectivity, and later, it was learned that accepting food and a bed from the Crandons was the least of the problems. One investigator had shockingly even borrowed money from Margery's husband, while another hoped to win his backing for a research foundation. Worse yet, the "distinguished" panel was not unaware of Margery's physical attractions. Years later, at least one committee member would tell of his amorous encounters with the shapely medium.

Mina Crandon certainly created a firestorm of controversy in the paranormal world of the early 1920s, but in truth, she was a rather unlikely medium.

MINA STINSON WAS BORN IN ONTARIO, CANADA, IN 1888, THE daughter of a farmer. She moved to Boston when she was 16, pursuing a career in music. She was talented with the piano, coronet, and cello, and she performed with many local bands and orchestras, although this seldom paid well. After working as a secretary, an actress, and an ambulance driver, she married a grocer named Earl P. Rand, with whom she had a son. They remained happily married until a medical operation introduced her to Le Roi "Roy" Goddard Crandon, a prominent surgeon and a former instructor at the Harvard Medical School. She divorced Rand in 1918 and married Roy Crandon a short time later.

Mina had no psychic experiences early in her life and, in fact, had no interest in the spirit world at all until her husband became enthralled with the paranormal around 1920.

One evening in May 1923, Dr.

Crandon invited several friends to his home to attempt a seance. The group gathered around a small table and soon had it tilting in response to the sitters' questions. Roy suggested that each person remove their hands from the table, one at a time, to see which individual was responsible for the paranormal activity. One by one, each of them took their hands away, but the table only stopped rocking when the last of the sitters lifted her hands. Dr. Crandon had solved the mystery -- the medium was his own wife.

Dr. Le Roi "Roy" Crandon posing for a "spirit photograph." It was his influence that pushed Mina into becoming a spirit medium and he defended her tirelessly against attacks by Houdini.

At first, the idea of being a medium seemed like a lark to the fun-loving Mina. Throughout the summer of 1923, the Crandons held numerous séances in their home. Each time, Mina seemed to be able to entice furniture to move and raps to rattle the wooden table. But after many nights of this, Roy proposed a new method of communicating with the other side. Knocks and raps would no longer suffice. Instead, he wanted Mina to go into a trance and vocally produce the spirit messages.

"I will do nothing of the sort," she told her husband.

This was the first time that Mina had protested her husband's ideas, so to settle the matter, Roy put the question to what seemed to be the dominant presence at their séances. Moments later, the spirit indicated through table knocks that it wanted to try the experiment.

For a while, all hands remained on the table, and the only sound was a faint series of taps. Then, as one, all heads turned toward Mina, who was making strange noises. She sighed and began to sway. Suddenly, a loud and guttural voice, nothing like her own, cried out, "I said I could put this through!"

According to the accounts of those present, when Mina came out of her trance that night, her face was damp, but not with tears or perspiration. She was secreting ectoplasm – the unexplained substance of the spirit world.

While nothing miraculous occurred that night, an important contact had been made, and from that point on, Mina began to exhibit new abilities at nearly every sitting. It seemed that Roy only had to read about some new manifestation of spirit before his wife could duplicate it.

Soon, the identity of the deep voice that had emerged that night was identified. It belonged to Mina's brother, Walter Stinson, who had been crushed to death in a railroad accident in 1911. From this point on, Walter's spirit was a regular presence in the Crandon séance room. He proved to have a strong personality, a quick wit, and was given to using salty language. Many visitors to the séance room became convinced of what they heard simply because they could not imagine that such coarse and vulgar language would come from the mouth of the pretty doctor's wife.

But that was the strange thing – many observers noted that Walter's voice did not seem to come from Mina at all. The sound

Mina's late brother, Walter Stinson, who became her "spirit guide" and a driving force during her seances, or so she claimed.

seemed to emanate from another part of the room, and it was claimed that the voice was often heard even when Mina wasn't speaking or when her mouth was filled with water. The effect seemed so remarkable that one skeptic, searching for a plausible explanation for what he had experienced, wondered if perhaps Mina was able to speak through her ears. Walter became well known as Mina's spirit guide and, along with his sister, began to get a lot of attention.

Within weeks, experts at Harvard got wind of the séances across the Charles River. Dr. A.A. Roback, who knew Roy professionally, was the first outside investigator to participate in the séances. Roback, a Harvard psychologist with a thick German accent, was told how the table had manifested incredible power, how it pushed into the laps of the sitters, and had chased one of them out of the study and into the hall.

Such things sounded ridiculous to Roback, and when Mina later brought the table to life, he ducked under the table with a flashlight to make sure the medium and her sitters were not using a hand or foot to cause the piece of furniture to vibrate and move.

There was no place in Dr. Roback's worldview for the occult, and yet he found no evidence of flim-flam or trickery. He turned to the chief of Harvard psychology, Dr. William McDougall – a member of the *Scientific American* panel – to help solve the mystery.

During the first few months of Mina's mediumship, the psychologists participated in many of her séances. Walter – the spirit guide – gladly welcomed them, claiming that both men were known on the higher plane for their work with mediums. Even so, in their attempts to establish a natural explanation for Mina's manifestations, the investigators found themselves in a sort of contest with the spirit, trying to prove that with their strict controls, the phenomena would stop. But for all their efforts, the activity continued.

Although Mina purportedly was unable to whistle, Walter usually announced his arrival in the séance room with a piercing

A photo of Mina during one of her seances, where word of her alleged skills began to spread to the scientific community in Boston

whistle. The sitters reported noises that sounded like dragging chains; raps on the furniture, walls, and floor; piano notes on the instrument on the home's first floor; and much more.

Unsettling as all this was, the table seemed to be where most of the action occurred. One night, Walter was challenged to cause the table to levitate. A tense wait began as the spirit gathered energy from the circle, and then with a wobble and a shake, it allegedly lifted a few inches off the floor. Over the next two months, Walter's strength seemed to grow, and after steady progress, he was able to raise the table for as long as a minute and at shoulder height.

And the table apparently didn't have to be empty. Reports claimed that on two occasions, a neighbor climbed onto the table in an attempt to stop its movements, but it bucked him off, like a horse would have done.

Soon, the regular séance attendees began utilizing most of the traditional articles used for séances, and Mina often sat in a curtained, wood-framed spirit cabinet, which provided the darkness and privacy needed for ectoplasm to materialize. Dr. Edison Brown, the husband of Mina's friend, Kitty, was cautious about attributing what he witnessed to true spirit energy, and it was often he who sat next to Mina and kept control of her hands and legs during séances. One night, Dr. Brown occupied the spirit cabinet with her, and it began to shake and move around the floor. Loud knocks were heard, and the curtain rod swung downward, inches from Brown's head. Then the entire structure simply broke apart.

It was rebuilt sturdier than before, and during a sitting one week later, with Dr. McDougall now controlling Mina inside the cabinet, the curtain rod again shot toward him with hostile force. When the sitters tried to replace it, they claimed to meet resistance from an invisible presence that shattered the cabinet a second time. The nine screws that held the structure together were soon discovered neatly stacked in the corner.

Dr. William McDougall

Despite what occurred that night, Dr. McDougall turned out to be a much tougher audience than Mina's friend, Dr. Brown. He had been present for dozens of séances during the summer of 1923, and by autumn, he had become suspicious about Mina's psychic abilities. He asked to meet with Mina on November 23 and informed her of his misgivings. He clearly wanted her to confess to some sort of mischief.

When she challenged his allegations, he patronizingly explained that he had been a major in the British Army during the Great War; it had been his duty as a psychologist to distinguish the disturbed cases from those simply shirking their duty. He was concerned about her well-being, he told her, and implied that the pressure that had been put on her to manifest spirits was pushing her to cheat.

Mina protested. She hadn't faked anything. How could she? She was unconscious during the sittings.

Disappointed by her lack of remorse, McDougall insisted she was not dishonest – it was only an innocent joke that got out of hand.

Again, Mina denied this. He'd been at her séances and had held her hands and feet, she reminded him. How was it possible for her to cheat?

The argument went back and forth until finally, McDougall told her that he would have to expose her to Roy if she didn't come clean. But Mina replied that no matter what Dr. McDougall did, she and her husband would continue to hold seances and converse with Walter. Smiling in bewilderment, she said that her brother's spirit was as real as any psychologist who had come to her home on Lime Street. At that moment, McDougall reached into his desk and brought out evidence that he claimed proved otherwise.

He held in his hand a piece of thread. The thread had been invisible in the dark room, but he claimed he had found it after the séance.

To the psychologist's irritation, Mina began laughing. She now realized that he had been hoping to lull her into a confession with a random piece of thread. But it was nothing more than a theatrical prop – Dr. McDougall had no other explanation for the things he'd seen.

As she walked out of his office, she was struck by the absurdity of the visit. No matter what McDougall tried to claim, Mina Crandon had not been caught doing anything that could be considered fraud.

She didn't know it yet, but the investigations – and the accusations – were just getting started.

ON THE SAME DAY AS THE CONFRONTATION WITH DR. McDougall, the Crandons picked up *Scientific American* associate editor Malcolm Bird at the Back Bay Station in Boston. Bird was struck by her appearance when he saw her. She was not at all what he'd been expecting. The female candidates that he'd considered for the panel so far had been middle-aged, stout, and unrefined. In contrast, Mina was a youthful blond with the stylish bobbed hair of a light-hearted flapper.

And Bird would not be the only investigator – well, male investigator -- to feel that way. Even Houdini conceded that she was an exceedingly attractive woman, and one psychic researcher warned his colleagues to "avoid falling in love with the medium."

She usually greeted the sitters at her séances wearing a flimsy dressing gown, bedroom slippers, and silk stockings. This attire, leaving almost nothing to the imagination, was supposedly intended to rule out the possibility of trickery or concealment, but it also tended to distract male visitors. Mina's slender figure, pretty face, and merry blue eyes made her, in

Malcom Bird would not be the only male investigator who was charmed by Mina Crandon, which had disastrous results

the words of one admirer, "too attractive for her own good." To make matters more titillating, it was rumored that it was not uncommon for her to hold sessions in the nude and, according to some, she was especially adept at manifesting ectoplasm from her vagina.

The Crandons returned to Lime Street with their guest, and Bird sat down for dinner with the Crandons and their friend, Aleck Cross.

Cross, a middle-aged victim of "shell shock" that the Crandons charitably employed, had been broken years earlier by the War. After witnessing one of Mina's séances, he became a Spiritualist overnight. He held Mina in affectionate awe, despite her being 19 years younger than he was and, he believed, a witch. He didn't believe she was a spell-caster, but he had noticed at one sitting that she had aurora-like flares shooting from her fingers, had heard her speak prophecies while in a trance, and was bewildered by her gift of automatic writing. Mina was now manifesting writings from spirits in English, French, Swedish, Dutch, Greek, and German – as well as a note in Latin that was translated by a blushing classics professor who said it was too obscene to repeat. She had also produced for Cross, who had spent almost 30 years adventuring in the Far East, a message in Chinese that had addressed him by a childhood nickname that schoolmates who thought he had the eyes of a "Chinaman" had given him while growing up in England. How could she know what they had called him as a boy?

The group had barely started the first course before Mina brought up her confrontation with Dr. McDougall. It sounded to Bird that Mina had gotten the better of the psychologist. She said he had subjected her to kindness, threats, and intimidation to try to persuade her to admit to trickery. She appeared to be hurt and confused, unable to understand what he thought she had to gain from faking psychic manifestations.

Bird later recalled, "It was impossible for her to talk about anything other than the allegation of fraud, or to listen to anything else for more than a minute at a time." She seemed to be reacting with genuine indignation, he thought, of someone falsely confused. But if this was – like the committee's other cases – another dead end, he didn't blame Dr. McDougall for wanting to discover this sooner rather than later. Bird was determined to find out if Mina was genuine or another imposter.

Bird told her that Harry Helson, a psychologist who'd assisted McDougall with his investigations, had discovered a thread attached to a stool that Walter was supposed to have moved across the room. Mina asked him what he would think if he found a piece of thread on the floor after a séance, and Bird said he'd likely think it had unraveled from a rug. But what about the matter of it being attached to the stool?

Mina's face reddened. Helson, she told him, had not found anything tied to a stool.

"He didn't?" Bird was puzzled.

Before she could say anything else, Roy interrupted and insisted that he was ready to accept a plausible explanation for his wife's effects. However, none of the psychologists had come up with one.

Then Aleck described how Walter tore apart the spirit cabinet with McDougall inside, and suggested there were bad feelings between the spirit and the psychologist.

While touring the house after dinner, Bird noticed a significant impediment to any investigation. The house, at No. 10 Lime Street, had an elaborate layout, and he knew it would not be easy to find a place for a controlled experiment. It had been turned into a complex piece of architecture because of extensive remodeling. He noted:

There are two flights of back stairs, affording four independent points of access to the front of the house; there is a butler's pantry with a dumb-waiter. The whole house fairly teems with curious closets, crannies, cubbyholes large and small, blind shaft ways, etc., the utility or necessity of which is now always apparent. The more mysterious ones doubtless occupy space that hung heavy on the remodeler's hands, but even when one has formulated this idea, some of them are very puzzling.

The Crandons' stylish home at No. 10 Lime Street in Boston

The Crandons, though, seemed less eccentric than their home. Even as the evening progressed and the conversation went naturally in macabre directions, Bird found the couple engaging and refreshingly rational.

Bird was perhaps more impressed with their social credentials than he should have been, in any case. He was of a much humbler origin. His roots were in Brooklyn, where his father had been a carpenter. It was only his gift for science and mathematics that got him to Cornell and Columbia, and now, he has a position at the magazine. As studious as he was, he quickly found himself charmed by the medium and her husband – more charmed than Houdini, as a serious investigator, would have liked.

He became so comfortable with the couple that Bird began explaining how magicians used horsehair to levitate objects invisibly – the way that McDougall had claimed she caused the table to rise – and so she led the search for threads and horsehairs by looking under ashtrays and teacups. "She has a sense of humor quite as wicked as my own," Bird said. "My visit was made into one continuous circus by the fashion in which that confederacy theory was batted about the house."

The hilarity continued as an amused Mina pulled Bird along with her as she threw open closet doors to look for accomplices and lifted rugs that might hide trapdoors. At one point, she dramatically pulled open drapes behind which someone might hide, though she claimed to have no idea who that person might be.

The Crandons' maid, Lydia, was too scatterbrained for flimflam, she told him. Lydia would walk into a séance and blurt to the Harvard investigators that she forgot to crank the Victrola that played the ghostly sounds. Aleck Cross was too clumsy to tiptoe around in the dark.

"If we cracked one joke about strings, we cracked a hundred," Bird wrote. He believed their horseplay was her way of dealing with the strain that came from her visit to McDougall, but it wasn't that simple. She captivated Bird like no medium had before – and that was the problem. Mina slowly and carefully got the editor on her side, recruiting him as an ally against the other investigators who were treating her so unfairly.

He laughed at her jokes, mooned over her good looks, and was drawn in by the elegance of Mina and her husband. When Dr. Crandon suggested that the Harvard researchers may have been in a hurry to expose Mina before Bird got the credit for revealing another hoax, he was flattered by how highly Roy seemed to think of him. He hadn't even seen Mina perform a séance, and he was already starting to believe anything the Crandons told him.

And he wasn't the only one eager to please the couple. Harry Helson stopped by Lime Street on the day after Bird arrived and said he wanted to make amends. He had been eager to solve the mystery and found the string on the floor. It wasn't attached to anything. He had been misquoted, he said. He apologized for offending the Crandons. Later, McDougall stopped by and he apologized, too. In return, the Crandons withdrew the ban on the Harvard men – they were welcome to return to Lime Street.

Later that night, Bird heard the hair-raising whistle in the séance room and was greeted by Mina's dead brother for the first time. Walter's voice was so different from the medium's that Bird couldn't imagine the same vocal cords producing both sounds.

At a sitting the following evening, nothing occurred for some time, and when the table did start to move, something seemed different. Walter typically turned the table in a circular motion, but this time, it moved in a straight, jerky fashion – a sign that an unfamiliar spirit was in control. It would only communicate using the old method, tilts, which spell out yes and no. However, it answered no to everything that was asked of it.

All were relieved when the energy seemed to change, and Walter returned. The table started twirling in the way that was his trademark. But he didn't stay, and soon, the other personality was directing the medium. A frightening male voice whispered, "Break the circle, quick!" and all the sitters pushed away from the table. Only Mina remained. She was oblivious to danger while in her trance and urged her friends back into the circle. Thinking this was a bad idea, Roy turned on the lights to wake her, and she abruptly went into a seizure. Her body contorted wildly, and her arms thrashed against the spirit cabinet.

According to Bird, her voice changed, and she began cursing loudly. As Walter tried to come through, the voice barked, "Get the hell out of here!" To all appearances, there was a struggle for control of the medium. This went on for several minutes, but the struggle eventually ended, as did the séance.

Malcolm Bird was almost sure that what he had seen that night had been real.

THE FOLLOWING NIGHT, THE HARVARD MEN WERE INVITED TO return to Lime Street for dinner and for a séance. Dr. McDougall thought it was improper to return so soon after offending the Crandons, but Helson was there, along with Gardner Murphy, an alternative judge for the Scientific American contest.

As the séance proceeded, the researchers realized the medium was not in good form. She demonstrated only the least impressive table effects. It seemed the mysterious intruder was still preventing her brother from manifesting. Bird found it more disturbing that the table kept moving toward him, confirming the suspicion of one of Mina's friends – that he was responsible for attracting this malevolent spirit. Their attitude took him aback since psychics had always considered him an energizing presence in the past.

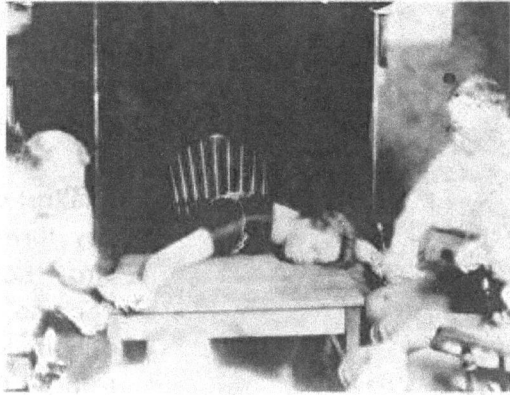

Mina performed seances for Boston scientists, as well as members of the Scientific American commission before Houdini became involved in the investigation

It was decided that Bird and the Harvard men should leave the house to see if Mina performed better without them in the room. They took a stroll while Mina's friends attempted to contact Walter. He soon returned and told them that the interfering force was on a lower plane, closer than he was, which was why it was easier for it to control Mina. Walter said the situation would only be dangerous if Mina slipped into a trance. It was safe to hold séances, but only if she was conscious. But if he told them to break the circle, they needed to do so immediately.

At the séance the following evening, Bird watched everything closely. At one point, the table moved slightly, and Helson spoke up, complaining that he was tired of that kind of phenomenon. "Let's get on to levitation and the music," he urged. It was a remark that Bird felt disqualified the Harvard man from psychical research – if his previous misconduct hadn't already done that.

In reply, Mina explained that she was helpless without her magic thread that lifted tables and pulled piano strings. They all laughed – even Helson. Moments later, Aleck Cross left the circle, and then so did Gardner Murphy, who needed to catch a train to

Mina Crandon posing for a "spirit photograph"

New York. The commotion led Mina to wonder if Walter had wanted them to break the circle, and yet, he had not returned.

All agreed they would make one last attempt to contact Walter. Roy turned down the lights, and Bird noticed that Mina had become silent. Someone announced that she was in a trance. Before they could wake her, the intruder spirit had returned. She made anguished noises, kicked over a chair, and toppled onto the floor, knocking over the spirit cabinet. At Dr. Crandon's command, four men struggled to get hold of Mina. She fought against them and then suffered another seizure, although it was shorter than the previous evening. She came out of it moaning, as if waking from a very disturbing dream.

If she was faking this, Bird thought to himself, she ought to be in the movies.

On his way back to New York the next morning, Bird mulled over what he had seen. Dr. McDougall had made it clear that he thought this case had more to do with abnormal psychology than the spirit world. As for Bird, however, he was impressed with the sincerity of the medium and found her unusually gifted, even if he had witnessed none of the physical effects that had baffled other researchers.

The one thing that worried him was Walter's open contempt for the Harvard team. "It takes a crook to catch one," the spirit said of the investigators trying to discredit his sister. It seemed that science was on the defensive this time, not the spirits. The Harvard investigators seemed out of their element, finding the idea that a ghost might really exist an assault on a scientist's beliefs and authority. They were willing to consider the reality of paranormal phenomena while doubting that spirits could be the cause.

Back in New York, he informed Orson Munn that there was a war raging between the Crandons and the Harvard scientists. Who was winning? Munn wanted to know.

Bird told him that the medium was winning.

WHILE MALCOLM BIRD HAD BEEN IMPRESSED WITH MINA, no one promoted her as widely and loudly as her husband, Roy Crandon. Believing that his lovely wife was a "remarkable psychic instrument," he took her abroad to build up a consensus of favorable opinion about her from European experts. One of these was Sir Arthur Conan Doyle, who declared her to be a "very powerful medium" and, he noted, "the validity of her gifts was beyond all question."

Dr. Roy Crandon

Meanwhile, in New York, Bird was writing a series of articles about Mina. All were lopsided enough in her favor that he could hardly be considered an impartial investigator.

At the behest of Orson Munn, *Scientific American* published in bold print the names of famous psychics that Bird was most interested in bringing to New York for testing. The magazine was willing to pay their way and put them up, but they needed to step forward now or not at all.

The only worthwhile reply came from Roy Crandon -- who had returned to America, even though his wife's name was not on Munn's list. Mina was willing to be tested; however, Dr. Crandon feared the New York setting would be a circus and was convinced nothing of merit could be determined there. Instead, he offered to bring the commission to Boston so that the séances could take place in a calmer environment. He even invited the judges to stay at Lime Street while they sat with Mina, just as Malcolm Bird had recently done.

The news that Mina was ready to step into the spotlight pleased Bird. He felt she was likely their last hope, he told Munn, for investigating a worthwhile psychic. Unlike other mediums, Mina never took payment for her work, and the Crandons had generously offered to fund the tests in Boston.

In return, Bird was willing to make special arrangements for them. Bringing mediums to the Scientific American offices, where they were expected to deliver, was not working; even Munn conceded that. So, what harm could it do?

The Crandons also wanted to avoid publicity – what other medium could say that? – To address their concern about appearing in the newspapers, Bird offered to give her a pseudonym. Mina's middle name was Marguerite, so why not call her Margery?

And it would be under this name that Mina's fame would steadily grow during and after the tests.

UNKNOWN TO HOUDINI, THE TESTS BEGAN IN APRIL 1924 WHEN Bird returned to Boston. He quickly discovered that the activity during Mina's séances had increased in power. Almost as soon as the night began with the ghost's eerie whistle, he saw things that he'd never seen before.

Walter had started to produce spirit lights that flashed and danced around the sitters. He warned the sitters not to be afraid or panic at their appearance. The lights often appeared in clouds of mist, while others were in the shapes of circles and diamonds. They were sometimes accompanied by cool breezes that were strong enough to move the curtains.

Following the light show were table manifestations, like when it clipped over and rotated back into its upright position. Then it tilted on two legs. Mina's spirit cabinet began to quake, shifting and tilting to the point that Bird had to join Roy and Dr. McDougall in keeping it steady.

Bird was also asked to help control the medium, to make sure that she wasn't physically responsible for the strange happenings in the séance room. He was able to keep her hands firmly gripped – yet to his shock, his hair was grabbed and pulled. Dr. Roback, whose job it was to catch anyone sneaking around in the room, swore that no one was standing behind Bird. Either the medium had used her teeth, or Walter was responsible for the attack.

Bird had little time to consider the assault before something more remarkable happened fully. Walter had apparently gotten hold of a curtain rod from the top part of the cabinet and slammed it onto the table with a hair-raising crack.

The next sitting was just as perplexing. The pole moved again, this time all over the room, and Bird could only say one thing for sure – that Mina, with all four of her extremities controlled, had not moved the pole. If there was a human culprit responsible, Bird could not identify them.

During the investigations, a guard – usually McDougall's assistant – was stationed at the door to prevent an intruder from sneaking into the séance room. And to ensure that none of the sitters were up to mischief, Dr. Roback continued to patrol the room quietly.

As the investigations continued. Bird and the others took full advantage of the Crandons' offer to accommodate any representatives of *Scientific American* and other judges of the contest, who wanted to stay with them. After the séances, large parties often went out to dinner, and Dr. Crandon always picked up the bill. Bird saw Mina's hospitality and the doctor's generosity as proof of the Crandons' dedication to the inquiry.

Others wouldn't see it quite that way.

Between April and August, Bird made eight separate visits to Boston. He wasn't alone. Other visitors included Hereward

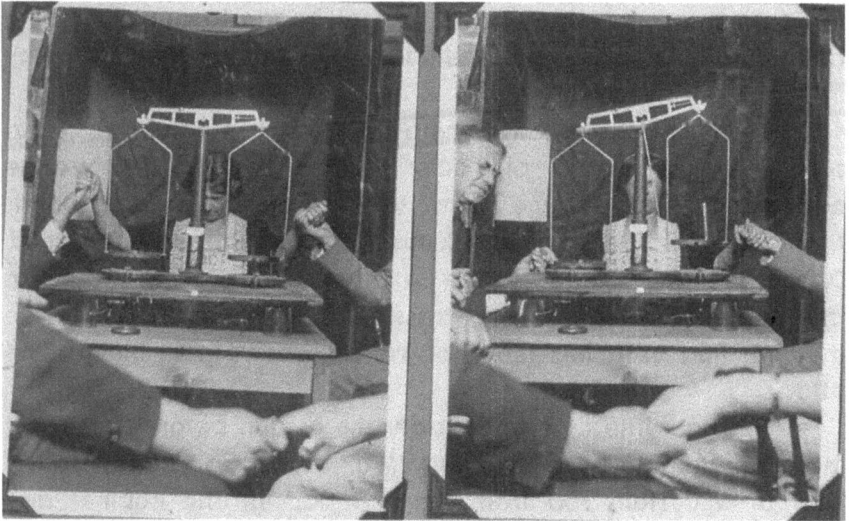

Seances with Margery were often conducted using testing equipment to determine if she was creating physical manifestations with psychic powers.

Carrington; Fred Keating, a magician and alternate judge; physicist Daniel Comstock; Walter Franklin Prince; and others. But Bird was the most frequent offender. During that spring and summer, Bird – neglecting his editorial duties – spent 57 days and nights at Lime Street.

Is it any wonder that he became one of "Margery's" great defenders? Nearly as dedicated was Hereward Carrington, who, like Bird, became fast friends with the Crandons. Both men felt this gave them some advantage in determining whether the mediumship was authentic, instead of making them look like fools.

Dr. McDougall was not so easily entranced. Despite months of trying, though, he had never caught the medium committing fraud. Regardless, the psychologist was never shy about theorizing aloud that strings were transporting objects during her sittings or that her spirit cabinet was destroyed by a stealthy intruder in the dark, not a ghost.

One of the cardinal rules of the *Scientific American* tests was not to condemn the psychic without ironclad evidence, but

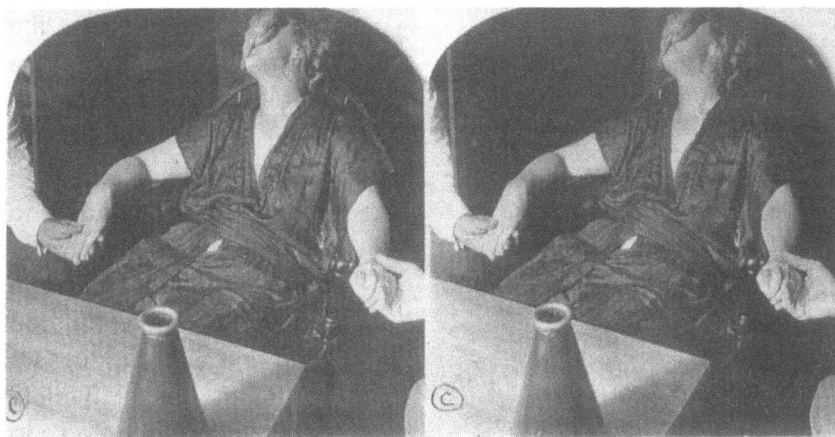

McDougall continued to voice whatever suspicions came into his head. It was difficult, though, to provoke real anger in Margery. She had forgiven him for the accusations in his office, and during the séances, a kind of banter developed between them, and she responded to his skepticism with humor.

And Margery would continue to laugh. She could afford to be funny when she knew that no one had the ammunition with which to expose her.

WEEKS PASSED AND THE SÉANCES CONTINUED. DR. CRANDON was fond of telling the investigators that Margery could produce exactly what the committee called for – fraud-proof yet straightforward exhibitions of her psychic power.

Daniel Comstock had invented a new device for the séance table with which the medium could be tested – a bell and a battery wired to a telegraph key that, when pressed down, caused the apparatus to ring. The challenge presented to Margery was to make the bell ring without touching it physically.

Margery had no idea that he was introducing the device into the séance on the night he appeared with it, and yet, on that same night, she mastered it convincingly. While Bird was in place, controlling Margery's movements, the bell rang suddenly. Bird

The bell and battery device that was created for Margery's seances by Daniel Comstock

believed this was "the climax of the mediumship, so far as sheer inescapable validity."

With her hands and feet controlled, she caused the bell to ring in long and short peals, one time and then repeatedly. Walter, her invisible companion, seemed to have complete control over its functions.

"You ask it to ring and it rings," Bird said. "You ask it to stop and it stops."

There were times when one of Margery's sitters, usually the farthest from her, grabbed the bell box and left the circle. It rang as he walked away. Her hands were held, and an investigator covered her feet, but it rang. The bell rang when she laughed. A sitter held the bell in his lap – it rang. A light was placed over the contraption to reveal any shadowy hand or device that might have caused the effect. None were spotted. The bell was secured inside a box – it still rang. In darkness, as well as in a lighted room, the bell rang.

Once, though not in the presence of the commission, a sitter asked Walter if he could reveal his own ethereal hand as he pressed the button. A friend of the Crandons, Dr. Mark Richardson, reported that a shaft of light, in the shape of a finger, suddenly appeared from Margery's lap, and when it reached the bell, it rang.

Even before these latest experiments with the bell, Dr. Crandon knew that Malcolm Bird believed in Margery's power. Bird believed that even if Margery's revelations were due to an unknown subconscious force and not her dead brother, she was the genuine psychic they had been searching for. It made no difference to Bird whether the spirits were present. What mattered was that Margery's abilities appeared to transcend known physical laws. And when the commission could not explain a medium's effects, she was supposed to be awarded the prize.

In Bird's opinion. Margery was authentic, trustworthy, and overwhelmingly convincing. While returning to New York, Carrington said that he felt the same way and that if a vote were held that day, his ballot would be cast in her favor. Keating, while not a voting member of the committee, was also a believer. He'd seen no sign of hocus-pocus in her abilities.

Bird believed that Comstock was on the verge of supporting her, and even McDougall seemed to be softening. But while Bird only needed four votes to declare Margery a winner, the idea was not for the committee to decide individually. They were supposed to render their decision as one unified panel.

And that left Houdini.

Woman Astounds Psychic Experts
- New York Times

Scientific Investigators Won by Demonstrations of Rich Woman Medium
- Brooklyn Eagle

Four of Five Men to Bestow Award
Sure She is 100 P.C. Genuine
- Boston Herald -

BIRD WASN'T INTERESTED IN WAITING ON HOUDINI'S DECISION about Margery. He went ahead and published his thoughts about the medium and the authenticity that he perceived in her skills. It had been an idea, Bird had once warned Orson Munn, to put

Houdini on the committee – a man that the spirits considered a mortal enemy.

Even though Bird knew the report on Margery would be controversial, he and his colleagues had still underestimated the interest in their story. Once the newspapers picked up the story, readers wanted to know more about the Boston lady who might be the world's first scientifically verified medium.

But Orson Munn was not crowning a winner just yet. A few newspaper stories had emphasized something that Bird had mentioned in passing – that definitive proof had not yet been given. Anyone following the story would have thought that it had, though. In July, the *New York Times* heightened expectations when it reported that the committee was "unable to find the slightest evidence of fraud" in Margery's séances. The headline of the story even reported MARGERY PASSES ALL PSYCHIC TESTS.

As Bird had expected, the most famous judge on the panel reacted strongly to the barrage of publicity. It appeared, to Houdini's dismay, that Bird spoke for the entire committee.

But Bird did not speak for Houdini. He had been left out of things. A vital inquiry was taking place, and he was the only member of the committee who had been excluded. Yet the newspapers were reporting that Margery had convinced the experts, which suggested she had also impressed him. When he read this, Houdini exploded. *Scientific American*, the committee, and the magician himself were "being made to look ridiculous." He wanted to go to Boston and put an immediate stop to this.

Bird responded to Houdini's irritation with a letter reminding him that the original idea was not to bother him with a new case "unless, and until, it got to the state where there seemed serious prospects that it was either genuine, or a type of fraud which our other committeemen could not deal with." As it had now reached that stage, Bird and Munn did, in fact, want to talk to Houdini. Could he come to New York at his convenience, to lunch with the publisher? There was no need to hurry, though; Munn was out of the office until next week. Bird would be busy for the next few days. It might be best to call first.

But when Houdini finally confronted Munn, the publisher told him that he had been trying to reach him for a week, but Bird had been "sidestepping the matter." Houdini was not surprised by this. He already suspected that he had been left out of the Margery tests so that Bird could push the other judges toward the verdict he wanted. Munn didn't believe this could be true, so he called Bird into his office to refute the charge.

Houdini was outraged to be left out of the Margery investigations when he learned that members of the panel were prepared to award her the prize.

When Bird walked in, he was asked directly if Margery was going to be awarded the prize.

"Most decidedly," Bird answered.

Houdini scoffed. "Mr. Bird, you have nothing to lose but your position, and very likely you can readily get another if you are wrong, but if I am wrong, it will mean the loss of reputation."

Houdini turned to Munn, whom he felt respected him as an expert on spirit shenanigans. He had to be permitted to sit with Margery, he told the publisher. If she were a genuine medium, then, given the reports he'd read, she had to be "the most wonderful in the world." But if she were given the prize and later found to be an imposter, then those who endorsed her "would be the laughingstock of the world."

Munn agreed. That was why they wanted to see him, he acknowledged. He wanted Houdini to go to Boston right away.

Bird tried to hide his displeasure at this. The other experts had worked with Margery for three months without detecting trickery. He wrote sourly, "He would not step in, locate in two sittings the deception that had eluded them in fifty, and with one magnificent gesture would save the committee."

After Houdini left the office, Bird had a private conversation with Munn. Houdini had just called the rest of the committee incompetent at best, dishonest at worst – and he seemed to have already formed the opinion that the medium was a fraud. Bird warned him that Houdini would wreak havoc on the Margery case. He would ruin everything, Bird insisted.

Realizing that the situation could be a concern, Munn decided to go with Houdini to Lime Street and make sure that he was "on his best behavior." So, on July 22 – after the *Times* ran its most positive story about Margery to date – Munn and Houdini traveled by train to Boston. Bird, who left immediately after he met with Munn, arrived there one day earlier.

When she heard that Houdini was on his way, Margery became noticeably nervous and excited. Dr. Crandon wrote to Sir Arthur Conan Doyle about the turbulent atmosphere at Lime Street:

Tonight, Houdini and Mr. Munn, owner of the Scientific American, *sit with us for the first time and will stay for several days. I think she is somewhat stirred by it internally because of Houdini's general nastiness. She is vomiting merrily this morning. However, some of her worst days have given the best sittings.*

Dr. Crandon had received alarming reports about Houdini, whom Doyle called a clever liar and medium baiter. Sir Arthur wondered if Walter could "rise above" Houdini's negative energy.

Whether Roy would work with Houdini was just as uncertain. Even before the magician came to Boston, something had shifted in the way that Dr. Crandon dealt with investigators. Feeling that some of them were out to persecute his wife, he was not as friendly as the tests continued. Now that Crandon believed Margery was on the verge of winning the contest, he required that investigators sign copies of their notes after every sitting and leave those notes with him, so that if they later made statements inconsistent with what they'd observed, he had the material to "crucify them."

He wrote to Doyle that he was finished "wasting my time in compliments and politeness. It is war to the finish, and they know I shall not hesitate to treat them surgically if necessary."

If this was how he felt about the investigators who shared some of his metaphysical beliefs, then prospects for a civil relationship with Houdini didn't seem likely. Houdini was a foe of Spiritualism and disdained the beliefs of people like the Crandons and the Doyles.

And besides that, he was a Jew.

Like men in his circle, Dr. Crandon was wary of immigrants, especially those who seemed to threaten to turn the United States into an Eastern European nation. At his yacht club, he was known to make severe remarks about Jews and expressed, before ever meeting him, the same hostility toward Houdini. He wrote to Sir Arthur – who did not share his opinions: "My deep regret is that this low-minded Jew has any claim on the word American."

ON JULY 23, HOUDINI AND MUNN ARRIVED AT THE CRANDON house. For all the reservations the couple had about Houdini's reputation, they couldn't ignore the fact that they were hosting two of the biggest names in the country when it came to entertainment and publishing. While Houdini's presence made her understandably anxious, Margery was proud to receive him in her home. She had only become aware of researchers within the last year, but Houdini had been a star since she'd been a child.

Oddly, he seemed, like her, a little out of touch with the intellectuals and scientists. He admitted that he didn't know McDougall until he became a member of the investigative panel. And it seemed that McDougall, like the other judges, was not eager to attend a sitting where Houdini was in charge. He had not responded to Bird's calls about the gathering. As for Carrington, he'd left Boston before Munn and Houdini arrived. Comstock had pressing business in New York and sent his assistant, Will Conant,

as a proxy for Houdini's first séance with Margery.

Given Houdini's reputation for trouble, Margery was pleased to find he was polite, curious, even enchanting. He had left all his disguises and tricks behind. He wanted to see Margery perform under the same circumstances that his colleagues had experienced.

Before her husband had arrived home from the office, she had given her New York guests a tour of the neighborhood, and despite their spiritual differences, she and Houdini appeared to get along famously.

During their walk, Houdini discussed the loss that had driven him to explore the spirit world. While Bird always found it maudlin when the magician spoke of his "beloved" and "Sainted" mother, Margery was sympathetic about Houdini's frustrations with the mediums who failed to contact his loved one.

Houdini and Munn booked rooms at the Copley Plaza Hotel, ignoring the offer that the Crandons had made for the two men to join the other members of the committee who had stayed at their home. They did accept a dinner invitation from the couple, however, and found Dr. Crandon to be a gracious host and a fascinating conversationalist. Margery, as they had heard, was a beautiful and confident woman. She liked the magician very much and, as far as she could tell, the feeling was mutual. In his diary that night, he praised the couple's good taste and noted Margery's beauty, which he said explained Bird's glowing reports of her mediumship.

Though determined to be the one investigator immune to the woman's charm, Houdini enjoyed his time at Line Street. He was amused when Margery – who had heard it from Sir Arthur – asked him if he was also a medium.

Houdini and Margery outside of the Line Street house. Malcolm Bird lurks in the background and publisher Orson Munn is standing at the right.

He denied the claim with good humor. Houdini also seemed impressed with Dr. Crandon, who had proudly shown him his private collection of Abraham Lincoln memorabilia.

It was hot in the house that evening, and the men – Roy, Houdini, Munn, Bird, and Will Conant -- removed their coats in the upstairs séance room. Bird confessed to Houdini that the room itself had never been thoroughly examined. Harry immediately went to work to remedy this sloppy oversight. There was no door to be locked between the room and the hallway leading to the stairs. He inspected the séance props -- a megaphone, the three-sided spirit cabinet, a phonograph which usually played Margery's favorite song "Souvenir," and the bell box. The 14-inch-long wooden box contained batteries and a bell. A slight tap on a lever on the top completed an electrical circuit and caused the bell to ring.

Margery and the four men sat in chairs forming a circle. She asked them all to link hands with one another. The medium was seated between Houdini and her husband. Bird sat outside of the circle, his right hand clasped around the linked hands of Margery and the doctor. Margery's right foot was pressed against her husband's left foot, and her left foot was pressed against Houdini's right foot. This proved Margery's hands and feet were "under control" when the manifestations began.

The dark gathering began with the usual disembodied whispers and the whistle. At one point, Walter called for "control!" and Margery shifted away from Roy and toward Houdini, so that he could control both her hands and feet. With the medium immobilized, Walter announced that the spirit megaphone was floating in the air.

"Have Houdini tell me where to throw it!" the voice said.

"Toward me," Houdini replied.

Instantly, the trumpet landed at his feet.

Walter then ordered Bird to guard the door against any intruders. Before he could, the cabinet was hurled "backwards violently," Houdini reported.

Although Margery and Houdini had met on agreeable terms, the ghost seemed to be having none of it. "You – Munn and Houdini – think you're pretty smart, don't you?" Walter hissed at them while assailing them with his antics. The Victrola slowed and stopped. The light that had been placed on the bell box rose, lowered, and moved back and forth. For the climax, the bell box rang – seemingly of its own accord – while Margery was held tightly by Houdini, who, she imagined, could feel every beat of her pulse and twinge of her nerves.

Houdini had not sat idly while Walter was active. During the séance, he had placed both of Margery's hands between his knees and explored the bell box for signs of manipulation. When he later put his hands back on hers, he then ran them up to her shoulders to make sure he was indeed holding Margery. She sensed he was uncomfortable with the intimate contact. He wasn't interested in any groping. Houdini was not one of the investigators who examined Margery's body in her lingerie or checked her vagina to make sure she wasn't hiding anything.

But while Houdini was less invasive with the medium, he had no hesitation about dominating the proceedings. Earlier in the night, he had snapped at Bird for releasing one of his hands from the circle. To Spiritualists, when a sitter breaks the chain, it can damage the séance battery, but Houdini had other reasons for ordering Bird to keep his hands away from Margery.

Aside from that, Margery had not found Houdini to be a hindrance. Afterward, the Crandons were pleased with Bird's report, which mentioned good control and a steady production of phenomena. The document was signed by Orson Munn, Bird, and, without disputing it, Harry Houdini.

Houdini made no statement when the séance was over, but appeared pensive, as if thinking deeply about what he had seen. The Crandons were hopeful that he had come to scoff but had left a believer, but he said nothing. He politely thanked his hosts and left with Bird and Munn.

Bird drove Munn and Houdini back to the Copley Plaza Hotel. No one got out of the car when they parked on Beacon Street. This was where the sitters planned to discuss what they had seen. Munn turned to face Houdini in the backseat and asked for his opinion about Margery.

"I've got her," he said. "All fraud, every bit of it. One more sitting and I will be ready to expose everything."

Houdini was impressed by what he had seen at the Crandon home and very impressed with the famous Margery --- though not by her supernatural powers, he quickly assured the other men. Although there was one thing he hadn't worked out yet. "I don't see how she did that megaphone trick," he admitted.

Bird refrained from speaking up and defending the medium. Instead, he offered a speculation that Walter Prince had made – if she were cheating, Margery might have balanced the megaphone on his shoulder while it was supposed to be floating. "It couldn't be on her lap, that was open to exploration," Bird said.

"It couldn't be on her shoulder either," Houdini told him. He had checked there during the manifestation. But the expression on his face quickly changed from confusion to excitement, and he blurted out that it had been the "slickest ruse" he had ever uncovered. Margery didn't have supernatural powers. She couldn't have suspended the megaphone in the air; that was certain, and she couldn't keep it on her shoulder. There was only one other possibility, and Houdini was convinced this was what she had done – Margery had balanced it on her head and then launched it toward him.

It was simple and yet genius, he told the others.

Bird found this absurd. How could a society wife pull off a trick that challenged an expert vaudeville performer like Houdini? If everything was fraudulent, he wanted to know, then how had she made the bell box ring? Sitters on either side of her held Margery's hands, and her feet were in contact with theirs. The bell box rang many times during the séance, so how was this done?

That was much simpler – with her foot, Houdini insisted.

Usually, the bell box sat on the floor between Margery's legs, but Houdini had insisted that it be placed on the floor at his own feet. Regardless, the bell rang repeatedly. Houdini had a ready answer for this. He explained that he had worn a rubbed bandage around his leg, just below the knee, throughout the day. By the time he arrived at Lime Street, his calf and ankle were swollen and tender.

"This gave me a much keener sense of feeling and made it easier for me to notice the slightest sliding of Mrs. Crandon's ankle or flexing of her muscles," he said.

During the sitting, he noticed her pull up her skirt well over her knees. Every time she slid her ankle or flexed a muscle, he felt the subtle movement through her silk stockings. He felt this happen precisely when the bell rang. It had been Margery's foot, and not a spirit, that had been responsible for the ringing of the bell.

Margery, Houdini assured them, was a cunning imposter.

Bird then asked him about stopping the Victrola. Margery could not have accomplished that. That was easy, Houdini dismissed. Someone got up and stopped it.

Bird had trouble restraining himself. It wasn't enough that Margery was balancing spirit trumpets on her head and ringing bells with her feet; now Houdini claimed she had accomplices who broke the circle and manipulated the phonograph.

"Well, it couldn't have been Dr. Crandon," Bird remarked. "I was controlling him myself during the sitting."

At this remark, Houdini bristled. Why had Bird broken the circle? He asked him. Bird claimed it was for exploring purposes, but, as Houdini hinted, the editor often seemed to have his hands on the medium when it was unwarranted. As the meeting ended, he made the strong suggestion that Bird was Margery's confederate.

Earlier that day, the two men had exchanged a cordial handshake when Houdini and Munn arrived at Lime Street, but by the end of the evening, they were open enemies.

It was a turn of events that, while not really surprising, almost undoubtedly had a great effect on the final outcome of Margery's tests.

THE NEXT DAY, HOUDINI AND MUNN RETURNED TO LIME Street, and while in the séance room alone, Houdini demonstrated for the publisher how he believed Margery's feats were achieved.

After the previous night's séance, Houdini refused to speak publicly about Margery – and there had been reporters at his hotel that morning, asking for a comment. He did not reveal his opinions about what had occurred that night. He only stated that he felt more stringent tests were required. This started the rumor that Margery had somehow outwitted Houdini and that her powers were genuine. But Houdini said nothing.

Despite his silence, he found himself confronted by Margery about something that – unless Walter was right and he really was everywhere – she should have known nothing about. Hurt and disappointed, she accused Houdini of making cruel statements about her. She warned him that it would only tarnish his own name if he followed through on his promise to try to expose her during the séance that evening.

Begging her not to attribute what she knew to her psychic sense, Houdini asked her who had been whispering in her ear. After admitting that her source was Malcolm Bird, she made Houdini promise to keep quiet about it.

But Houdini went directly to Munn and Bird and accused the editor of compromising the investigation by informing Margery of the committee's discussions. Bird denied saying anything to the Crandons and demanded to know who had accused him. Reluctant to completely break his promise to Margery, Houdini simply said that he had connected the dots after seeing her and Bird talking privately.

Bird snorted and told him he was wrong – but he wasn't.

If Houdini planned to spring his trap on July 24 at the Lime Street house – where Margery worked her magic best – he was reluctant to find that the next séance would take place in Dr. Comstock's apartment at the Charlesgate Hotel on Beacon Street.

Gladys Wood, Comstock's secretary, was tasked with searching Margery before the evening began. She later wrote, "She removed most of her clothes and I examined her and them carefully. She wore a loose green linen dress into the séance room, and I examined this carefully before she put it back on. She also removed her shoes, and I examined her feet and shoes carefully. She then put her shoes on again. She also took down her hair, which I searched."

She also searched her genital region, probed her vagina, and found nothing in her mouth. Assured that Margery was clean, Houdini and Dr. Crandon, waiting in the makeshift séance area, clasped her hands when she was seated in her cabinet.

Also present in the locked room within the suite were Munn, Bird, Comstock, Conant, and Walter – if one believed in his

The Charlesgate Hotel in Boston -- a perfect gothic setting for the seances

existence. "Haha, Houdini!" the spirit cackled when Houdini reported that something had touched his knee.

After the spectral contacts came a series of Margery's effects – the cabinet quaked and moved across the floor, the table rose, the megaphone moved, the Victrola behaved erratically, and raps were heard. At a moment when Houdini, Conant, and Bird declared the medium was in control, the table became animated and turned over, knocking the bell box to the floor. Minutes later, Walter shouted for Munn to straighten up. The publisher admitted that he had been slouching. Walter then instructed Munn to say how many times the bell should ring, and it chimed five times at his suggestion.

Walter bid the sitters good night, and the séance was abruptly over.

A dramatic effort to prevent or expose the phenomena had been expected from Houdini, but he had not interfered with the test. Deferring to Comstock, he hadn't snapped at Bird this time. After the Crandons left the hotel, Houdini told Comstock that Margery had again performed every trick in her repertoire. He explained that during the séance, he had released his grip on Munn's hand in the dark and had reached under the table when it was tilting. He felt Margery's hand underneath the table, lifting it. He had quickly pulled his hand away and leaned over to Munn to whisper, "Shall I denounce and expose her now?" The publisher whispered back that he should wait. The time was not right.

He had been surprised when the bell box took a long time to ring, and Houdini said that Margery revealed her predicament to him when she asked him if he had garters holding up his socks. He replied that he did and asked the reason for her question.

"The buckle hurts me," she said.

It was then that Houdini realized the buckle had snagged her stocking, so her ankle was pinned to his. When he unfastened the buckle, he said her foot shifted, and the bell soon rang.

By this point, Harry wanted to go directly to the newspapers and tell them all about Margery's slippery feet, as well as how he had caught her with her head under the table – she said she was looking for a hairpin – and the other ways that he had caught her cheating. The other men, though, voted him down. Unhappy, Houdini wanted to know why it was suitable to expose the other candidates but not Margery.

"It's different this time," Bird replied.

Later, Houdini handed Munn a letter that he had written, stating that Margery was "one hundred percent trickster or fraud." Bird was outraged by this statement, saying that Houdini had not kept his promise to catch the medium because he could not. The Crandons also felt vindicated by the two seances performed for Houdini and the New York men. In their view, Houdini had come to Boston determined to discredit her. "He said many nasty things behind the psychic's back," Dr. Crandon wrote to Doyle – and yet he'd left without stopping her work. To counter Houdini's accusations, Roy had his signature on séance reports that said the magician had the medium under control when the manifestations occurred.

"The clouds break a little since yesterday," Dr. Crandon wrote to Sir Arthur. "Houdini and Munn have signed the complete notes of both their sittings without reservation. These sittings are so full of clean-cut psychic phenomena that any subsequent denial would indict these men before all the world."

In the wake of the contentious tests, it was evident to Margery's supporters that she had survived Houdini's first challenge. Dr. Crandon added in his letter to Sir Arthur: "Houdini is apparently all you and other gentlemen have ever said of him, to which I should be pleased to add a choice collection of adjectives which you may assemble from the Whitechapel and the East End. Nevertheless, I think we have him."

If Houdini could not stop the phenomena – and he had abstained from trying this time – Margery would receive the prize. As final proof, Crandon suggested to Bird and Doyle the possibility of "the one-man circle." He wanted Margery alone in the dark with Houdini – and let him stop her if he could. "Who knows, perhaps we shall add Houdini to this list of magicians who have become Spiritualists," he said.

In the end, though, Crandon decided that Houdini – who was not only crooked but an unsavory Jew – would probably cheat himself to keep Margery from succeeding. It was better, he felt, to have other judges present so that both Houdini and the medium could be supervised.

Another round of sittings, this time for the entire jury, was arranged for the end of the summer. Bird expressed confidence to Roy that Margery would do just fine when they all came together again at the end of August..

MUNN AND HOUDINI HAD TAKEN THE MIDNIGHT TRAIN BACK to New York after the second sitting, and when they parted ways at Grand Central Station, Munn felt the shift the entire investigation had taken. He knew things had reached a crossroads, and the credibility of his family's publication was now at stake. He would be 41 years old the next day, far younger than the magazine that had been entrusted to him.

He knew that the wrong decision could destroy the *Scientific American* for good.

Munn had a decision to make. Though he respected his editor, Houdini's suspicion that he was passing on information to Margery disturbed him. The September issue was supposed to contain another report on the medium – Bird's most positive article yet about her talents. It would be a great embarrassment if Bird praised Margery just as Munn's leading expert exposed her as a charlatan. Houdini had advised him to pull the article, even though the issue had already gone to press. It would be expensive to do it, but endorsing a medium that turned out to be a fraud would be more costly in the end. So, at no small cost, Munn decided to pull the story from the issue.

The whole thing came to a head at the *Scientific American* office days later – when Houdini showed up with a report on Margery that he withheld from Bird. The editor was incensed. During an exchange that followed, Houdini got Bird to admit to Munn "that she wormed things out of him by cross-examining."

As it turned out, Houdini was not the only member of the committee bothered by Bird's actions and writings. Dr. Walter Franklin Prince was also disturbed by Bird's early articles in *Scientific American* lauding Margery's gifts. He and Houdini were even more annoyed by his statements to the press. Bird was not a committee member -- he was an employee of the magazine. Both men believed that the committee should be independent of the publication. They met with Munn and voiced their complaints.

Even though Houdini said he had no issue with Bird's presence at the séances, Munn, fearing more conflict, decided to ban him from the next round of tests. He feared that Bird had become too close to Margery and her husband, compromising Bird's reputation as a neutral observer, which compromised the magazine's reputation by extension. If *Scientific American* was going to err, Munn wanted it to be on the side of caution.

The final contest now belonged to Houdini.

Bird was unhappy. "Houdini and Price simply constituted

themselves the mouthpieces of the committee," he later recalled. "The dictators got together, agreed on a program, and jammed it through as far as they were able."

Houdini knew this was his last chance to expose Margery for what she was. Knowing that manual control of the medium wasn't working, he and his assistant, Jim Collins, designed a mechanism for restraint – one that would prevent her from using her head, hands, and feet in the way that he knew she had been.

Houdini wrote: "We are going to have a final séance with her – and in this séance she is to be stopped."

THE SHOWDOWN BETWEEN HOUDINI AND MARGERY QUICKLY became an international story. According to many reports, *Scientific American* judges had decided to award the prize to the Boston medium unless Houdini could change their minds – and their upcoming encounter would not be as friendly as the one in July. The newspaper did all it could to create conflict for the eventual showdown in the séance room.

Despite the provocation, though, Margery and Houdini remained on good terms. Their battle over Spiritualism had not bled into their private relationship. "I have been hearing some very nice things

Despite their public battle, Houdini and Margery were on good terms in person–perhaps, too good. He later claimed that she tried to seduce him to go easier on her during the tests.

about you lately," she wrote to him, "so I am glad to be able to say I know 'The Great Houdini.'"

Margery apparently did not share the same opinion as he

husband when it came to the Jew who could not be trusted and shouldn't be able to call himself an American.

While Dr. Crandon intercepted most letters written to Margery, Houdini and Margery maintained a personal correspondence that had begun when he sent her some of the snapshots he had taken at Lime Street. Most of them were photographs of the two of them together, seemingly enjoying each other's company.

But the newspapers were relentless, printing Margery's real name and displaying photos of Mina Crandon side-by-side with Houdini fettered by chains. The couple refused demands for interviews, and while Houdini – who never minded the publicity – respected their privacy. He was often forced to defend his need to put Margery to further tests, for even though he was not convinced, the New York and Boston newspapers had already crowned her as the real thing.

Houdini told the *New York World*: "The woman may be genuine, as they say. I will not commit myself until the tests are over. But there will be further tests. A case of this kind excites too many people, disturbing them, and giving them hope for communication with the dead. If Margery can give that communication, all right; but if she can't, I want to do something more for humanity than entertain it."

As the date for the final tests drew closer, Houdini and Orson Munn decided to curtail their interviews with the press, so Houdini was rankled that Margery's supporters were continuing to speak to the papers. Even more irritating was a Margery feature in his favorite paper, the *New York World*, by Fred Keating, a fellow magician and alternate jury member, which praised Margery. Other laudatory reports, by reporters who had never been to Lime Street – with statements like "Psychic Power of Margery Established Beyond Question" – did little to deflate the hopes of her more devout followers.

Houdini, meanwhile, was being presented as the devil for believers in Spiritualism. One publication, the *National Spiritualist*, made it clear he was "racially a Jew" and referred to him as Weiss – a name he hadn't used since he was a teenager. The magazine stated, "Mr. Weiss may pass as an expert conjurer or ephemeral importance to humanity, but he cannot qualify as an expert on matters belonging to the realm of spiritual powers. His special sphere is trickery for his own financial gain."

This was ironic considering how many fraudulent mediums had been exposed since the start of the movement, who had specialized in "trickery for financial gain."

From another direction – if you believed he was real – Walter, the spirit guide, said that defeating Houdini mattered more than the outcome of the contest. At one of Margery's seances, he allegedly said, "More important than to get a favorable award is forever to wipe Houdini off the map as a ghost hunter."

The voice warned that the magician was plotting a dastardly trick – he was going to conceal an obstructive object in the bell box so that Walter would not be able to ring it. Margery's followers needed to be on guard.

It seemed that enemies from two worlds were after Houdini. Upon his arrival in Boston, "he was shadowed by hostile interests," a Boston tabloid reported. "He refused to be seen at his hotel. Meeting a friend at the Back Bay railroad station, he held his conversation in a telephone booth, declaring that he was being watched and that they might be overheard."

That same night in the séance room, Walter's voice was heard whispering, "I will take care of Houdini."

BY THE TIME THE DATE FOR THE FINAL TESTS ARRIVED, TENSION had ratcheted up to an uncomfortable level. Some of the members of the committee, as well as alternate judges, still believed that Houdini had no place in a scientific trial. He was too volatile, they said, and too slippery. But Houdini had promised he would not hinder the medium in her performance. As he said in an interview, "I want to give Mrs. Crandon every possible chance to make good, and if she possesses any psychic power, I will be the first to assist her in proving her genuineness." He and his assistant, Collins, had developed an apparatus for control that would be "comfortable for Mrs. Crandon."

He told Dr. Crandon that he hadn't "the slightest wish to interfere with anything."

But his promises weren't enough for some of the investigators. Hereward Carrington, who had already made up his mind about Margery, saw no point in disrupting the atmosphere of the séance by knocking heads with Houdini. He left Lime Street just before Houdini arrived in Boston. Once again, McDougall was out of town. Despite Munn's hopes, Margery would not perform for the full panel.

Munn and Comstock had asked Houdini to develop a method of restraint for Margery that was both foolproof and humane – an apparatus that wouldn't inhibit the delicate formation of ectoplasm. To that end, Houdini – master of escape from trunks, water cans, and torture cells – drew on his regular line of work to design Margery's "cage." He built what became known as Houdini's Box.

Houdini and Collins built a new kind of spirit cabinet – one that allowed the darkness and privacy deemed necessary for the medium while eliminating any impulse to cheat. They presented an oak box that sloped upward at the top, like the roof of a house, with openings at the top and sides for the medium's head and arms. Once locked inside, Margery's movements -- and her chances of deception -- would be severely limited.

Bird, along with others, feared the design was too restrictive: "The use of this cage involves the assumption that the psychic force either issues from the medium's head, or else is capable of penetrating an inch of wood." Dr. Prince also thought it might be impossible for the medium to perform in the box.

Margery, though, reluctantly agreed to conduct a séance from inside the cabinet, but not before Houdini and Dr. Crandon exchanged such harsh words that they nearly came to blows.

Munn suggested that Bird transport Houdini's "fraud-preventer" box to Boston in his car, but Harry, trusting no one, replied that he would transport it himself. He was sure that Bird would allow the Crandons to examine the box and find a way to undermine it. He didn't want to give them access to the box until Margery was locked inside it. He transported the box to Boston by train, and then he and Collins lugged it to Dr. Comstock's apartment and assembled it on the morning of August 25, 1924.

The box into which Margery was clapped by Houdini to prevent any possibility of fraud.

Margery fastened into Houdini's "fraud-preventer" box to see if she could still perform as a spirit medium under confined conditions

It was an odd-shaped box that might have been a storage crate for a roll-top desk. There was ample room inside for the medium to sit comfortably on a chair. Semicircular holes were cut out of the hinged front and top panel so that when the cabinet was closed, a hole was created to circle the occupant's neck. Her hands were extended through holes in the cabinet sides so that committeemen could "control" them. Provision was also made for wood panels that could be nailed over the side openings should the committee wish to test her with her hands inside the box.

In front of the box was a six-inch-wide screen, and this became the first problem with the box after Margery inspected it.

She asked that a piece of wood replace the screen. Houdini was unhappy with this. The screen, he explained, was in line with the medium's lap and was designed to allow her ectoplasm a point of release into the room. Margery countered that Comstock had said that if she were a fraud, she could extend wires through the screen to ring the bell box. Each time Houdini made a case for the screen, the medium repeated, "Comstock said, perhaps I could stick out wires." She said that when the phenomena occurred, she wanted no talk of threads, concealed wires, or anything else that critics could use to discredit her.

Houdini suspected that she knew the real reason he had installed the screen – to give him a window into the part of her body where the tools of a false medium's trade were often hidden. Part of the answer to the Margery mystery, he believed, lay in the inventive use she made of her anatomy. He doubted the secretaries and wives who searched her before her séances looked very carefully between her legs.

But since Margery's argument was a sound one, Houdini relented. There would be no screen in the box.

The Crandons inspected the box a little more and then withdrew for a hasty conference. When they returned, the doctor insisted that Margery be allowed to try out in the device during a séance with her friends before she submitted to the committee's test. Without Walter's consent, after all, there would be no tests.

Houdini agreed to this as long as he and the other judges could stay until she was securely locked in the box. While he didn't say so, he believed that Margery was angling for time and privacy so she could figure out how to defeat the fraud-proof cabinet.

Margery and her supporters – Dr. Crandon, Aleck Cross, Roy's sister, Laura, and friends named DeWyckoffs – agreed, and the medium stepped into the box. Houdini lowered the flaps on the top, and he gently helped her to extend her arms through the side holes. He fastened a padlock into place, and then Munn, Comstock, Prince, and Houdini quietly left the room as the lights were being lowered.

Just over 30 minutes later, Margery's "friendly circle" exited the séance room. Walter had okayed the use of Houdini's box – the sitting could start immediately. The panel members entered and formed around the table. Houdini controlled Margery's left hand, Roy her right. Seated outside the circle, Dr. Prince grasped the handhold between the Crandons, while Comstock and Munn completed the chain. The table was arranged, and the lights turned off.

Bird, who was not present at the séance, wrote one account of what happened next. Houdini offered a different version. Just eight minutes after the séance began, a loud and violent sound was heard. Both Bird and Houdini agreed that the noise was the front of Margery's box being broken open in the dark.

Houdini immediately spoke up – the fixture had been secured with brass tacks. Anyone who leveraged their shoulders could sit in the cabinet and muscle it off. Exasperated, Dr. Crandon stood up. Neither Houdini nor Price, he stated for the record, had given any indication that they felt the medium tense or strain, as she would have had to do to cause the phenomena to occur. Besides that, Houdini has already admitted that any effects occurring while Margery was in the fraud-proof box had to be genuine. If the box was secure, then how could he accuse Margery of shenanigans? He stated that Walter had been responsible.

But Houdini doubted this to be the case. The Crandons and their friends had access to the box for nearly 30 minutes before the séance began. They could've easily loosened the nails. Houdini's offer to demonstrate how easy it was to force open the front of the box did little to mollify the doctor.

Comstock now joined in, too. He was miffed that the supposedly stalwart oak box could be so easily manipulated.

The argument became so heated that Walter ordered the committee to leave and the friendly circle to return. Margery's friends rushed into the room to replace the investigators, and "psychic harmony" was temporarily restored. When the committee members were invited to return, Dr. Crandon asked Houdini if he had a flashlight on him. He warned that any white light could endanger the medium. Houdini assured him that he had no flashlight and offered to be searched if anyone doubted it. Crandon dropped the issue, but there was more awkwardness when the Crandons finally realized that Bird, whom they assumed was characteristically late, wouldn't be attending the séance at all. They were given no reason for his removal from the tests.

The séance began again, and a few minutes later, there was another disturbance when Walter demanded to know how much Harry was being paid to stop the phenomena in the séance room.

Houdini replied, "I don't know what you're talking about. It's costing me $2,500 a week to be here." He said that he'd given up theater dates in Buffalo, New York, to be in Boston.

Dr. Comstock interrupted. "What do you mean by this, Walter?" he asked. "This talk isn't psychic research."

The voice responded: "Comstock, you take the box out into white light, examine it, and report back. You'll see fast enough what I mean."

After doing this, Comstock announced that a rubber eraser had been wedged against the clapper of the bell, rendering it inoperable. The Crandons would later blame Houdini for trying to sabotage the proceedings – precisely the way that Walter had predicted he would do several days earlier.

However, I think we can all agree that it's just as likely that the Crandons had wedged the rubber piece into the bell so that Houdini could be blamed.

At this point, though, no accusations were made, aside from those by Walter. Houdini swore he hadn't tampered with the box. When he asked Walter for proof of his accusation, a stony silence lasted until the séance ended at 11:01 P.M.

The committee was unhappy with how the night had turned out. Even if Houdini had not sabotaged the bell box, it was clear that he hadn't managed to build a "fraud-proof" box as he claimed he would do. Harry replied that he hadn't expected Margery to break out of it. He vowed that he would have the box in proper condition for the séance the next night.

The next day, he and Collins reconstructed the box in Comstock's apartment, adding thick metal staples, hasps, and new padlocks. As they were working, a man entered the apartment and approached the séance room. Entering the hallway to see who it was, Houdini encountered Comstock's assistant, Will Conant, who was used to coming and going from the apartment as he pleased. Accused of spying for the Crandons, Houdini chased him out. He trusted no one who was friendly with Margery – least of all those who lurked outside the séance room while he was working on the fraud-proof box.

Despite his rift with Dr. Crandon, Houdini found that Margery rarely made anyone feel unwelcome at Lime Street. After his run-in with Conant, Houdini stopped at the Crandon home to inform them that all was ready for the séance that evening. The relationship between Margery and Houdini was refreshingly pleasant away from the Charlesgate Hotel. Margery even asked Harry, who admitted he was exhausted, if he wanted to take a nap upstairs instead of going back to his hotel. After accepting the offer, he followed her upstairs to her absent son's room. John was staying with his father during the tests.

She told him that the boy would be thrilled to know the Handcuff King had slept in his bed. Houdini replied that he would like to meet John someday and entertain him. Privately, though, he couldn't understand why the Crandons had sent their son away from home while people like Malcolm Bird were allowed to stay there.

HOUDINI ARRIVED ON TIME FOR THE SÉANCE SCHEDULED THAT night at the Charlesgate. However, when he met the other committee members, he discovered that Bird had unexpectedly arrived for the session. Munn had told him to stay away from the hotel, and Bird wanted to know why. Houdini and Dr. Prince were more than happy to enlighten him -- Bird had given the Crandons information about the committee's findings in July and had also released unauthorized statements to the press. Munn told him that it was better for Bird not to participate in the séances. Before he was escorted from the hotel suite, Houdini said that Bird immediately resigned from the committee, realizing that no one trusted him.

Bird, of course, told it differently. He said he resigned because the situation had become untenable – he could not continue to function as the committee's secretary and still oppose Houdini. Bird said that he found himself in the humiliating position of having to abandon the enterprise that he, more than anyone else, had created and advanced.

"When do you leave for New York?" Houdini asked him.

"You go to hell!" Bird snapped, then left after saying goodbye to the Crandons.

Margery was shaken. She now believed she was seeing the commotion that Sir Arthur had warned would ruin the *Scientific American* tests. But she was ready to attempt another demonstration for the panel. Going into Comstock's bedroom, she removed her dress, slip, and stockings. Standing naked, she was examined by a female stenographer, who vouched that she was hiding nothing on her body. Then, after slipping back into her clothes, she entered the séance room and stepped into Houdini's Box.

The same group as the night before – Dr. Crandon, Comstock, Prince, Munn, and Houdini – surrounded her, while the stenographer sat in an adjacent room with the sliding doors partially open so she could hear Munn dictate what occurred.

The locks on the cabinet were examined by the jury, and the bell box by Houdini, who stated that Margery could not reach it. Then came a reshuffling of the circle, a game of musical chairs that would have been amusing if it weren't so volatile. Houdini refused to allow the doctor to control his wife any longer, so Prince took over Roy's customary position on Margery's right. In reaction, Dr. Crandon insisted on strict control over Houdini. When he seated himself on Margery's left and grasped her hand, Comstock, the sitter most sympathetic to the Crandons, was placed in control of Houdini's left hand, left foot, and head. To accomplish this, he put his foot on top of Houdini's, then held the magician's hand high in the air, resting his elbow on Harry's shoulder and leaning their linked hands against his head.

Although the Crandons claimed this was to prevent Houdini from planting anything in the bell box or the fraud-proof box that might incriminate Margery, Houdini suspected it was to restrict his movement so that he couldn't detect her trickery.

To Munn, it appeared as if both Margery and Houdini were on trial.

After he locked the door to the hallway and the lights were turned out, the most controversial of Margery's séances began. Houdini had a hunch that she might attempt to smuggle something into the box to ring the bell, which she could access while the box was being locked and before her hands were restrained. As the sitters linked hands, he watched her face carefully. By her expression and the way she tensed her neck, he determined she was reaching for something she had dropped on the floor of the locked cabinet. Thanks to this, he repeatedly irritated Prince and offended Margery by reminding him not to let go of her hand.

"What's the matter with you that you keep saying that?" she demanded.

"Do you really want to know?" Houdini asked.

"Yes," she replied.

"Well, I will tell you. In case you have anything smuggled in the cabinet box, you could now conceal it."

"Well, do you want to search me?" she asked him.

"No, never mind, I am not a physician."

With Margery's permission, Houdini stuck his hand into the box, discovering nothing suspicious, though he could not reach the floor, where he believed she had something stashed.

But if Margery was cheating, she now demonstrated why she was the match of any sideshow trickster who made their living pulling the wool over the eyes of rubes on the Midway.

Almost immediately, the medium went into a trance, and as soon as Walter's shrill whistle signaled his arrival in the room, he began his attack. The voice rang out: "Houdini, you are very clever indeed, but it won't work... I suppose it was an accident those things were left in the cabinet?"

"What was left in the cabinet?" Harry asked.

"Pure accident, was it? You were not here, Houdini, but Collins was."

Before Houdini could say anything else, the voice flew into a rage: "Houdini, you god damn son of a bitch! Get the hell out of here and never come back! If you don't, I will. What did you do that for, Houdini? You're a bastard for putting up a plant like that on a girl. There is a ruler in the cabinet!"

A collapsible ruler would be just the thing for Margery to use to ring the bell box that was out of her reach. Houdini already suspected that the earlier "prediction" Walter had made about a rubber eraser jamming up the bell was a sign that the medium was frustrated and trapped. He now believed that a ruler had been planted as a distraction – one more thing to be blamed on the "nefarious" magician who was out to make Margery look bad.

But what Margery's brother said next was chilling: "You won't live forever, Houdini, you've got to die. I put a curse on you now that will follow you every day until you die. Then you'll know better!"

Houdini didn't react to the curse, but he did respond to the fact that Walter – or whoever was providing his voice – had called him a bastard. As he later said, "If a man would have said that to me, I would clean up the floor with him." No one was allowed to talk about Harry's mother that way.

But right now, Houdini, of course, denied placing the ruler inside the box. As far as he was concerned, this was a triumphant moment in his campaign against fraud. Margery was still in her box, most likely with a pilfered device on the floor. She was trapped red-handed, Houdini believed.

No one seemed to dispute the idea that a ruler was in the

box – but who had put it there was the real question.

It was Dr. Comstock who spoke up and stopped the threats and recriminations from Walter. He reminded the voice that his behavior was detrimental to the psychical researcher. He also reminded everyone that a ruler had been used to construct and to repair the box and could have easily been left there by mistake. Since Walter had accused Houidni's assistant of planting the ruler, Orson Munn summoned the old stagehand to answer the charge. When he arrived, Collins produced his own folding ruler from his pocket. To bolster his statement, Houdini made him swear on the life of his mother that he had nothing to do with the one in the box.

Houdini believed the ruler had been part of Margery's attempt to cheat, and when she found out she was unable to do so, she used "Walter" to accuse Houdini of putting it there. The Crandons accused Houdini of leaving it there so that he would have an excuse when he was unable to discover the source of Margery's phenomena.

Houdini blamed the Crandons, and they blamed him.

No one knows how the ruler ended up in the box. In his biography of Houdini, author William Lindsay

Braves Curse

MRS LE ROY CRANDON
HARRY HOUDINI

Harry Houdini, magician and exposer of fake mediums, was skeptical that the curse of death, called down on his head by Margery (Mrs. Le Roy Crandon) would be effective.

Gresham quoted Collins, who he stated had confessed years later to hiding the ruler in the box because Houdini told him to do so.

Gresham's source for the quote? Magician Fred Keating, an alternate judge and supporter of Margery. It's a story that needs to be taken with a very large grain of salt, especially since other biographers, including Milbourne Christopher, called Collins' alleged confession "sheer fiction."

But whatever was in the cabinet, Houdini quickly stopped worrying about it. The ruler would have no bearing on any effects that might occur the rest of the night, he promised; the controls created to prevent fraud were too tight.

Once again, hands were linked and, at 9:45 P.M., the lights turned off and the séance continued. Comstock later said the atmosphere was "volcanic" with the entire circle "on edge." When Walter returned, he apologized for his nasty words and asked them to be removed from the record, although, "being the brother of the kid," he said he had to defend her.

In the meantime, Margery was sweltering in the box without ventilation. She struggled to do anything but sweat.

Houdini wasn't surprised, and he couldn't help but gloat. He said aloud that he could be stripped nude, searched, and locked in the box with his hands held by Margery and Dr. Crandon, yet could still ring the bell box, tie knots in a handkerchief, and shake a tambourine.

"That would not prove anything," Comstock retorted.

"It would prove these things are done by trickery," he replied.

Margery insisted that Houdini would have to smuggle a tool into the box to perform in such a way, and Houdini likely thought to himself, "Like you did, you mean?" He maintained, though, that he could perform such marvels without concealing any device. He said to the medium, "Your husband, Dr. Crandon, can search me as only a surgeon can, and I will guarantee to do these things. Do you want me to do it?"

She did not. She only said that if Houdini could do such wonderful things, then he must possess psychic powers of his own.

"I wish I did," he sighed.

Later, when it was clear the séance would be uneventful, Margery became irritated. She accused Houdini of trying to ruin her for his own financial gain. She knew he was going to give a performance at Keith's theater after the test séances were over. It had been theatrical motives that had drawn him to her work, she claimed.

Houdini responded that he had booked the show in June, long before the sittings were arranged. Furthermore, he was "in demand all over the world" and could dictate his own dates. He offered to change his local dates if she wanted him to.

Not long after this exchange, which was around 11:00 P.M., Houdini finally suggested that the lights be turned on and Margery be released from the box. After she stepped out of it, he found the disputed ruler at the bottom of it. According to Dr. Crandon, Houdini told him that he said he was willing to forget about the ruler if the Crandons were. He implied that Houdini was admitting his guilt, but anyone who knew Houdini doubted the doctor's story. But neither Houdini nor the Spiritualists were going to let it be forgotten.

The next morning, Houdini wrote a letter to his friend Walter Lippmann, who was also an editor at the *New York World*. He wrote that he had unmasked the medium whom Bird "failed to detect" in 40 sittings. He had stopped her manifestations and was convinced she was a fraud.

But Margery had one more séance with which to prove him wrong.

ON THE DAY OF THE THIRD AND FINAL SÉANCE, THE GROUP that had been attending the sittings together also dined together – albeit somewhat reluctantly. Despite the tension at the Charlesgate Hotel, Margery, Houdini, Munn, and Prince had dinner in the private room of a restaurant, which kept them from the prying eyes of both the public and the press.

This time, though, the bad feelings between Margery and

Houdini had not dissipated overnight. Dr. Crandon sat next to his wife during séances because she said it calmed her, but that afternoon, he was away, tending to his medical practice. This left Margery feeling agitated about being at a dinner that didn't include any of her supporters.

By Houdini's account, she brought up his upcoming show at Keith's and was sure that he was going to denounce her to his audience. She warned him that her supporters would turn violent if he attacked her during the show. She told him, "If you misrepresent me from the stage, some of my friends will come up and give you a good beating."

Houdini shook his head. "I am not going to misrepresent you. They are not coming on the stage, and I am not going to get a beating."

But Margery was not satisfied. She repeatedly told him that she did not want her son to grow up and read that his mother was a fraud.

Houdini, who usually had a soft spot for mothers, was unmoved by her words. "Then don't be a fraud," he told her.

When the Crandons arrived at Dr. Comstock's apartment that night, Margery seemed refreshed in a green kimono, and she expressed the hope they might have a "good-natured séance."

Houdini, meanwhile, had arrived with an athletic suit and seemed ready for a physical contest. He wanted to prove that he carried nothing on him – no flashlights, no rulers, nothing – that would concern the Crandons. But Margery smiled and told him that his usual clothing would be sufficient.

While the circle waited in the darkness for the bell to ring and other manifestations to occur, Dr. Crandon spoke up. "Someday, Houdini," he said, "you will see the light, and if it were to occur this evening, I would gladly give $10,000 to charity."

Harry replied, "It may happen, but I doubt it."

The doctor repeated. "If you were converted this evening, I would willingly give $10,000 to charity."

It was unusual to say, and some would later wonder if it had been made out of desperation—the promise of a bribe of Houdini would simply say that Margery was a genuine medium.

If it was, though, Houdini didn't bite, and he couldn't have proclaimed anything that happened that night to be authentic. The group sat for more than two hours while Margery moaned and perspired in her box, but there were no manifestations – no whistle, no raps, no shaking cabinet, no ringing bell.

Houdini had apparently won the contest. He had proved that when he applied his controls, the manifestations ceased. Margery had been so inhibited by Houdini's box that nothing happened. Even Walter failed to show up.

The final séance at the Charlesgate was a night of silence and darkness.

THE AFTERMATH OF THE MARGERY SÉANCES WAS TROUBLING for everyone involved. Unsurprisingly, there were two perspectives on the sittings – those of Houdini and of Dr. Crandon. Some newspapers reported that the Crandons were depressed after the three sittings, yet, by Roy's account, it was a triumphant group that gathered at Lime Street on the night after Margery's last encounter with Houdini.

Those who supported the Crandons claimed that it was Houdini – not Margery – who cheated at the Charlesgate. He was discredited in predictable circles after Dr. Crandon began spreading his version of events. "Surely the committee will not stand for this," Sir Arthur complained in a letter to Malcom Bird," and will protect a very self-sacrificing lady against such attempts upon her honor. I trust the matter will be most fully ventilated in the press. It is a complete exposure, but not of the medium."

"I have never heard such terrible stuff in my life!" Hereward Carrington wrote to Dr. Crandon.

Malcom Bird claimed that Houdini's thick oaken box hadn't accomplished anything but to temporarily cut off the medium's psychic current. But, since Margery didn't live up to Bird's many

MARGERY GENUINE, SAYS CONAN DOYLE; HE SCORES HOUDINI

MEDIUM AND HER NEW CHAMPION

MRS. MINA CRANDON
Who, as Margery, Is Storm Centre in Psychic Controversy

SIR ARTHUR CONAN DOYLE
Who Comes to Defense of Mrs. Crandon
(Bain News Service)

CRITICIZES THE EXPERT BODY IN SEVERE TERMS

All but Bird and Carrington Derelict in Silence Under Attack

HE ANALYZES ALL EVIDENCE ADDUCED

Surprised American Gentlemen Should Tolerate Wizard's Conduct

Using the methods of deduction made famous in his Sherlock Holmes stories, Sir Arthur Conan Doyle analyzes the phenomena shown by Mrs. Le Roi G. Crandon, the famous medium "Margery," and vigorously defends their authenticity in a statement which he sent to The Herald yesterday.

He finds after a minute examination of the proceedings of the Scientific American investigating committee, which held more than 90 seances with the wife of the Boston surgeon, that the charges of fraud made by Houdini, the magician, were entirely groundless, that the other experts, with the exception of C. Malcolm Bird and Hereward Carrington, were derelict in remaining silent after the handcuff king's attack. He also declares that Dr. Crandon was entirely too forbearing in permitting the tests to continue after his wife's honesty was impugned.

MAKES COUNTER-CHARGES

Counter-charges against the members of the committee who opposed Bird's and Carrington's proposal of a favorable report and a sense of amazement at their stubborn incredulity characterize Sir Arthur's message. He states that a cabal, headed by Houdini, was undoubtedly organized against Bird and finally resulted in his removal as secretary of the body.

He is particularly bitter in his criticism of Houdini and states that "he left Boston a very discredited man so far as psychic research is concerned." In conclusion he expresses his "amazement" that the committee, consisting of "honorable gentlemen" should permit the attack on the reputation of a lady and permitted a man "with entirely different standards to make this outrageous attack," and adds that by doing so they practically make themselves responsible for it.

By SIR ARTHUR CONAN DOYLE

It is Christmas morning and I sit at a table which is heaped with documents and photographs. They are the dossier of the Crandon case. Perhaps one should not work upon Christmas day, and yet surely there is no day so holy that one may not use it for the fight for truth, the exposure of evil and the defence of the honor of a most estimable lady.

The Margery case will live in history and perhaps it is fitting that I should have some hand in the record since the matter was in a double sense of my begetting. In the first place the committee of the "Scientific American" newspaper was instituted in consequence of my psychic lectures of 1922. In the second it was I who, with her consent, introduced Margery to their notice.

CHARMING, CULTIVATED

Margery is a most charming and cultivated lady. A year or two back she found that she possessed certain psychic powers which ran in the direction of physical phenomena. Her husband, as a man of science, was naturally interested in this development. Hearing that the committee of the "Scientific American" found it hard to get the services of professional mediums, Margery took the heroic resolution of presenting her powers for examination.

Sir Arthur Conan Doyle was, of course, quick to champion Margery in the battle between the medium and Houdini

claims, the *Scientific American* and its editor had some explaining to do. Though they had promised more reports on Margery, the September issue – for the first time in more than two years – carried no psychic story of any kind. Instead, Bird wrote in his column that two of the judges from the panel (Houdini and Prince) had threatened to quit if the magazine continued to publicize Margery before the verdict was delivered. He accused the "scandal sheets" of causing misunderstandings, while also refuting the rumors that Bird had been banned from the contest.

The newspapers, afraid to lose a good story, tried to keep the controversy alive by declaring the result of the tests a "hung jury." To Houdini's displeasure, one headline declared "MARGERY STILL HAS A CHANCE." To bolster her case, Margery gave her first interviews, complaining that it had not been a fair test because Houdini's box had prevented her psychic current. The image of the obliging medium locked in Houdini's box made many feel sympathetic toward her, but Houdini wasn't concerned. He was convinced about what had occurred – or rather, not occurred – at the séances and, in the end, he emerged on top.

Eventually, *Scientific American* declined to grant the prize to

Margery, in large part because of Houdini's exposure. Bird, whom Houdini continued to believe colluded with the Crandons, remained angry and kept insisting that Houdini should have been disqualified from the sittings at the very beginning.

Houdini further outraged Bird, the Crandons, and their supporters when he published a small book called *Houdini Exposes the Tricks Used by the Boston Medium Margery*. He was adamant that Margery was doing nothing more than offering clever tricks. In his final verdict on the medium, he wrote: "My decision is that everything which took place at the séances which I attended was a deliberate and conscious fraud..."

DESPITE HOUDINI'S CRITICISM, MARGERY EMERGED FROM THE controversial events relatively unscathed. She continued her séances and by the end of 1924, had begun to produce even greater manifestations, including "spirit arms" that rang the bell box and caused objects to fly about in the séance room.

In 1925, Malcolm Bird published a book that supported Margery. After becoming the research officer of the American Society for Psychical Research, he was able to sway many other ASPR members to her side. They became her greatest supporters and devoted hundreds of pages in the ASPR journal to her séances.

Eric J. Dingwall, an officer of the Society for Psychical Research in England, read of his American colleagues' support and decided to investigate the medium for himself. He wanted to see the ectoplasm that Margery was manifesting, and Dr. Crandon allowed him to view it by the light of a red lamp, which Crandon flashed on and off to reveal quick glances at the phenomenon. Too much light, Dr. Crandon said, would have an inhibiting effect on the mysterious material, which is said to be the manifestation of spirit emanations. Dingwall wrote to a friend: "The materialized hands are connected by an umbilical cord to the medium. They seize upon objects and displace them."

Later, when he was permitted to grasp one of the "ghost hands," he described it as feeling like "a piece of cold raw beef or

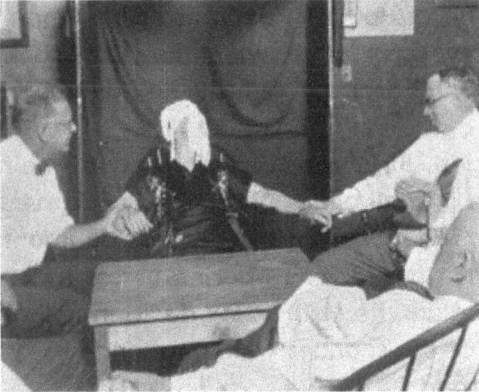

After the controversy with Houdini, Margery continued to perform as a medium. In these photos, she is seen blowing masses of ectoplasm from her nose and ear during different sessions.

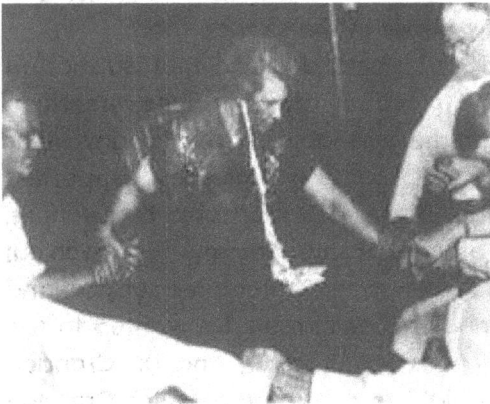

possibly a piece of soft, wet rubber."

Halfway through his investigations, Dingwall began having doubts. Dr. Crandon's red lamp never allowed him to see the ectoplasm emanating from Margery's body. He had only seen it after the fact. Odder still, many of the photographs revealed that many of the emanations seemed to be hanging from slender, almost invisible threads. Others who looked at the photos said that the "hands" looked suspiciously like animal lung tissue, a substance that Dr. Crandon could have obtained through his work at Boston hospitals. Dingwall's final report on the case was inconclusive.

As usual, Margery was unconcerned. Sitters continued to file into the séance room at the Crandons' Lime Street home. One investigation after another raised allegations of fraud, but no one was ever able to make the accusations stick. Even J.B. Rhine, who would later become one of the most prominent personalities in paranormal research, was intrigued by Margery but was unimpressed with what he saw.

As always, though, Conan Doyle defended the medium. When

Rhine published an unflattering account of his experiences with Margery, Doyle bought space in several Boston newspapers to run a reply. The black-bordered message read simply: "J.B. Rhine is an ass."

In 1928, Margery began to develop a highly unusual manifestation that made her even more widely known in Spiritualist circles. Two dishes were placed on a table in front of her during séances. One contained hot water, and one contained cold water. In the first dish was a piece of dental wax. When the wax was softened, it was claimed that Walter would make an impression of his thumb on it. Then, the thumbprint was put into cold water to harden. The prints appeared mysteriously, and a fingerprint expert called in by the Crandons stated that the thumbprint matched one that was taken from an old razor that once belonged to Walter Stinson.

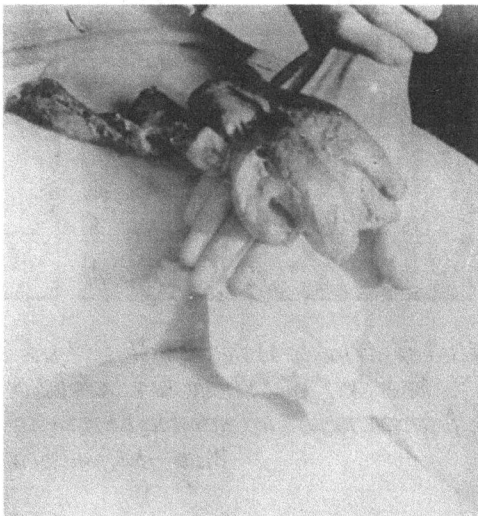

Margery also continued her reputation for holding sexually charged seances. In this photograph of Margery's vagina -- discreetly covered by a handkerchief -- it is seen to exude a dark-colored ectoplasm.

Below, Margery has her dress raised and her stockings rolled down so that she could exude ectoplasm from her vagina.

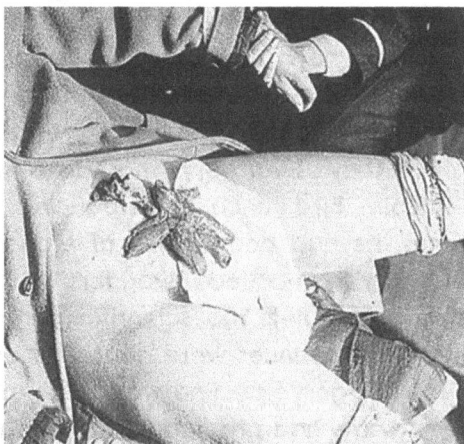

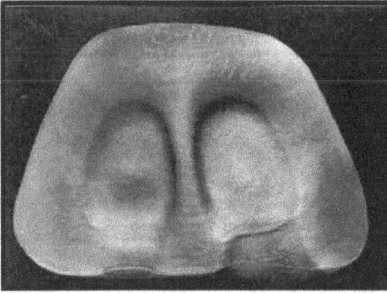

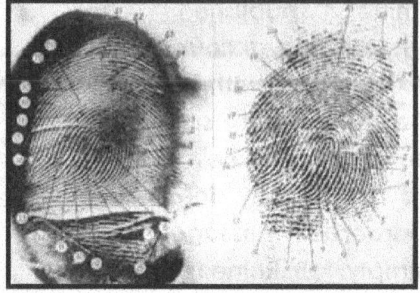

Margery had confounded the skeptics again, and this new manifestation enthralled believers. It was almost as if the spirit was leaving a calling card, but even better.

The excitement soon came to a crashing end, however.

Psychic researcher E.E. Dudley set out to compare Walter's wax print with those belonging to regulars at Margery's séances and made a surprising discovery -- Walter's thumbprint was identical in every way to that of Margery's dentist, Dr. Frederick Caldwell, from whom she had gotten the wax that she used for this feat. Dr. Caldwell created a sample thumbprint to show the Crandons how the wax could be used, and a metal die-stamp of his fingerprint was created to make more impressions of the wax.

This discovery marked the end of the ruse.

Many of Margery's most devoted followers drifted away. Even Malcolm Bird, once her staunchest defender, admitted that, at times, he had been guilty of elaborations and half-truths about Margery's so-called "wonders." Sir Arthur Conan Doyle was strangely quiet. The scientific community let it be known that Margery's séances were no longer of interest.

Margery's decline was quick and tragic.

Some had predicted that the Crandons' marriage would end

with the crash of Spiritualism, and while they led independent lives, they maintained a tattered bond until the end of the decade. Margery was deeply concerned when Roy fell in front of their home and fractured his pelvis on December 22, 1939. He died five days later, at age 66, of bronchial pneumonia.

Margery never really recovered. The home that had once been the center of an unusual mix of gaiety and spirit communication, reporters found to be a

Dr. Crandon and Margery toward the end of his life.

"hushed and darkened place" where Margery grieved. She told the newsmen that Roy's health had been declining for two years, and in that period, the couple had largely abandoned their efforts in psychic research. More surprisingly, she stated, "I do not contemplate making any efforts to communicate with him in the afterlife."

In the months that followed, Margery retreated from her friends, grew deeply depressed, and turned to consolation. She began to look older than her years as her beauty slowly faded away.

Despite what she said at the time of Dr. Crandon's death, she did return to the séance room. There were still those who believed in her, and she was willing to reach out to the spirits on their behalf. But even they disappeared after she grew so distraught during one sitting that she climbed to the roof of her home and threatened to throw herself off.

By 1941, she had become estranged from even those to whom

The end came for Margery on November 1, 1941, when she was only 54.

she had once been close and was often alone at No. 10 Lime Street. The séances were over. Walter, the spirit once known around the country, now only had an audience of one. Many evenings, Margery sat with a notebook in hand, scratching out messages from him. By then, she had come to the realization that only the dead were still there for her.

In October, when she knew that she was dying, investigator Nandor Fodor tried to get her to reveal her methods and admit her deceit, but Margery only had one statement to make. With a flicker of her old humor, she forced a smile and told him," Why don't you guess? You'll all be guessing for the rest of your lives."

When Fodor stood to leave, she croaked out something else, so faint that he could barely hear her. He asked her to repeat herself, and Margery whispered, "Go to Hell. All you psychic researchers can go to Hell."

Margery, like Houdini, seemed ready to depart this world on Halloween, but she hung on until the following afternoon, when she died at home from cirrhosis of the liver.

Mina "Margery" Crandon was dead. She was only 54.

NO REST FOR THE WICKED

THE ACCUSATIONS MADE AGAINST HOUDINI BY MALCOLM Bird, the Crandons, and others had little effect on the magician or on his career. His shows continued, and for the remainder of 1924, he embarked on a national tour, performing illusions and escapes, while continuing to try to put fraudulent mediums out of business.

The tour took him to small towns where he had never played and to big cities where he was already a vaudeville favorite. His contract paid him $1,500 per week, plus transportation, although in the larger cities he also received 50 percent of the net receipts. In various cities, he also battled with mediums who wanted to challenge him. Harry was always happy to oblige them.

In Denver, he was challenged by the Reverend Josie Stewart, who had earlier been exposed as a fraud in New York by the *Scientific American* committee. She wanted to take the stage and prove to her hometown audience that her gifts were genuine. She specialized in spirit messages that mysteriously appeared on previously blank cards – or that was how the act was supposed to work. When she had performed for the committee, the cards that were given to her were secretly identified with pinpricks. When the "spirit writing" appeared, the pinpricks vanished, proving to the

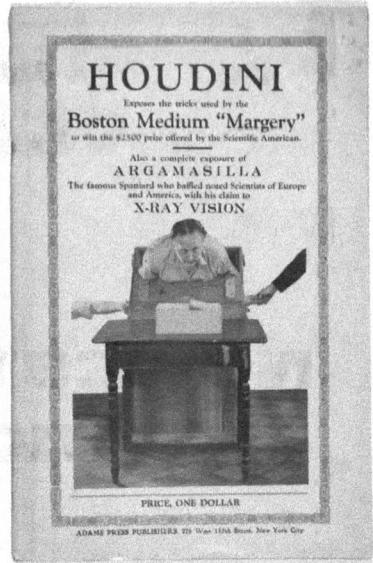

In the aftermath of the battle with Margery, Houdini published a "tell-all" book about how he believed she performed her act. It was filled with illustrations and step-by-step articles about how she fooled investigators for years.

committee that the medium had switched the cards.

When she came onstage in Denver, Houdini announced that he would give her the entire night's show receipts if she could produce any spirit phenomena that he couldn't duplicate. She produced no manifestations, but she put up quite a verbal battle, during which some of her followers got into a fistfight with Houdini's crew. The next day, the *Denver Post* ran a story headlined, "HOUDINI STARTS A RIOT."

In January 1925, Houdini returned to Boston on tour for the first time since the Margery debacle. Harry handed the city's mayor $5,000 in bonds as photographers snapped photos. The bonds were to be awarded to any medium -- Margery included -- who was able to produce physical phenomena that Houdini could not reproduce. Symphony Hall, where Sir Arthur Conan Doyle had once presented lectures endorsing Spiritualism, was packed for Houdini's performance. Occupying 100 chairs on the crowded stage was a committee that Houdini had invited as guests -- ministers, reporters, fellow magicians, and esteemed community members.

This night, a Houdini was introduced to Bostonians, who was unlike the man they knew so well from his many performances at Keith's. This Houdini was a little stockier and a little more serious. His once-dark, disheveled hair was now peppered with gray. His bright, hypnotic eyes hadn't changed, though. He spoke slowly, making his words very clear.

He had no intention of attacking anyone's religion, he told the audience. Everyone should be allowed to worship as they see fit, so long as they remain within the laws of the country and don't hurt anyone.

Houdini told them that he was not an unbeliever. He longed to believe in the spirit world, and more than anything else, he longed for some word from his late, beloved mother -- or from any of the friends with whom he had made pacts before they died.

His enemies, he complained, dismissed him as a mere magician, a showman. But he had spent nearly 35 years studying Spiritualism and had investigated scores of mediums. Like his father, he was a scholar. He had an immense library in New York, one of the largest in the world on the occult and magic. Anyone could talk to the dead, he said, but as far as he could tell, the dead did not answer. Inmates of lunatic asylums heard strange voices and saw phantoms, but this did not make them real. Millions of dollars had been spent on psychical research without producing any solid results. In 1854, Harvard University established a $500 fund that would be given to anyone who performed a genuine psychic event.

That very day, Houdini reminded them that he had given $5,000 to the mayor with instructions to award it to any authentic medium in the city of Boston, but there had been no takers. Not even from the same mediums who regularly demonstrated their manifestations, under their own fixed conditions, to their followers for a dollar or two.

Men like Sir Oliver Lodge and Sir Arthur Conan Doyle were menaces to mankind, Houdini firmly stated, eliciting a gasp from

the audience. They were great men and deserved to be respected in their fields, but were not qualified to say that any medium was genuine. Most of these so-called "psychics" were nothing more than escape artists and thieves. Houdini could perform feats of phony spirit phenomena that would defy scientific explanation, but it was nothing more than trickery. He even confessed to posing as a medium himself, as a foolish and poverty-stricken young man, and told how he had faked a message from a murdered man in Kansas that caused a panic in a theater.

He showed the audience a letter from Lady Emily Shackleton, widow of Sir Ernest Shackleton, who died in the Antarctic of a heart attack aboard his ship *Quest* in 1922. The letter denied that Sir Arthur Conan Doyle could have heard from the late explorer, as he claimed that he had. Harry told the audience about how, in Atlantic City, Lady Jean Doyle had written page after page of messages that supposedly came from his dead mother. Cecilia, who had been educated in Europe, could speak five languages, but very little English. Sir Arthur, when he learned this from Houdini, had laughingly asserted that his mother had gone to college in heaven and had learned English.

After this lengthy introduction, the house lights were turned down, and slides of famous mediums like the Fox sisters and the Davenport brothers appeared on screen. Houdini summarized their careers and explained how their feats were mere tricks, stage hocus pocus, not psychic powers.

After the lights came back up, Houdini demonstrated how those mediums performed their fraudulent activities. A man from the audience was invited onto

Houdini shows how phony "spirit hands" were created for seances

the stage, and Houdini had him sit down at a table, like one that would have been used in a séance, and had him examine a slate that Harry handed to him. The slate was blank, but after the man held it under the table, writing appeared on it. A medium, Houdini told the audience, would call this a spirit message -- but it wasn't. He showed how he had switched slates under his chair before the man grasped the slate beneath the table. The audience howled with laughter.

Houdini then recounted his version of events in the Margery tests, stunning the audience as he explained how he had discovered the trickery that occurred during her séances. Two spectators were invited to the stage, sitting on either side of him. Both had their heads covered with hoods to simulate the dark conditions of the séance room. Each man held one of Houdini's hands, each controlled one of his feet. Houdini asked one of the men if a megaphone was sitting on the floor next to him. The man reached out his hand, touched the megaphone, said that it was there, and retook Houdini's hand.

Harry then bent forward, put his head under the table in

front of him, and lifted it so that only two of the legs were on the floor. Then he pulled his head back, and the "levitated" table thumped back into place. The audience once again laughed loudly. "That's exactly how Margery did it," he exclaimed.

Once more, Harry asked the man on his right to make sure the megaphone was next to him. The man again released his hand and verified the position of the trumpet. In the few seconds this action required, Houdini picked up the megaphone as soon as the man's hand left it, jammed it on his head, and had his hand ready for the volunteer to take hold of it again. Neither of the volunteers was aware that anything out of the ordinary had occurred. With the hoods over their heads, it was the same as being in a dark séance room.

The man to Houdini's left was told that the megaphone was floating through the air above his head. Did he wish for it to fall near him? The man said that he did, and so Harry turned in his direction and, with a shake of his head, made the megaphone fall into the hooded volunteer's lap. The audience broke into gales of laughter once more.

Houdini also demonstrated how the bell box on the table could be rung with his forehead while his hands and feet were held in place.

The enclosure he had built for Margery was brought on stage. This was the first time it had been seen in Boston since the controversial series of séances. He talked about Walter and showed how "spirit hands" were made and how, using long metal tongs, the hands could touch the faces of séance attendees sitting some distance away.

He invited another man up from the audience, and the man sat at one end of a table with Houdini at the other. The man put his feet on Houdini's under the table and held Houdini's hands across the top. A dinner bell rang under the table. A tambourine jangled. Control had not been broken; the volunteer insisted that he could still feel Harry's hands and feet. Houdini's assistant lifted the cloth over the table, and the audience laughed. The man's feet were still on Houdini's shoes, but Harry had slipped his foot out of the right one. He was able to grab the bell with his toes, and as he shook his foot, the bell rang.

After taking questions from the audience, Houdini closed the show. It had been a resounding success, and it was repeated again and again across the country. The show cast him in three roles -- magician, escapologist, and debunker of mediums. The performances sold out in every city, and Houdini found himself extending tour dates because the demand for tickets was so high. Reporters from newspapers in the cities he played joined his corps of psychic investigators, which until then had consisted of his wife, Bess; Julia Sawyer, Bess' twenty-two-year-old niece; his stage assistants, and his friends and fellow magicians. He hired not only Rose Mackenberg -- his "secret weapon" – but also other private detectives who devoted their time to exposing spirit fraud.

During an engagement in Cleveland, Harry, wearing shabby clothes and thick glasses as a disguise, went with County Prosecutor Edward B. Stanton and reporter Louis B. Seltzer to the home of a medium named George Renner on Superior Avenue. In his séance room on the second floor, the medium showed his clients four spirit photographs. Houdini's name was mentioned, and Renner called the magician a fraud.

"I once paid two and a half dollars to see him," Renner said. "He's a big fraud and a faker. They chased him out of Massachusetts. When he says Spiritualism is a fake, he lies, folks. Tonight, we will prove that Spiritualism is genuine, and Houdini is a faker."

Three other visitors -- not members of Houdini's group -- joined the circle around a large table. Renner instructed them to place their hands on the knees of the persons on either side of them, checking to make sure his instructions were carried out. Then he turned to the reporter, Louis Seltzer, and said, "Young man, you look a little frightened. There is no need to be. If the spirits brush your cheek, don't be afraid. If the guitar or trumpet floats over your head, keep quiet. They will not harm you."

The medium stood at the end of the table and announced, "Folks, you will hear tonight from Jimmy Nolan of Anderson, Wisconsin. Are you ready?" Renner fastened two frames covered with opaque paper to the windows, then draped rugs over the three doors to the room. He took his seat in the circle and switched off the lights, plunging the room into darkness. Soon, a booming voice broke the silence, announcing that it was "Jimmy."

There were raps, and then they heard a voice claiming to be the father of one of the sitters. Another voice followed him, this one claiming to be a Native American "chief." Then a guitar began to play, apparently floating around the room in the darkness. It returned to the table, and after the music stopped, the lights were turned on again. Renner was in his seat, his hands on the knees of those next to him, as they had been earlier.

Rising to leave, Seltzer said that he wanted to pay for himself and his two friends. Renner accepted the $3 but protested that the séance had only just started. Once more, the room was darkened. A spirit voice sang "Nearer My God to Thee" and "Jerusalem," and the sitters joined in. A whooshing sound indicated that the trumpets were now hovering above the table. They clanked as they dropped back to the table. A flashlight was switched on, and a bright light was suddenly trained on the medium. He blinked his eyes. His hands were covered with soot, and there were dark streaks on his face.

Houdini's voice called out, "Mr. Renner, you are a fraud. Your hands are full of lampblack. The trumpets are also full of lampblack. That's how you got it on your hands."

Seltzer switched on the lights, and Houdini explained how the medium had taken a can of lampblack – a pigment made from soot -- from his pocket in the dark and coated the trumpet with it so that it wouldn't reflect any light in the dimly lit room.

Renner shouted angrily. "I have been a medium for 40 years, and I have never been exposed!"

Houdini smirked, "Well, you are now."

"Who are you?" Renner demanded to know.

"My name," said the shabby little man, removing his glasses, "is Houdini." He then introduced the county prosecutor and Seltzer, whose story appeared on the front page of the *Cleveland Press* the next day.

Renner was arrested, tried, and found guilty of obtaining money under false pretenses. He was fined $25 and sentenced to spend six months in jail.

In Pittsburgh, the Reverend Alice S. Dooley, of the Pittsburgh Church of Divine Healing, volunteered to be tested at the Alvin Theater in September. Harry sealed three questions in envelopes and hung them on a string suspended across the stage. The psychic asked for music to put her in the mood so that she could "commune with her astral influences." The orchestra obliged with a slow waltz.

She pointed to the first envelope. "All is well. March 30, 1894," she said.

No vibrations were produced by the second envelope.

Her answer to the third question was, "It is possible."

A committee of judges and clergymen opened the first envelope. The question was, "What Pittsburgh chief of police did I meet in Europe? When, how, and where?" The psychic's reply had not answered any part of Houdini's query. The date she had given was meaningless. He had not gone to Europe until 1900.

The third question was, "What was the name of the Hindu who taught me the East Indian Needle Trick? Where and what year, and the circumstances?" Her reply of "it was possible" was scarcely an answer at all.

The critic in the *Cincinnati Commercial Tribune* wrote that the show "was good fun from start to finish... Houdini manages these magical shows just a bit better than anyone else. There's one big difference between Houdini on a vaudeville bill and Houdini in his own show. In the latter instance, there's more of him. Ergo, the show is better."

During a week in Syracuse, Julia Sawyer and Rose Mackenberg went on a special mission to Lily Dale, the famous Spiritualist summer camp. At Lily Dale, the curious could patronize

Lily Dale in New York, Spiritualist settlement

clairvoyants, message-readers, and various physical mediums. Many believers spent their vacations there. In 1916, the Fox family farmhouse, where Kate and Maggie Fox had started producing the phenomena that gave birth to the Spiritualist movement, was moved to the Lily Dale grounds, where séances continued to be held in the house.

Julia masqueraded as a curious teenager and Rose as a housewife. For $3 each, a medium named Pierre Keeler admitted them to a slate séance. Keeler produced a spirit message for Julia from a sister she never had, as well as communication from her mother and brother, who were said to be happy in the spirit world.

This was quite a shock to Julia since they were both still alive.

After the séance, Keeler was taken to meet Julia's elderly uncle, who sat slumped in a wheelchair under the care of a nurse. The "elderly uncle" was, of course, Houdini, who whipped off his disguise and announced that he had the goods on Keeler. The medium admitted his deceptions but pleaded with Houdini not to expose him. They were, after all, in the same business.

"Not so, "Harry replied, "I'm a legitimate entertainer, you're a cheat."

HOUDINI BEGAN A RUN ON BROADWAY AT THE 44TH STREET Theater near the end of 1925 and then played in Brooklyn and Manhattan before traveling to Hartford, Connecticut, for an engagement. It was snowing heavily when he arrived, and he went straight from the station to speak before 400 men at the Advertising Club. He then addressed a radio audience on WTIC.

Hundreds were in line in front of the theater an hour before the show. Despite the storm, the house was sold out when the curtain went up.

During Houdini's three-week run in Philadelphia, he took the night train to Washington. On the morning of February 26, 1926, he testified before a House of Representatives committee in support of bill H.R. 8989, which would ban fortune-telling in the District of Columbia. This bill, and two similar ones introduced in the Senate, had the magician's complete approval.

The Spiritualists, as well as their associations and publications, were as vehemently against the bills as Houdini was in favor of them. The room where the Subcommittee on Judiciary of the District of Columbia held its public hearing was jammed. Among the spectators were Spiritualists, as well as palm readers, crystal gazers, and clairvoyants.

Houdini addressed the committee:

Please understand that, emphatically, I am not attacking a religion. I respect every genuine believer in Spiritualism or any other religion. But this thing they call Spiritualism, wherein a medium intercommunicates with the dead, is a fraud from start to finish. There are only two kinds of medium: those who are mental degenerates and who ought to be under observation, and those who are deliberate cheats and frauds. I would not believe a fraudulent medium under oath; perjury means nothing to them.

How can you call it a religion when you get men and women in a room together, and they feel each other's hands and bodies? The inspirational mediums are not quite as bad as that. But they guess and by "fishing" methods and by reading obituary notices, they get the neurotics to believe that they heard voices and see forms. In thirty-five years, I have never seen one genuine medium.

Washington abounded with fortune-tellers, lucky charm sellers, card readers, and mediums of every kind, Houdini claimed. For $25, anyone could buy a clairvoyant license, then point to it

Houdini with Senator Arthur Capper. Houdini had endorsed anti-fortune-telling legislation in Washington in 1924. Neither the bill proposed to a Senate Committee, nor the one considered by the House passed.

and say: "If I were not genuine, I could not get a license."

Harry repeated his offer of $10,000 for proof of mediumship. He took a telegram from his pocket, crumpled it, and threw it on the table. He dramatically looked back at the audience. "Read that, you clairvoyant mediums, and show me up. Tell me the contents of that telegram." The Spiritualists remained silent.

Representative Frank Reid, a Republican from Illinois, broke in: "I will tell you what it says -- please send more money."

Houdini replied: "You can make your own deductions. You are not a clairvoyant."

"Oh yes, I am," Reid quipped, setting off a round of laughter.

Houdini smiled and crumpled up another telegram and tossed it on the table. "All right, if you're a clairvoyant, tell me what this wire is."

"Is it asking if it didn't come?" Reid said.

Houdini shook his head. "No, sir. Everyone guesses at it."

Although these statements came from the official proceedings of the committee, newspapers gave varying accounts of what occurred that day. Different statements were made about what Representative Reid said, and some even claimed that he jumped out of his seat and shouted, "That's an invitation to you to appear before the committee this morning. I win the $10,000!" This didn't happen.

The *New York Morning Telegraph* account included an incident that was not mentioned anywhere else. When Houdini challenged any of the mediums in the room to tell him the name his mother called him before he was born, a palmist, standing just outside the door, was said to have remarked, "She probably called him an incipient damn fool."

Jane B. Coates, one of Washington's best-known mediums, took the stand. She was asked to define the term mystic. "A mystic, "she replied, "is a person who has evoluted [sic] certain senses within themselves which bring them knowledge from the world beyond."

A congressman asked her if Houdini was a mystic. Mrs. Coates replied, "I think Mr. Houdini is one of the greatest mystics in the world today." The hearing was adjourned until May 18.

When the session resumed, Houdini returned to Washington to be the star witness for the bill's supporters. For three days, he attacked the mediums, and they lashed back at him when they took the stand. Harry showed how he could produce a "spirit" voice from a trumpet without moving his lips and caused a message to appear on a pair of blank slates. When the Spiritualists called him "vile" and "crazy," he asked Bess to come forward.

Harry said to her, "I want the chairman to see you. On June 22, 1926, we celebrate our thirty-second anniversary. There are no medals and no ribbons on me, but when a girl will stick to a man for thirty-two years as she did, and when she will starve with me and work with me through thick and thin, it is a pretty good recommendation. Outside of my great mother, Mrs. Houdini has been my greatest friend. Have I ever shown traces of being crazy, unless it was about you?"

"No," Bess quietly replied.

"Am I brutal to you or vile?"

"No."

"Am I a good boy?"

"Yes."

"Thank you, Mrs. Houdini."

The hearings ended on May 21. Despite Houdini's testimony and best efforts, no bill to ban fortune-telling was ever passed.

DURING THE EIGHT WEEKS THAT HOUDINI PERFORMED AT THE Princess Theater in Chicago, he and his assistants investigated more than 40 mediums who operated in the city. One night, eight of the 19 sitters at the home of a medium named Minnie Reichart were members of Houdini's team.

Before the séance began, Mrs. Reichart unplugged the only lamp in the room. Aware that Houdini was in town, she wasn't taking any chances. No lights were going to interrupt her séance, which included spirit voices that sang songs that varied between "Nearer My God to Thee" and "Yes Sir, That's my Baby."

Later, her spirit guide, Chief Blackhawk, was speaking through her spirit trumpet in a guttural tone when a flash illuminated the room. A *Chicago American* photographer had taken a picture. One man pulled up the shade, and another threw open a window, which was the quickest exit route. Five men jumped to the lawn outside. The séance room had been plunged into chaos.

"Where's the outlet for the floor socket?" someone shouted.

A female voice screamed, "Don't put on the lights. Do you want to kill our medium?"

Mrs. Reichart's supporters rushed the sitters -- including Houdini's crew -- out of the house. The sister of the medium slapped the photographer, knocking off his hat. Another swing sent the flash equipment tumbling from his hands onto the grass. He clutched his camera firmly in his other hand and fought his way to his car. His hat, his camera case, and his flashgun were lost in the scuffle.

The photographic plate was developed in the newspaper

darkroom, showing that the single image had captured the medium holding the trumpet to her lips with a handkerchief-wrapped hand so no fingerprints would appear on the shiny surface. The photograph, four columns wide, titled "Picture Bares Fraud," appeared on the front page of the March 11 issue of the *Chicago American*.

The lengthy run in Chicago produced one unexpected event. Harry was visited in his dressing room by an elderly couple, Mr. and Mrs. Ernest Benninghofen. They complimented him on his exposures of fraudulent mediums, and Mrs. Benninghofen explained that she had once been known as Anna Clark, the "mother medium," because she had developed so many young psychics, including Mrs. Cecil Cook, then a leading figure in the movement. She said that 20 years earlier, Mrs. Benninghofen had sold Mrs. Cook her North Side apartment and her list of wealthy suckers.

She told Harry, "When I reformed, I had no intention of going before the public and showing how tricks were done. But I will come any time or any place to help you, as I now see the great good that is being done."

Harry was overwhelmed by the visit. He had an ally, ordained by the National Spiritualist Association, who would stand before an audience, confess her sins, and demonstrate the feats that had fooled hundreds of those who had believed in her. He arranged a press conference at the Sherman Hotel and promised reporters one of his greatest revelations ever.

By coincidence, the twenty-seventh annual convention of the Illinois State Spiritualist Association was in progress on Chicago's West Side at the time. During the convention, John Slater, who was said to have made over 1 million dollars with his séances, ridiculed Houdini's stage exposures – not realizing what was then happening at the Sherman Hotel.

At the hotel, Houdini was introducing Mrs. Benninghofen to the press. He announced that she would showcase her entire repertoire – and explain how the phenomenon was produced. The

Reformed spirit medium, Annie Benninghofen, appeared with Houdini in Chicago and explained to reporters how she had produced "spirit voices" from "floating" trumpets during her sittings.

lights were switched off, and prayer and song ushered in the "ghostly" phenomena. Trumpets rose and floated in the dark room. Ghostly hands appeared and disappeared. Spirits talked through the trumpets in the air, and those "spirits" included a little girl named Rosie, a deep-voiced Uncle John, elderly Aunt Susan, and even Chief Big Elk, a war cry-whooping Native American.

After astounding the reporters with what seemed to be genuine psychic activity, Mrs. Benninghofen revealed the trickery behind her antics. Voices seemed to come from distances far beyond the length of an ordinary spirit trumpet. She showed how this was accomplished by attaching two trumpets together -- mouthpiece to mouthpiece -- in the dark room. She whispered at one end of the two trumpets, and her voice came out of the far end of the other, creating the eerie effect. She also exhibited her vocal range, showing how she could speak in many voices and many tones, including those of a child and an adult man.

Houdini helped her reveal the secret of "ghostly" hands. A glove coated with luminous paint was glued to a piece of black cardboard. When the luminous side was turned toward the spectators, the hand appeared in the dark. When it was turned away, the hand vanished. By moving the cardboard quickly from one area to another, he produced what seemed to be two hands in different places. Mrs. Benninghofen confessed that she concealed the hand-producing device under her skirt.

She also demonstrated how she was able to free one of her hands in the dark -- even when the sitters on either side of her believed she was being controlled. She released her right hand momentarily, "to brush back her hair," and then clasped hands again with the man on her right. Only this time, she clasped his hand with her left hand, which was held at the wrist by a man to her left. Neither man realized that one hand was being "controlled" rather than two. With her free hand, the medium could swing trumpets in the air, could speak through them, and could even tap people on the head at a distance with the end of the trumpet.

As Houdini had promised, it was an amazing and eye-opening press conference.

Mrs. Benninghofen explained her motives:

I really believed in Spiritualism all the time I was practicing it, but I thought I was justified in helping the spirits out. They couldn't float a trumpet around the room; I did it for them. They couldn't speak, so I spoke for them. I thought I was justified in trickery because, through trickery, I could get more converts to what I thought was a good and beautiful religion. When people asked me if the spirits really moved trumpets, I told them to judge for themselves. So, while I acted a lie, I didn't tell one.

Houdini only had one comment to make when it was all over, and he was bidding Mrs. Benninghofen goodbye. "It was a shame," he said, "that more mediums couldn't say the same.

BURIED ALIVE

HOUDINI ENDED HIS WINTER SEASON ON THE ROAD IN Harrisburg, Pennsylvania, in May 1926. He returned to New York with the intention of spending the summer months relaxing and devising new mysteries for his upcoming fall season. He was also working on a book about witchcraft and planning the next stage of his career. Starting in 1927, he was supposed to begin teaching a magic curriculum at Columbia University.

But he couldn't spend as much time relaxing as he wanted because he was soon confronted with what was alleged to be a new psychic sensation. Hereward Carrington, the only *Scientific American* committee member to continue endorsing Margery, began trumpeting about a new medium -- the "Egyptian Miracle Man," Rahman Bey.

The slender, bearded mystic claimed to be able to influence his body with his mind, slowing the pulse in one of his wrists while increasing it in the other, thrusting steel needles through his flesh, and resting with a sword blade under the back of his neck, with another under his heels, as a man holding a sledgehammer cracked a stone slab on his chest. As a climax to his show, he went into a trance and was buried in a coffin under a mound of sand.

While he was in the coffin, Carrington lectured for 10 minutes about suspended animation and living burials, and then the sand was shoveled away, and Bey was removed from the coffin. He revived himself enough to walk unsteadily to the footlights each night and accept thunderous applause and curtain calls.

In July, Bey announced that he was going to perform his greatest feat yet. He was to be enclosed in a metal box like usual, but instead of being buried in the sand, the coffin would be submerged in the Hudson River. Bey would attempt to stay underwater in the coffin for an entire hour.

On the day of this stunt, Bey mentally prepared himself. Two doctors took his pulse and measured his heartbeat. Bey pressed his fingertips to his temples, shut his eyes, and lowered his head. He swayed and then fell backward into the arms of his assistants, who lifted him into a bronze coffin. The inner lid was bolted, and the outer cover was soldered shut.

The coffin, lifted by a hoist, swung over the water, but before it was lowered into the river, an electric alarm bell rang. The bell was part of a safety device controlled from inside the box. The hoist brought the coffin back, and workmen feverishly hacked away at the cover, tearing away the lid with chisels and hammers.

Just 19 minutes after Bey was sealed into the coffin, he was set free and lifted out. His body was covered with sweat, and his face was twisted angrily. After emerging from the trance, he explained -- through an interpreter, since he allegedly spoke no English -- that he had not rung the bell. Someone offered the theory that perhaps when the coffin had been lifted, his body had shifted against the buzzer and rang the bell.

Two weeks later, he was ready to try the underwater stunt again. This time, the coffin was lowered into the waters of the Dalton Hotel swimming pool on 59th Street. He stayed, sealed inside the bronze coffin, for the entire hour.

When he emerged, his supporters, including Carrington, bragged that he had used his psychic abilities to slow his pulse and his breathing to allow him to survive under impossible conditions.

"Impossible," it would turn out, was an overstatement.

Rahman Bey's most vocal critic was, of course, Houdini. He was familiar with most of the man's stunts from his dime museum days. There was nothing paranormal about them. It was all simply a matter of knowledge and training. Harry could do the same stunts -- except for being buried alive. He had been buried in California once, and he had been locked in boxes and coffins underwater countless numbers of times, but his intention was always to try to free himself as quickly as possible. It wasn't to stay underground for an hour – or any longer than he had to.

Houdini's criticisms eventually reached Bey's manager, and in late July, he publicly challenged Houdini to duplicate the water endurance feat. Although he'd never attempted to stay underwater or underground for such lengthy periods of time, Harry's ego made it impossible for him to ignore the challenge.

On the day of his attempt, he was sealed into a container the same size as Bey's and was lowered into the pool at the Shelton Hotel. An hour and a half later, assistants hauled the box from the water and opened it. Tired, but otherwise in good condition, the magician told reporters that there was nothing supernatural about the stunt. The secret, he explained, was to remain calm, move as little as possible, and breathe with short, regular intakes of air.

Hereward Carrington and some of his supporters,

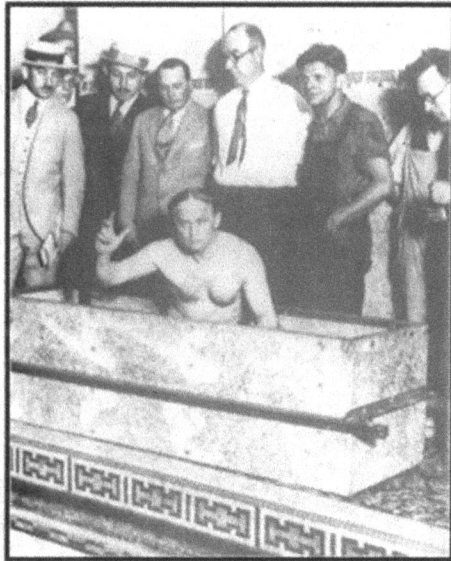

Houdini in his "coffin", just before his underwater stunt in the Shelton Hotel swimming pool

who were present at the pool, discounted Houdini's controlled-breathing explanation. They believed, never having attempted the feat themselves, that a trick had been used to supply Harry with oxygen, either a false compartment in the box or a secret flow through the telephone line that had been installed in the coffin as a safety precaution.

They were wrong.

Houdini later told his friend and fellow magician, James S. Harto, that he had trained for weeks in water to get his lungs accustomed to breathing very little air. Houdini had always been able to hold his breath for extended periods of time, and the stunt simply required him to train a little harder. He told Harto that he merely had to lie on his back and take very shallow breaths. "There is no doubt in my mind, "he said, "that anyone can do it."

Houdini's explanation was validated in 1958 when James "The Amazing" Randi demonstrated on British television his ability to survive under almost the same circumstances. Randi was younger and weighed less than Houdini, but the box he used was the same size. He stayed underwater in the coffin for two hours and three minutes.

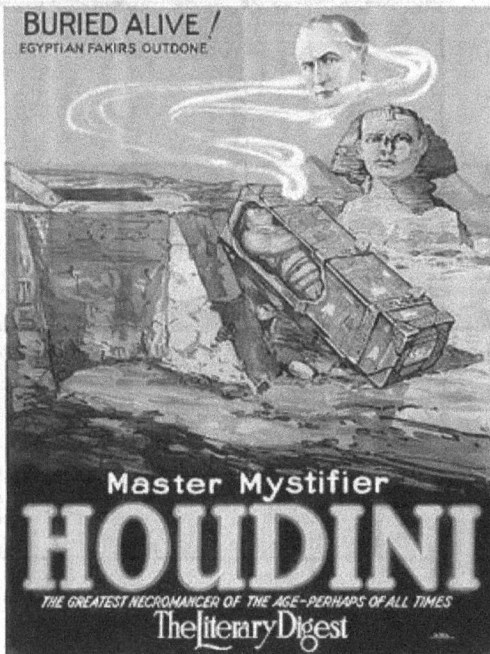

BURIED ALIVE /
EGYPTIAN FAKIRS OUTDONE

Master Mystifier

HOUDINI
THE GREATEST NECROMANCER OF THE AGE – PERHAPS OF ALL TIMES
The Literary Digest

Having been successful with the makeshift iron box, Houdini bought a $2,500 bronze casket -- just like the one that Rahman Bey had used -- and planned to perform the feat as an attraction during his fall tour, much as he had suspended himself in a straitjacket above the city streets in the past.

A new lithograph poster was printed to publicize the stunt: "Buried Alive! Egyptian Fakirs Outdone! Master Mystifier Houdini, The Greatest Necromancer of the Age -- Perhaps of All Time." The poster depicted a coffin, with a cutaway section that showed Houdini tied up inside, resting against the edge of an Egyptian burial chamber. To the right was the Sphinx, and above it, in a swirl of mist, was Harry's face.

Houdini's fall season began in September in Paterson, New Jersey, but nothing seemed to go smoothly, and problems and mishaps constantly plagued the show.

No one knew it when the tour began, but soon, the curtain was going to fall on Houdini for the last time.

THE END OF THE SHOW

HOUDINI KNEW HIS DAYS WERE NUMBERED.

That was according to Fulton Oursler, anyway. The head of the McFadden publishing empire and a medium-busting ally of the magician recalled that before Houdini left New York for the start of his fall tour, he said he had been "marked for death" by spirit circles everywhere.

And there may have been something going on, because his second stop on the tour marked the start of a series of misfortunes.

In October 1926, Houdini began a week-long engagement in Providence, Rhode Island. When Bess awoke sick and feverish one morning, Harry, who never consulted a doctor himself unless Bess cried and threatened to leave him, had a physician at her bedside within the hour. The doctor pronounced ptomaine poisoning as the source of her illness, and Harry put in a hurried call to New York to summon a nurse to come and travel with her. On Friday evening, Bess' temperature climbed, and Houdini sat with her throughout the night.

On Saturday morning, the fever finally broke. Harry managed a few hours of restless sleep between the matinee show and the evening performance. After the last show, he loaded Bess, her nurse, and the troupe onto a train bound for Albany, while Harry climbed aboard the last train to New York City. He dozed occasionally in his seat, but the stops and starts of the train at various stations kept him awake for most of the journey. By the time he reached Grand Central Station, he was exhausted.

Harry had returned to the city for a meeting with Bernard Ernst, but when he arrived at the Ernst home, the family's maid told him that his friend had not yet returned from a trip. Knowing he would arrive soon, the maid invited him to wait. He dozed on a couch in the living room until Ernst returned.

A few hours later, he called the hotel where the company was staying in Albany, and the nurse reported that his wife's condition was unchanged.

Houdini's next stop was the magic shop he had once owned. His friend – and the new owner – Frank Ducrot arranged to have several pieces of apparatus shipped out for the show.

When he arrived home, he telephoned Albany again. There was still no change, but the nurse told him not to worry. She would be staying with Bess through the night.

On October 11, Houdini took the early morning train to Albany, again unable to sleep for most of the trip. He dashed to the hotel to see Bess and found her condition improved, although she had been ordered to stay in bed. Harry managed a short nap before that night's performance, which would be marked by the next mishap.

During the show, a chain slipped during the famous Chinese Water Torture Cell escape and fractured Houdini's ankle. A doctor in the audience advised him to end the show and go to the hospital, but he refused. Harry didn't want to disappoint the audience. He finished the performance painfully hopping on one foot, good-naturedly poking fun at himself. When the show ended, he was taken to Albany's Memorial Hospital for X-rays and treatment. The doctors there told him to stay off his feet for at least one week, but Harry declined and made plans to continue

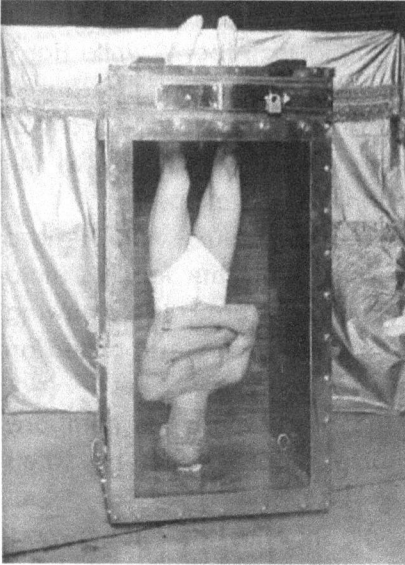

Houdini in the Chinese Torture Cell. A slip when he entered the tank caused an ankle fracture on October 11, 1926. He finished the rest of the show hopping on one foot. Although ordered by a doctor to stay off the foot for at least a week, Harry continued to perform.

performing.

Newspapers that reported the injury predicted cancellations and a delay in the tour, but they underestimated Houdini. It would take more than a broken bone to keep him off the stage. Harry fashioned a leg support for himself, and the tour continued, going first to Schenectady and then to Montreal, where he visited another doctor about his ankle. After an examination, he told Harry the same thing the doctors in Albany did – stay off his foot for a week and allow the bone to heal.

But Houdini was not going to let down the excited crowds that turned out for his October 18 show at the Princess Theatre or for his lecture at McGill University.

Although Houdini limped slowly to the podium for his lecture, he came alive when he began to speak, explaining that people who embraced Spiritualism simply lacked the ability to see things clearly. If people would educate their eyes and minds, they could easily see through practically every "miracle" performed by psychics like Margery, whose greatest power was her sexual charm. "Margery handed out applesauce to the investigators," he told the students. "I know this because I have walked through the apple orchards myself." While he had resisted the fruit, she was only one of his many enemies.

"If I should die tonight," he declared, "the Spiritualist mediums would hold a national holiday."

Among those cheering for him at the McGill student union was a junior named Samuel Smilovitz. He was one of the many students who surged forward to meet him after his lecture. The young man showed Houdini a sketch he had made while Harry had been talking. The magician pronounced it as an excellent likeness.

While Samuel had been sketching Houdini, another member of the audience took notes while watching the magician as he spoke. A curious young man, Jocelyn Gordon Whitehead, liked to get to the bottom of things. He loved details and hidden meanings. While reading the newspaper at home, he always kept a dictionary on one side of the table and an atlas on the other. Six-foot-two and muscular, he didn't look like a scholar, and at 31 years old, he didn't look like a freshman, but officially, he was one. Even at a glance, there was something a little off about Whitehead. It's unknown why he started college in his thirties. He claimed to be studying religion and at other times, medicine or engineering. He had studied boxing, too, and he had battered enough opponents to prove he was skilled. A loner, Whitehead slipped out of the student union when Houdini finished the lecture.

McGill University students Samuel Smilovitz and (below) J. Gordon Whitehead.

Meanwhile, two of Sam Smilovitz's fraternity brothers convinced Houdini to autograph the sketch that had been made of him. And then Houdini had a message for their friend, the artist – would he be so kind as to come to the Princess Theatre and make another drawing?

On Friday, October 22, Sam, along with his friend and fellow student Jack Price, met Houdini outside the theater around 11:00 A.M. There was a crowd at the ticket window when Harry arrived with Bess, her nurse, and a secretary. Sam heard the nurse impatiently urge Houdini to go inside and eat. Replying that he wasn't hungry but could always get something, Harry made a hot dog appear from the lapel of one of his startled female fans. While others applauded, the magician greeted Sam and his friend and escorted them to his dressing room.

Harry hung up his hat and overcoat, took off his jacket, rolled up his sleeves, and removed his tie. After opening his shirt collar, he reclined on the sofa. He apologized to them for lying down, saying that he was not in the best of health. Houdini seemed tired, but he was in a fine mood as he chatted with the young men and flipped through a stack of mail that waited for him on a small table. He continued talking, regaling the boys with stories from his career, as Sam sketched a new portrait.

While Houdini was talking and Sam was drawing him, there was a knock at the dressing room door, and Gordon Whitehead, who seemed to know Houdini, was allowed inside. He was wearing a blue gabardine suit that looked to be a size too small for him. He was carrying three books – one of which Houdini had apparently loaned him – when he walked into the room. Whitehead spoke with an exaggerated Oxford accent, and while he spoke softly, to Sam's irritation, he spoke too much. After sitting down, he began to dominate the conversation with Houdini.

Soon, the two began a contest. Houdini claimed to be able to solve the mystery in any detective story after hearing only a few sentences read aloud to him. Whitehead had brought along a pulp novel with him and, after reading a few excerpts, Houdini successfully figured out the stories. When Sam and Jack complimented him, Houdini grinned.

Whitehead then steered the conversation in another direction – one about which Houdini preferred not to discuss. "What is your opinion of the miracles in the Bible?" asked Whitehead. Houdini said that he preferred not to answer, but he wondered how his own stunts would have been received in biblical times. Would they have been seen as miracles?

Whitehead looked shocked and bothered by the statement. He again changed the subject, this time to Houdini's famous stamina. As if out of nowhere, he asked, "Is it true, Mr. Houdini, that you can resist the hardest blows struck to the abdomen?"

Houdini sidestepped the question, calling attention instead to his iron arms and back muscles. He invited the students to touch them, and Sam and Jack expressed admiration.

But Whitehead just repeated his question. He persisted – could Houdini sustain solid blows to the abdomen? Houdini nodded absently. He was still stretched out on the sofa, though, and had not braced himself before Whitehead suddenly attacked with "four or five ferocious blows to his lower abdomen."

"Are you mad?" Jack Price cried out. "What are you doing?"

Jack and Sam grabbed Whitehead and pulled him away, but Houdini stopped them with a painful wave. "That will do," he said. Although the other two visitors were disturbed by the sudden violence, nothing seemed immediately wrong with Houdini. He smiled at Sam and watched as he finished his portrait.

IN THE AFFIDAVIT THAT HE SUBMITTED LATER, WHITEHEAD claimed that Houdini had given him a copy of the new November issue of Scientific American, calling his attention to an article titled "How Death Deals Its Cards: Death in a Thousand Shapes Is Knocking Eternally at Everyman's Door."

It was certain that it was knocking at Houdini's door, and he was wrong to assume that Whitehead was just another of his fans. Whitehead remains a mystery. For years, sympathetic accounts of

his actions that day insist that he apologized profusely for misunderstanding Houdini's agreement that he could withstand hard blows to the stomach as permission for Whitehead to try it, but this wasn't true.

Whitehead dropped out of school a few months after Houdini left Montreal and then disappeared, as elusive as a fugitive from the law. He was arrested once for theft after stealing books on boxing and palmistry, and much later ended up living in a dank apartment with magazines and books stacked to the ceiling. His only company by then was two eccentric women who delved into mystical arts like numerology and the "Science of Being."

By that time, he had been existing on disability payments that he received for a head injury he suffered working as a day laborer on a construction site. He had a plate in his skull and claimed to have no memory of being, as many people called him, "the man who killed Houdini."

He died from malnutrition on July 5, 1954.

AFTER WHITEHEAD LEFT THE DRESSING ROOM, HOUDINI TOLD his niece, Julia, that due to a "misunderstanding of his remarks," a student had assaulted him before he could stand up and prepare for it. He complained of stomach pain but tried not to let it bother him. He was, however, seen wincing in pain several times during his performance that evening, and when it was over, he was too weak to undress himself.

He continued to perform the next night, even though he was in agony. During the intermissions, he fell into a restless sleep and

The Garrick Theater in Detroit, Houdini's final venue.
On the right is a newspaper ad for what turned out to be Harry's final show.

had to be roused to continue. After his final show, he told Bess what had occurred in his dressing room. On the train to Detroit, his next engagement, the pain became so intense that Bess insisted a wire be sent to a doctor who would meet them when they arrived at their hotel.

The train arrived late, and Houdini went straight to the Garrick Theater rather than to the Statler Hotel, where Dr. Leo Dretzka was waiting in the lobby. When the doctor finally got to the theater, he found Houdini busy helping his assistants with props for the evening show.

Though the doctor diagnosed appendicitis, Houdini refused to cancel the sold-out show. It was a full house, he said, and added, "They're here to see me. I won't disappoint them."

By the time that he took the stage, his fever had gone up to 104 degrees. He was tired, feverish, and tormented by abdominal pains, plus he was hobbling on the broken ankle from two weeks earlier. He somehow managed to perform the entire show, although his terrified assistants were constantly forced to complete some motion that Houdini couldn't manage. Spectators reported that he often missed his cues and that he seemed to hurry the show along.

He fainted between the first and second acts and had to be taken to his dressing room so that he could be revived with ice packs, which would also hopefully cool his fever.

He returned to the stage and changed his routine to feature what he called "little magic" with silks, coins, and sleight-of-hand card tricks. He also accepted questions and small challenges from the audience. He remained on the stage throughout the evening, but just before the third act, he turned to his assistant and murmured, "Drop the curtain, Collins, I can't go any further."

When the curtain closed, he collapsed where he had been standing. Houdini was helped back to his dressing room, where he changed his clothes but still refused to go back to the hospital.

He went to his hotel, still convinced that his pain and illness would subside. It was not until the early morning hours – after Bess threw a tantrum -- that the hotel physician was summoned. He contacted a young surgeon named Dr. Charles Kennedy, who arrived just after 3:00 A.M. When told of the punches that Houdini had received, Dr. Kennedy pleaded with him to go to the hospital. He still refused. It took a call from his doctor in New York to finally convince him.

Examined at Grace Hospital, the surgeons determined that Houdini had peritonitis. The punches, they said, had burst his appendix.

They gave him 24 hours to live.

But the doctors had not taken into account the strength and sheer will of their patient. For six days, Harry hung on, even after enduring two operations. The pain was excruciating, and his bowels were paralyzed, but no one heard him complain. He was polite, smiling, and kind to the nurses and attendants, and happy to see the family members who rushed to his bedside.

Houdini's dire condition was not a secret. The nation closely followed the press releases from the hospital, which detailed the rise and fall of his fever, the time he spent in and out of consciousness, and the visitors who arrived to see him.

But by the afternoon of October 31, Houdini began to fade. Finally, he turned to Bess and his brother, Theo, and spoke quietly: "Dash, I'm getting tired, and I can't fight anymore. I guess this thing is going to get me."

Grace Hospital in Detroit

It had been a sunny day, yet Dash recalled that just as Harry closed his eyes, "the heavens clouded over, and it poured rain like I have never seen it pour before."

Houdini was declared dead at 1:26 P.M. on Halloween 1926 – stepping through the curtain between this world and the next.

VOICES IN THE
SÉANCE ROOM

ALL THE PROPS FROM THE SHOW HAD BEEN CRATED UP AND shipped to New York when Houdini was taken to Grace Hospital, but Jim Collins was notified by the Detroit Transfer Co. that one crate had been accidentally left behind. When investigated, he discovered that it was the box containing the bronze casket that had been used for the Rahman Bey exposure. Houdini's attorney, telephoning from New York, disclosed that one of the first provisions of his will was his desire to be buried in this casket in the event of his death.

It was the first trick of fate that followed Houdini's death.

Harry's body was placed in the bronze casket for the train journey to New York. He had left detailed instructions about his funeral. It was held at the massive Elks Lodge Ballroom on West 43rd Street with two rabbis officiating. More than 2,000 people were in attendance.

Houdini had belonged to more than a dozen clubs, societies, and lodges, and all of them took part in his funeral. A cedarwood wand was broken in half over his casket to the funeral chant of the Society of American Magicians. There were tributes from the National Vaudeville Artists, the Jewish Theatrical Guild, and rites by the St. Cecile Masonic Lodge, the Mount Zion Congregation, and the Elks. The procession that took his body to Machpelah Cemetery was 25 cars long, and the pallbearers and honorary pallbearers included authors, showmen, magicians, vaudevillians, and movie producers. As

Thousands streamed past Houdini's casket at the Elks Lodge Ballroom on West 43rd Street in New York

the coffin was lowered into the ground, one pallbearer whispered to another -- impresario Florenz Ziegfeld – "Suppose he isn't in it!"

Jim Collins and his other assistants lowered the coffin into its place next to his mother. As he had requested, his head rested on a black bag containing the letters Cecilia had written to him.

Houdini had finally been reunited with his beloved mother.

MYSTERIES SURROUNDED HOUDINI AFTER HIS DEATH.

Even the circumstances of his death were – and remain – somewhat mysterious. Some of those mysteries surfaced thanks to the *seven* different versions of his death that emerged. They included him dying in the arms of Bess in either Boston or Chicago; dying while hanging suspended upside-down in a glass tank; dying while performing at the bottom of a river; dying while trapped in a locked casket; and the list went on.

What really happened is clear, sort of – he died of peritonitis brought on by a ruptured appendix. But how did that appendix rupture in the first place?

In 1926, it was assumed that the punches to the stomach were what caused the rupture, but the medical consensus is that this

HARRY HOUDINI IS TAKEN BY DEATH IN HOSPITAL AT DETROIT

HARRY HOUDINI
Houdini, Famous Magician, died yesterday in a hospital at Detroit, a victim of peritonitis.

Miss Mabel Schultheiss of Marietta

isn't possible. According to medical literature, there has never been an instance of acute appendicitis caused by physical injury. Such a trauma can rupture the large intestine, and this was, in fact, the initial diagnosis of Dr. Kennedy, the surgeon who examined Houdini at his hotel and later operated on him. What he found, though, was a ruptured appendix. He said, "It is the only case of traumatic appendicitis I have ever seen in my lifetime, but the logic of the thing seemed to indicate that Mr. Houdini died of appendicitis, the direct result of the injury."

What seems most likely is that Houdini was already suffering from appendicitis before the Whitehead incident. This condition was likely aggravated by the punches or prevented him from realizing that his condition was something more than pain from the attack until it was too late.

Jack Price noted that "at the time Whitehead was hitting Houdini, the latter looked as though he was in extreme pain and winced as each blow was struck."

After Houdini's death, Professor William Tait, who had introduced him at the McGill lecture, remarked how carefully Houdini sat down at its conclusion, as though he was in pain. Tait assumed it was pain from his ankle, but his abdomen might have caused it.

This possibility is given further credence by a letter from Gertrude Hills to the *New York Sun* after his death. She described how Houdini had taken part in a fundraising show late in the summer in the letter:

He was delighted to be of assistance and promised to perform his 'straitjacket' act to try and

DEATH SHACKLES FOIL PAST MASTER

HARRY HOUDINI

DETROIT, Nov. 1.—Harry Houdini, master of the black art and known as the king of shackles, died here last night, following a second operation in an effort to save his life from acute peritonitis which developed after an operation for appendicitis.

beat his own record in escaping. In attempting to do so, he hurt himself so badly that for a number of days, he suffered pain in his side. Closely following upon this injury, he had an attack of what was diagnosed as 'ptomaine poisoning.' From this, he never really seemed to recover. When he left on his tour, he told me that the effects of the injury and the 'poisoning' were still evident.

As is likely apparent to those with any knowledge of history, appendicitis was a common and often fatal condition in the 1920s. When it ruptured, it was a serious, life-threatening medical emergency, with a high death rate. Houdini was not the only celebrity to die from the condition at the time. Rudolph Valentino, the silent film star, died just a few months earlier in August 1926. Eugene Gaudio, the acclaimed cinematographer, died during surgery in 1920.

While doctors began accepting (probably incorrectly) the concept of traumatic appendicitis following Houdini's death from a ruptured appendix, the primary treatment for the condition at that time was surgical removal of the appendix. The mortality peaked in the 1920s and 1930s before eventually declining after the introduction of antibiotics.

Houdini had simply been born too soon to be saved.

THE BLAME FOR MOST OF THE OTHER MYSTERIES THAT followed Houdini's death can be laid at the feet of the hundreds of clairvoyants who claimed to have predicted his death or to have witnessed signs and omens in advance.

A man named Gysel stated that at 10:58 P.M. on October 24, 1926, a framed photograph of Houdini suddenly slipped off the wall of his home and "fell to the ground, breaking the glass. I know now that Houdini will die," he allegedly said at the time.

Gysel's prediction was no surprise to Houdini's Spiritualist adversaries, who had been predicting his death for years. Sooner or later, they were bound to be correct.

According to Sir Arthur Conan Doyle, he and others in his

"home circle" had recorded an ominous message about the magician several months before his death. The message read: "Houdini is doomed, doomed, doomed!"

And on October 13, a medium named Mrs. Wood wrote a letter to Fulton Oursler. It referred to the late psychical investigator Hames H. Hyslop when she wrote: "Three years ago, the spirit of Dr. Hyslop said 'the waters are black for Houdini' and foretold disaster would claim him while performing before an audience in a theatre. Dr. Hyslop now says the injury is more serious than has been reported and that Houdini's days as a magician are over."

According to some accounts, Houdini himself had premonitions of his death. Among his clippings was one from 1919 that described the onstage collapse of a vaudeville comedian named Sidney Drew. The performer had taken ill in St. Louis, but had continued to play, against all advice, until in Detroit, when he could simply go no further. Those who discovered this clipping among Houdini's archives must have found the death of the comedian eerily like that of Houdini himself. Why he saved the clipping is unknown.

His friend and fellow magician, Joseph Dunninger, also told an eerie story after Houdini's death. He said that one early morning in October 1926, Houdini called him in New York and asked him to bring his car to his home on West 113th Street. He apologized but said he was in a hurry and had to move some things. When the car

Houdini's brownstone on West 112th Street, where Joseph Dunninger claimed his friend had a premonition of his death

was loaded, he asked Dunninger to drive through the park.

Dunninger said that as they got to the exit on Central Park West, around 72nd Street, Houdini grabbed him by the arm and urged him to go back to his house. Puzzled, Dunninger asked him if he had forgotten something.

"Don't ask questions, Joe," Houdini replied, "Just turn around and go back."

Dunninger drove back to the house, and when they arrived, Houdini climbed out of the car and stood looking at the brownstone in the rain. He stayed that way, water dripping down his face and soaking his clothing, for a few minutes, and then he got back into the car without saying a word. Dunninger drove away, and when the two men again approached the western exit of the park, he glanced over and saw that Houdini's shoulders had started to shake. He was crying. His friend asked him what was wrong, and Houdini gave a rather cryptic answer: "I've seen my house for the last time, Joe. I'll never see my house again."

"And as far as I know," Dunninger later wrote. "He never did."

ON HALLOWEEN NIGHT 1926, ONLY HOURS AFTER THE NEWS OF Houdini's death had stunned and saddened most of the country, a séance was held at a house on Lime Street in Boston.

When Walter arrived that night, he was whistling in a minor key, then communicated that Houdini's crossing would not be an easy one. He was, Walter said, "much confused and resistant to the idea of death." Without gloating over Houdini's passing, the spirit – or the other part of Mina Crandon's personality, if you prefer – Waqlter indicated that he would have one more encounter with his old foe: "I am not sure but that I will have something to do with Houdini and his admission."

Dr. Crandon observed that Walter had foretold Houdini's death many times over the last year by saying," Give Houdini my love and tell him that I will see him soon." The sitters on that Halloween night wanted to know whether Walter had caused the tragedy.

But the spirit cautioned them about becoming superstitious, because spirits had nothing to do with a human death, but "sometimes we can see a little farther ahead than you can."

If Walter sounded less vindictive toward Houdini than he had in the past, there was a sense from Margery's supporters that a higher justice had been served. In a letter to Dr. Crandon, scientist Robin Tillyard noted, "Well, Walter has got Houdini, and I hope Houdini is enjoying it. His 'sainted mother' will have something to howl about now." He also speculated that Gordon Whitehead had been operating under Walter's influence when he assaulted Houdini.

In Boston, Margery ally Joseph DeWyckhoff expressed satisfaction that the men he referred to as a "Jew reneged" had entered the fourth dimension, where he told Dr. Crandon that it was "an eye for an eye."

This was not, however, an attitude ever expressed by Margery herself. She seemed genuinely saddened by Houdini's death. In her statement to the press, she praised his virility, determination, and physical courage. She said that she had enjoyed entertaining him in her home, though, "at other times and places we had our differences."

To Margery, Houdini had been a man of action among the old men and fools on the committee that had investigated her abilities. "He sat with us four times, and his behavior here was a pleasant contrast to that of certain men high in academic circles." Surprisingly to some of the reporters, Margery stated that his death was a "serious loss" to psychic science, since wherever he went, he created an interest in spirit mediumship.

But the newspapermen refused to let go of their rivalry. When one asked if she had "willed" his death, Margery looked at the man, shook her head, and walked away.

The interview was over.

THE DEATH OF HOUDINI "WAS MOST CERTAINLY DECREED from the other side," Sir Arthur Conan Doyle told the press and believed it.

If that were true, however, the police couldn't investigate a spectral curse or a warning. However, Dr. A.A. Roback, the first Harvard psychologist to ever sit with Margery, wondered if the Spiritualist movement had somehow "gotten rid of its more formidable foe" by eliminating Houdini. No one ever found out if Whitehead was acting out of impulse or if he perceived some higher calling when he assaulted him. There was no police investigation. What voices, if any, the religion student heard were never determined. Sir Arthur, though, knew what he had heard from his spirit guide before the tragedy. He had been warned, and the next day, Houdini had been attacked.

Although Sir Arthur and Houdini had a falling out, neither man remained angry enough at the other to forget the bond they'd once shared

At some point before that, an angry Doyle told Dr. Crandon that Houdini had "a payday coming soon." But despite the harsh words and hard feelings, Sir Arthur was shaken and upset by the tragedy. He told the press, "His death is a great shock and a deep mystery to me. He was a teetotaler, did not smoke, and was one of the cleanest living men I have ever known. I greatly admired him and cannot understand how the end came for one so youthful. We were great friends. He told me much in confidence but never secrets regarding his tricks. How he did them, I do not know. We agreed upon everything excepting Spiritualism."

In truth, they had not been "great friends" for some time, although neither man ever lost the affection for the other, even when they were fighting a proxy war over Lime Street. When the spirits had warned of great tragedy, Sir Arthur hadn't tried to warn him. "He would have only mocked at them, and us, if we had sent them on," he sadly wrote to Bess.

The author and the widow bonded over their grief and their mutual love for the enigmatic magician. Her husband, she told Doyle, had admired him immensely and "would have been the happiest man in the world had he been able to agree with your views on spiritism."

Sir Arthur knew this, even in his angriest moments. As he wrote to Bess, "His crusade was a general wild attack upon all that we hold dear, but beyond all that, I can see quite a different person – a loving husband, a good friend, a man full of sweet impulses. I have never met anyone who left so mixed an impression upon my mind."

And yet, as soon as Houdini's casket was lowered into the ground, Sir Arthur hoped to hear from him again.

Bess desperately wanted her own reunion with Houdini. His death sent her into a prolonged period of despair, and she would soon attempt to find solace in séances.

Before that, though, she was startled by a crashing sound that turned out to be caused by the spontaneous shattering of a mirror. She took it as a sign from her dead husband. On his deathbed, he had vowed to try to return to her, and Doyle assured her that he would.

But with no message as yet, Bess found a little peace in a more traditional form of communication. She wrote to Sir Arthur, "When I next go to my dear one's last resting place, I will place a flower for you."

SPIRITUALISM, IT TURNED OUT, WAS MUCH MORE APPEALING to the bereaved than it was to the bankrupt. By 1930, in the wake of America's stock market crash, public interest in the other side finally began to fade.

In that year, J.B. Rhine and Joseph McDougall founded the Parapsychology Laboratory at Duke University, effectively removing psychical research from the séance room. Rhine's experience with

Margery had contributed to his mistrust of any case that depended only on spooks and spirits. As far as he was concerned, the era of the physical medium was over. His interest was in parapsychology – a term he and McDougall coined – and where Rhine led, most of the rest of the psychic research community followed.

It was also in 1930 that Malcom Bird vanished.

One night, Bird brought an "immoral woman" to Lime Street, and the Crandons turned him away. He became angry and made insulting remarks about the couple's sexual habits, but there was a deeper issue between them. Bird was then preparing a new volume on the Margery case for the ASPR journal, but this one was not entirely positive.

He had been preparing for a possible falling out with the Crandons for years and had kept a blank check that Margery had written to use against them if he needed it. Bird had finally admitted that while he still believed Margery to be a genuine medium, he knew she used trickery when she was under pressure to create manifestations. He had also recently gone to the trustees of the ASPR to tell them that before Margery's final séance with Houdini, "she sought a private interview with me and tried to get me to agree, in the event that phenomena did not occur, that I would ring the bell box myself, or produce something else that might pass as activity by Walter."

To the trustees, this was damning information. Most physical mediums were believed to cheat when under duress, but Bird had always presented Margery as the exception. Even now, his descriptions of her authentic abilities outnumbered his negative observations, but even so, this was shocking news. They refused to let Bird publish his critical report, and they smeared him by making it appear that his "frequent trips to Boston were for a series of illicit affairs."

And then they fired him.

There would literally have been no Margery if not for Malcolm Bird, who publicized her and provided her pseudonym. As an ASPR officer, he presented the case for her mediumship to more than 200 audiences. However, the powers at the ASPR were themselves Spiritualists who tolerated no criticism of Margery. Their mission was to develop her phenomena further, not draw attention to the rare occasions when she cheated. Bird had always been her stalwart advocate, but he had never embraced Spiritualism. Sensing that Margery had been, over time, resorting more to trickery, he knew that trouble was coming.

When the ASPR refused to publish his report, Bird crossed enemy lines and tried to get Walter Prince to publish it through the Boston Society of Psychical Research. However, Prince refused to get involved. The new policy of his society was to simply ignore Margery.

Bird quietly withdrew from the research community, and his subsequent activities became a mystery. Two years later, Prince visited him without coming away with any idea of how he occupied himself. Prince's secretary, Eleanor Hoffman, suggested that Bird became involved in bootlegging, but no one really knew. All that anyone could say for certain was that, with his reputation ruined, a once significant figure in the hunt for spirits abandoned the field and never returned to his former professions of academia and journalism. He seemed to just disappear, fading away like the importance of Spiritualism.

Bird lived out the rest of his life with a small income from the estate of his half-sister. Whatever else he did, he did it inconspicuously. His wife, Katherine, left him, and they never had children. He died on October 20, 1964, at Kings County Hospital – just 10 days after being hit by an automobile while crossing a street in Brooklyn.

IT WAS ALSO IN 1930 THAT A LEADING LIGHT IN THE HISTORY of Spiritualism took his last breath.

After he collapsed, clutching his heart after a walk in his rose garden, Sir Arthur Conan Doyle, whose health had been frail, was confined to his bed. He told his family he didn't want to die there, so in his last days, Lady Jean and the children helped him into a chair next to the window, where he could look out on the scenic Sussex woodlands

On July 7, he died with his family beside him. He spoke his last words to Jean: "You are wonderful," he whispered.

And the great man of letters and the leading proponent of Spiritualism was gone.

THE HOUDINI SÉANCES

I TOOK PART IN MY FIRST HOUDINI SÉANCE IN 1995. IT WAS held in a theater that had a reputation for being haunted, which seemed a suitable place for such an event. There were 12 participants besides myself and the medium, and we were trying on Halloween night – the anniversary of Houdini's death – to contact the great magician.

We sat around a table on the stage of the theater, in full view of nearly 200 people who had come to watch. In the middle of the table was a photograph of Houdini, a pair of handcuffs, a tambourine, a bell, and an envelope that contained the message he once promised to send to Sir Arthur Conan Doyle, if possible. The message was never transmitted.

Most of the participants seemed to assume that a manifestation of Houdini was unlikely, but they were willing to try. The medium directed us to relax, and we closed our eyes. The theater was silent, except for the low murmur of music. The medium, a woman I had known for some time, intoned from time to time, "Houdini, are you there?"

We kept our eyes closed. Nothing happened.

The medium called for Houdini for many long minutes before

The "Houdini Seances" began soon after Harry's death and continue today, although evidence that Houdini has actually been contacted seems slim

changing her attention to other spirits that she claimed surrounded us, drawn by the séance in this cavernous old building.

While I experienced nothing, several of the sitters – reasonable people I knew personally – stated they felt cold chills. Another said she'd been touched. I expected very little from the event, and yet, when I opened my eyes, I saw something that I couldn't explain. And so did the rest of the sitters around the table, as did many of those in the seats that were closest to the stage.

Before our eyes, a handful of white feathers appeared out of thin air and floated down to land in the center of the table. I don't know where they came from. I couldn't explain it – I've tried many times since then. *Something* happened at that séance. It may not have been Houdini, but something very strange had occurred.

THE "HOUDINI SÉANCES" BEGAN SOON AFTER HARRY'S DEATH. They continue today, although the official sanction of the Houdini estate ended years ago. They began with Bess trying to honor her husband's request to contact him in the spirit world, if it was possible to do so.

But this may not have been the only reason that she began seeking out the secret code that he promised to send her from beyond the grave.

Like her husband had been at the death of his mother, Bess was at a loss as to what to do with her life with Houdini gone. They had been together since Bess was 18, and she had been living inside his closed world – filling the role of wife, assistant, and maternal figure – for decades. She had never lived her own life. She was simply a player in Houdini's universe, although he never failed to refer to her as his "beloved wife... and the only one who had ever helped me in my work."

Their life may not have been perfect – they'd never had the children they wanted – but it had never been dull. As big as Houdini's ego had been, he never made it a secret that he depended on her completely. With Houdini gone, Bess drifted, her life hollow and empty. It's no surprise that she wanted desperately to speak with him again.

The same could be said for Theo. The brother he loved, who he called "Dash,"

Houdini's brother, Theo, continued to perform as Hardeen after his brother's death and became, at least in advertisements, the man who now kept the many secrets of Houdini

and who performed in Houdini's shadow as "Hardeen." But Theo never left that shadow. It was too late for him to reinvent himself, he believed. He inherited all of Houdini's illusions and apparatus and even his assistant, Jim Collins. Together, they finished Houdini's unfinished tour and started tours of their own. Eventually, he became, as his brother had been for so many years, president of the Society of American Magicians.

From time to time, Theo tried to contact Houdini, although he never really believed he would succeed. He remembered that after the death of their brother, Bill, in 1925, Harry and Dash had tried many times to reach him. They'd heard nothing but, during these attempts, the brothers had forged a pact – whichever passed away first, they would wait for a code to be delivered to them by a medium. But if it did not contain any of the 10 words that had been agreed upon between them, they would know it wasn't real.

But in 1935, he told a reporter: "This was 10 years ago, and up to the present time, I have not had as much as a peep from Houdini."

For Theo, though, séances to reach his brother were only a small part of a hectic life. He had his family, and he had his work. But for Bess, she only had emptiness. She had not only lived with her husband – she had lived through him. Their life together had revolved around Houdini – his work, his performances, his books, his investigations, his feats of daring. She didn't always find that life easy, and she sometimes resisted. There were her tantrums, the disapproval he dreaded, and the grumbling in the dressing room. But in the end, life went on, and Bess followed in his wake.

Now he was gone, and there was nothing for her to do. She could hardly go on tour with Theo or carry on Houdini's act as Adelaide Hermann had done with much success after the death of her husband, Alexander Herrmann. It had never been that kind of an act – she had always been the secondary performer.

But her life moved unsteadily on. While she was not rich, Houdini had left a trust fund for her, and his life had been heavily insured. She paid thousands in inheritance taxes, paid for books that Houdini had bought before his death, but never paid for. All the real estate they owned was in her name, and she had more than enough money to live comfortably for the rest of her life.

In time, she sold their brownstone on West 113th Street to Rose Bonnano, whose father had looked after the place for years while the Houdinis were away. As time went on and the neighborhood got rougher, Rose's connection to the infamous Bonanno crime family served her well. She lived in the basement, along with trunks of neatly stacked photographs, and did nothing to dispel the legend of Houdini's secrets. She never opened the padlocked attic because "Mrs. Houdini wouldn't like it." And there were all Houdini's mahogany bookcases, with their extra-deep tops and thick bases. What was hidden inside them? Rose didn't know, or wasn't telling, and the mystery went with her to the grave.

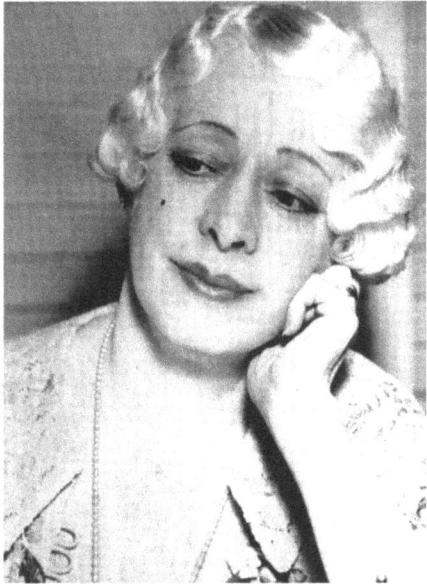

Bess struggled after Harry's death, searching for purpose and continuing the seances to try and reach her husband, who'd promised to reach out from the other side

Bess moved to a new house on Payson Avenue in another part of the city and lost herself in alcohol and misery for a while. A glimpse into her sad life during this time can be found in a diary entry from 1927. She wrote: "One of the few happy days." She had spent it visiting her husband's grave. "How peaceful. Home early, only one drink."

It eventually became clear to her that life couldn't continue in this way. She opened a tea room for a short time and thought of taking a vaudeville act on the road, but none of these projects ever really got off the ground.

Instead, her life continued to revolve around her husband. She commissioned and helped with the preparation of his biography, which appeared in 1928. But mostly, she spent a great deal of time trying to contact him. Every Sunday at the hour of his death, she would shut herself in a room with his photograph and wait for a sign. She confirmed that she was waiting for a secret message from her husband, and word spread far and wide that Bess had offered $10,000 to any medium who could deliver an actual message from Houdini.

Almost weekly, another medium came forward claiming to have broken the code. It was clear that anyone who could come up with the message would make much more than $10,000. The publicity alone was worth many times that amount.

However, none of the messages rang true until 1928, when famed medium Arthur Ford announced that he had a message for Bess. He told her that the message had come from Houdini's mother, Cecilia, and consisted of a single word, which was "forgive." After this news was delivered, Bess made a startling announcement, claiming that Ford's message was the first that she had received which "had any appearance of the truth."

"Forgive" was the one word that Houdini had always hoped to hear from his mother in the séance room. The reason for this was an incident that had happened many years before. When his brother Nat's wife, Sadie, abandoned him to marry another Weiss brother, Leopold, Houdini was shocked and angry. The once close-knit harmony of the family had been destroyed. Harry could not bring himself to forgive his brother unless his mother told him to. She died before he could discuss the family crisis with her – one of the reasons why he had

Medium Arthur Ford claimed to have reached Houdini and provided the code that Bess was waiting for, although controversy followed his announcement

searched so tirelessly for a genuine medium and was so infuriated when he found nothing but fakes.

In November 1928, another message came to Ford, this time, he claimed, from Houdini himself. In a trance, the medium relayed a coded message:

Rosabelle. Answer, tell, pray, answer, look, tell, answer, answer, tell.

After this information was relayed to Bess, she invited Ford to her home, and he asked her if the words were correct. She said they were, and Ford asked her to show off her wedding ring and tell everyone present what "Rosabelle" meant. Bess took off the ring and, holding it in front of her, she sang softly:

Rosabelle, sweet Rosebelle,
I love you more than I can tell;
O'er me you cast a spell,
I love you! My Rosabelle!

"Rosabelle" had been the word that made the message authentic -- a secret known only to Bess and Harry themselves. It was the title of the song the Floral Sisters had been singing at Coney Island on the night she first met the Houdini brothers.

But Ford wasn't finished. He explained the code passed on in the next nine words for the message spelled out the word "BELIEVE." The code was one that the Houdinis had used during the "mind-reading act" they perfected in their early days touring with the circus.

The message seemed to be authentic – the final clue that Houdini promised to relay from the other side. The next day, Bess signed a letter that three independent people witnessed:

Regardless of any statement made to the contrary, I wish to declare that the message, in its entirety, and in the agreed-upon sequence, given to me by Arthur Ford, is the correct message pre-arranged between Mr. Houdini and myself. Beatrice Houdini.

The message from Ford was widely publicized, but then two days later, a reporter from the *New York Graphic* tabloid named Rae Jaure created an even bigger sensation. Jaure had been trying to dig up dirt on Houdini since his death and had published several articles claiming he'd been involved in a string of affairs with various women. After crossing Bess one too many times, Bess stated she would have nothing else to do with the *Graphic.* Jaure was furious, and she swore revenge.

A January 10 article written by the reporter was headlined "HOUDINI HOAX EXPOSED! SÉANCE PREARRANGED BY MEDIUM AND WIDOW." It was alleged that Bess had given the code to Arthur Ford, and Jaure had found this out by eavesdropping on Ford, who admitted to the hoax and allegedly said he and Bess were planning a vaudeville tour together. He would finance it, and Bess supplied him with the code as her part of the bargain.

This, of course, caused an uproar, as it was supposed to do. Bess indignantly denied passing him the code, and in a statement to famed newsman Walter Winchell, she said:

I wish to tell you emphatically that I was no party to any fraud. When the real message, THE message that Houdini and I had agreed upon, came to me, and I accepted it as the truth, I was greeted by jeers. Why? Those who denounced the entire thing as a fraud claim that I had given Mr. Arthur Ford the message. If Mr. Ford said this, I brand him as a liar. Mr. Ford has stoutly denied saying this ugly thing, and knowing the reporter as well as I do, I prefer to believe Mr. Ford. However, when anyone accuses me of giving the words that my husband and I labored so long to convince ourselves of the truth of the communication, then I will fight and fight until the breath leaves my body.

But how else would Ford have known the code?

Houini's friend, Joseph Dunninger, entered the fray and pointed out some possibilities. The code, he reminded everyone, had been printed in the earlier biography of Houdini. As for "Rosabelle, believe" – Mrs. Houdini had not been alone with her husband when he murmured it to her. A nurse was also in the room, and she might have repeated it to someone, and that might have reached Arthur Ford.

The press, the skeptics, and Houdini's friends refused to accept the idea that Ford had broken the code. On Joe Dunninger's advice, Bess withdrew her reward offer.

Regardless, Arthur Ford always maintained that he had broken the code. He went to his grave in 1974 still claiming he'd received a message from Houdini.

In 1928, Ford was the pastor of the First Spiritualist Church of Manhattan and was a respected member of the psychic community. He had also recently distinguished himself by challenging the magician Howard Thurston to a debate at Carnegie Hall, which Ford won. Thurston, who had been carrying on Houdini's tradition of exposing fraudulent mediums, was unable to explain some of the effects that Ford produced. After he came forward with the code, jealous colleagues turned on Ford, and newspaper reporters and debunkers began to charge him with perpetuating a hoax, despite his claims of innocence. Shortly afterwards, Ford was expelled from the United Spiritualist League of New York but was later reinstated "on the grounds of insufficient evidence."

But was he a fraud?

Most believe so, and that he found the code in the book. Even if he didn't, the code had not been created by Houdini. It was an old code that had been around for years, so Ford could have found it somewhere.

The question, though, is did he? That remains a mystery.

BESS CONTINUED TO BE PLAGUED BY SPIRIT MEDIUMS AND disappointment for a few more years. More séances were held in hopes of reaching Harry, but as time passed, she began to lose hope that she would ever hear from him.

After 10 years had passed, Bess made plans for what was billed as the Final Houdini Séance. She was assisted in her effort by Eddy Saint, a former carnival and vaudeville showman who had also worked as a magician. Everyone found him to be a charming, amiable, and dignified figure. He had been recommended to Bess a few years before to act as her manager, although concerned friends had quietly hired him to watch over her and to protect her from being taken advantage of. A genuine affection developed between them, and eventually they began sharing a Spanish-style bungalow in Hollywood, a place where Bess had enjoyed living during her husband's brief movie career.

The séance was scheduled for Halloween night 1936, -- the tenth anniversary of Houdini's death -- and was held on the roof of the Knickerbocker Hotel. Coverage of the event, broadcast live on the radio all over the world, was enormous. Eddy Saint assembled a scrapbook of the publicity for the event that was three feet by two feet, six inches thick, and could barely be lifted. Every page was thick with clippings. One picture of Bess and Eddy appeared in 70 different publications.

Bess preparing for the Final Houdini Seance, which was held on Halloween night 1936.

A radio commentator described the scene:

Over 300 invited guests formed the outer circle, while 13 scientists, occultists, newspapermen, world-famous magicians, spiritual leaders, boyhood friends of Houdini joined Madame Houdini in the Inner Circle.

Bathed in the weird glow of ruby light, trained observers and spirit mediums joined under controlled conditions to evoke the shade of the late mystifier.

Eddy Saint took charge of the proceedings and started things off with the playing of "Pomp and Circumstance," a tune that Houdini had used to start his act in the later years. Eddy noted for the radio listeners: "Every facility has been provided tonight that might aid in opening the pathway to the spirit world. Here in the inner circle reposes a "medium's trumpet," a pair of slates with chalk, a writing tablet and pencil, a small bell and in the center reposes a huge pair of silver handcuffs on a silk cushion."

Eddy continued as everyone waited. He cried out, trying to make contact with the late magician:

The Knickerbocker Hotel in Hollywood

Houdini! Are you here? Are you here, Houdini? Please manifest yourself in any way possible... We have waited, Houdini, oh so long! Never have you been able to present the evidence you promised. And now, this, the night of nights... the world is listening, Harry... Levitate the table! Move it! Lift the table! Move it or rap it! Spell out a code, Harry... please! Ring a bell! Let its tinkle be heard around the world!

Eddy and the rest of Bess' inner circle attempted to contact the elusive magician for over an hour before finally giving up. Saint finally turned to Bess: "Mrs. Houdini, the zero hour has passed. The ten years are up. Have you reached a decision?"

The mournful voice of Bess Houdini then echoed through radio receivers around the world. "Yes, Houdini did not come through," she replied. "My last hope is gone. I do not believe that Houdini can come back to me --- or to anyone. The Houdini shrine has burned for ten years. I now, reverently... turn out the light. It is finished. Good night, Harry!"

But it wasn't finished at all.

THE OFFICIAL SÉANCE CAME TO AN END, BUT AT THE VERY moment the light went out, a rumble of deep thunder shook the building. A flash of lightning illuminated the night, the sky opened,

Bess and Eddy Saint at the last official Houdini Seance comes to an end

and violent rain began to fall. The terrifying storm drenched the séance participants, sending them running for the exit doors leading down from the roof.

The rainstorm seemed incredibly close to the hotel – because it was. It was later learned that the mysterious storm sprang up from nowhere, vanished just as quickly, and did not occur anywhere else in Hollywood.

It had only been above the Knickerbocker Hotel.

It's been speculated that perhaps Houdini did show up that night after all. He was too big a performer – with too big an ego – to just levitate a table or ring a bell.

He would do something big – like conjure up a thunderstorm.

Did he? Who can say for sure?

Even though the 1936 event was billed as the Final Houdini Séance, it wasn't the last one. Almost every year since, séances attempting to reach Houdini have been held across the country – hosted by famous magicians, skeptics, actors, and even William Shatner.

And it's likely they'll continue because even after all these years, we remain fascinated by Houdini. He is still a mystery and a puzzle that we cannot solve.

On one hand, he was an open-minded seeker of truth, but on the other, he was a rabid non-believer in all things supernatural. Houdini may be gone, but he has never been forgotten. He is, like Spiritualism itself, an American original who left a mark on our history that will never fade away.

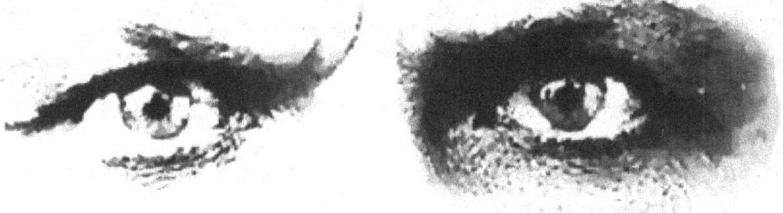

BIBLIOGRAPHY

Ackroyd, Peter H. – *A History of Ghosts*, New York, NY, Rodale Books, 2009

Bechtel, Stefan and Laurence Roy Stains – *Through A Glass Darkly*, New York, NY, St. Martins Press, 2017

Begley, Adam – *Houdini: The Elusive American*, New Haven, CT, Yale University Press, 2020

Bell, Dan - *The Man Who Killed Houdini*, Montreal, Canada, Vehicule Press, 2004

Bird, J. Malcolm - *Margery, the Medium*, Boston, MA, Small, Maynard & Co., 1925

Blum, Deborah - *Ghost Hunters*, New York, NY, Penguin, 2006

Bradbury, Will – *Into the Unknown*, Pleasantville, NY, Readers Digest Books, 1981

Brandon, Ruth - *Life and Many Deaths of Harry Houdini*, New York, NY, Random House, 1993

------------------------ - *The Spiritualists*, New York, NY, Alfred A. Knopf, 1983

Brown, Slater - *The Heyday of Spiritualism*, New York, NY, Pocket Books, 1970

Cannell, J.C. - *Secrets of Houdini*, London, UK, Hutchinson, 1932

Carr, John Dickson – *The Life of Sir Arthur Conan Doyle*, New York, NY, Carroll & Graf, 1949

Carrington, Hereward – *Modern Psychical Phenomena*, New York, Dodd Mead, 1929
------------------------------- - *The Story of Psychic Science*, London, UK, Rider and Company, 1930
------------------------------- - *Psychic Oddities: Fantastic and Bizarre Events in the Life of a Psychical Researcher*, London, UK, Rider and Company, 1952

Christopher, Melbourne - *Houdini: The Untold Story*, New York, NY, Simon & Schuster, 1969
----------------------------------- - *Houdini: A Pictorial Life*, New York, NY, Simon & Schuster, 1976

Christopher, Milbourne & Maurine - *Illustrated History of Magic*, New York, NY, Simon & Schuster, 1976

Dingwall, Eric – *Revelations of a Spirit Medium*, New York, NY, Arno Press, 1922

Doyle, Sir Arthur Conan Doyle:

MEMOIRS:
The Wanderings of a Spiritualist (1921) *Our American Adventure* (1923), *Our Second American Adventure* (1923), *Memories and*

Adventures (1924)

SPIRITUALISM:
History of Spiritualism (1926), *The Edge of the Unknown* (1930), *The New Revelation* (1918), *The Vital Message* (1919); *The Coming of the Fairies* (1921), *The Case for Spirit Photography* (1925)

Dunninger, Joseph - *Houdini's Spirit Exposes*, New York, NY, Experimenter Publishing Co., 1928
-------------------------- - *Magic & Mystery*, New York, NY, Weathervane Books, 1967

Ebon, Martin – *They Knew the Unknown*, New York, NY, World Publishing Company, 1971

Ernst, Bernard & Hereward Carrington - *Houdini & Conan Doyle: The Story of a Strange Friendship,* New York, NY, Albert and Charles Boni, 1933

Ford, Arthur - *Nothing so Strange,* New York, NY, Joanna Cotler Books, 1958

Garland, Hamlin – *Forty Years of Psychic Research*, New York, NY, MacMillan, 1936

Gibson, Walter - *Houdini's Escapes, New York, NY, Dover Publications,* 1930
--------------------- - *Houdini On Magic, New York, NY, Dover Publications,* 1932

Gresham, William Lindsay - *Houdini: The Man Who Walked Through Walls,* New York, NY, Holt, Rinehart & Winston, 1959

Haining, Peter - *Ghosts: The Illustrated History,* UK, Sidgwick & Jackson Limited, 1974

Hall, Trevor - *The Spiritualists,* London, UK, Gerald Duckworth Publishing, 1962

Houdini, Harry - *Handcuff Secrets,* Boston, 1907
-------------------- - *Magician Among the Spirits,* New York, NY, Harper and Brothers, 1924
-------------------- - *Miracle Mongers and their Methods,* New York, NY, E.P. Dutton, 1920

Jackson, Herbert G., Jr. – *The Spirit Rappers,* New York, NY, Doubleday & Co., 1972

Jaher, David – *The Witch of Lime Street,* New York, NY, Crown Publishers, 2015

Jolly, Martyn – *Faces of the Living Dead: The Belief in Spirit Photographs,* New York, NY, Mark Blatty Publisher, 2006

Jones, Kelvin I. – *Conan Doyle and the Spirits,* Northamptomshire, UK, Aquarian Press, 1989

Kalush, William & Larry Sloman - *The Secret Life of Houdini,* New York, NY, Atria Books, 2006

Kellock, Harold – *Houdini, His Life Story from the Recollections and Documents of Beatrice Houdini,* New York, NY, Harcourt, Brace & Co., 1928

Kendall, Lace - *Houdini, Master of Escape,* New York, NY, Macrae Books, 1960

Loomis, Bob – *Houdini's Final Incredible Secret,* Magic Circle UK, 2016

Lycett, Andrew – *The Man Who Created Sherlock Holmes: The Life and Times of Sir Arthur Conan Doyle*, New York, NY, Free Press, 2007

Manseau, Peter – *The Apparitionists*, New York, NY, Houghton, Mifflin, Harcourt, 2017

Maxwell-Stuart, P.G. – *Ghosts: A History of Phantoms, Ghouls, and Other Spirits of the Dead*, Gloucestershire, UK, Tempus Publishing, 2006

McHargue, Georgess - *Facts, Frauds and Phantasms,* New York, NY, Doubleday Books, 1972

Meyer, Bernard C. – *Houdini: A Mind in Chains*, New York, E.P. Dutton & Co., 1976

Miller, R. DeWitt - *Impossible, Yet it Happened,* New York, NY, Ace Books, 1947

Montague, Charlotte – *Houdini: The Life and Times of the World's Greatest Magician*, New York, NY, Chartwell Books, 2017

Morton, Lisa – *Calling the Spirits: A History of Séances*, London, UK, Reaktion Books, 2020

Moses, Arthur - *Houdini Speaks Out!* Xlibris Corporation, 2007

Pearsall, Ronald - *The Table Rappers,* New York, NY, St. Martins Press, 1972

Permutt, Cyril - *Photographing the Spirit World,* Chichester, Sussex, UK, Aquarian Press, 1983

Picknett, Lynn - *Flights of Fancy,* New York, NY, Ballentine Books, 1987

Posnanski, Joe – *The Life and Afterlife of Harry Houdini*, New York, NY, Avid Reader Press, 2019

Proskauer, Julien J. - *Spook Crooks*, New York, NY, A.L. Burt, 1932
-------------------------- - *The Dead Do Not Talk*, New York, Harper & Brothers, 1946

Roach, Mary – *Spook: Science Tackles the Afterlife*, New York, NY, W.W. Norton & Company, 2005

Robinson, William E. – *Spirit Slate Writing and Kindred Phenomena*, New York, NY, Munn & Company, 1898

Rosenstock, Barb – *American Spirits*, New York, NY, Astra Publishing, 2025

Sandford, Christopher – *Masters of Mystery: The Strange Friendship of Arthur Conan Doyle and Harry Houdini*, New York, NY, St. Martins Press, 2011

Somerlott, Robert - *Here, Mr. Splitfoot*, New York, NY, Viking Press, 1971

Silverman, Kenneth - *Houdini!* New York, NY, Harper Collins, 1996

Spraggett, Allen - *Arthur Ford: Man who Talked with the Dead* (1973)

Stashower, Daniel - *Teller of Tales: Life of Sir Arthur Conan Doyle*, New York, NY, Penguin Books, 1999

Steinmeyer, Jim - *Hiding the Elephant*, New York, NY, Carroll & Graf, 2003

Tabori, Paul – *Pioneers of the Unseen*, London, UK, Souvenir Press Ltd, 1972

Tait, Derek – *The Great Houdini: His British Tours*, South Yorkshire, UK, Pen & Sword History, 2017

Taylor, Troy – *American Hauntings*, Jacksonville, IL, American Hauntings Ink, 2015
---------------- - *Ghosts by Gaslight*, Decatur, IL, Whitechapel Press, 2007
---------------- - *Houdini Among the Spirits*, Decatur, Il, Whitechapel Press, 2007

Tietze, Thomas R. – *Margery: An Entertaining and Intriguing Story of One of the Most Controversial Psychics of the Century*, New York, NY, Harper & Row, 1973

Underwood, Peter – *Ghosts and How to See Them*, London, UK, Anaya Publishers Ltd, 1993

United States Congress – *House Committee on the District of Columbia, Fortune Telling, H.R. 8989*, February 26 / May 18, 20, 21, 1926

Vimpany, Nicky (Editor) – *Unseen World*, Pleasantville, NY, Readers Digest Books, 2008

Weisberg, Barbara – *Talking to the Dead*, New York, NY, Harper Collins, 2005

MAGAZINES AND PERIODICALS

American History / August 1999: The Medium & The Magician (Daniel Stashower)
Fate / March 1960: Margery was a Fraud (Alson Smith)
Fate / September 1961: When Congress Investigated Spiritualism (Richard Saunders)

Fate / August 1963: Mystery of Houdini's Death (Vincent Gaddis)
Fate / November 1971: Arthur Ford Goes a Round with the Magicians (Arthur Ford)
Fate / April 1985: Margery Mediumship (Marian Nester)

SPECIAL THANKS TO

April Slaughter: Cover Design
Becky Ray: Editing
Samantha Smith
Athena & the "Aunts" - Sue, Carmen & Rocky
Orrin and Rachel Taylor
Rene Kruse
Rachael Horath
Bethany Horath
Elyse and Thomas Reihner
John Winterbauer
Cody Beck
Trey Schrader
Tom and Michelle Bonadurer
Lydia Rhoades
Cheryl Stamp and Sheryel Williams-Staab
Joelle Leitschuh and Tonya Leitschuh
Scott and Hannah Rob
Victoria & Reese Welch
And the entire crew of American Hauntings

ABOUT THE AUTHOR

Troy Taylor is the author of books on ghosts, hauntings, true crime, the unexplained, and the supernatural in America. He is the founder of American Hauntings Ink, which offers books, ghost tours, events, and the Haunted America Conference, as well as the creator of the American Oddities Museum in Alton, Illinois. He was born and raised in the Midwest and divides his time between Alton, Illinois and wherever the wind decides to take him. See Troy's other titles at: www.americanhauntingsink.com

* 9 7 8 1 9 5 8 5 8 9 2 7 4 *